Palgrave Studies in Technology and Innovation in Africa

Series Editors

This book series will explore the nuanced perspectives of technology and innovation adoption on the African continent in a post-Covid-19 era. It will cover contemporary topics such as digitalization, digital finance and social inclusion, the internet, social and mobile marketing, innovations such as artificial intelligence, the metaverse, virtual reality (VR), and Internet of Things (IoT). It will also include entries on various settings and contexts, including the public sector, hospitality and tourism, trade, energy and education.

The series will explore strategies that African countries can adopt to leverage technology and innovation to enhance trade and economic growth on the continent, in the context of the still-emerging African Continental Free Trade Agreement (AfCFTA). Apart from the theoretical and empirical contributions this series proposes to make, the series will also have books with appropriate case studies and best practice guidelines, will offer practical insights and recommendations that can be applied by policymakers, industry leaders, and other stakeholders to facilitate trade and economic growth within an Africa that is rebuilding post COVID-19.

The series will welcome submissions from students and scholars in fields which will showcase scholarly discourse, and present compelling case studies from North, West, East, Central and Southern Africa. It will be a valuable compendium of principles and best practice on innovation and technology deployments under compelling conceptual, empirical and theoretical topics, providing an authoritative guide for researchers, students, practitioners and policymakers, with particular interests in Africa and related emerging economy contexts.

Patient Rambe · Robert Ebo Hinson
Editors

The Future of Entrepreneurship in Southern Africa

Technological and Managerial Perspectives

palgrave
macmillan

Editors
Patient Rambe
Faculty of Management Sciences
Central University of Technology
Bloemfontein, South Africa

Robert Ebo Hinson
Department of Marketing
and Entrepreneurship, Rooftop
Offices
University of Ghana Business School
Accra, Ghana

Palgrave Studies in Technology and Innovation in Africa
ISBN 978-3-031-55934-1   ISBN 978-3-031-55935-8 (eBook)
https://doi.org/10.1007/978-3-031-55935-8

This Palgrave Macmillan imprint is published by the registered company Springer Nature Switzerland AG
The registered company address is: Gewerbestrasse 11, 6330 Cham, Switzerland

Paper in this product is recyclable.

Foreword

Both my parents were born in Africa, but I grew up overseas—with my parents always talking about how they missed the people, culture, food, music and everything else with which they grew up. When, as a young child, I asked my paternal grandmother, "Where was our family before Africa?" she explained that we had ancestors in Africa since time immemorial and that Africa was the cradle of civilisation. She sat me down and told me that I was living in an age of technology and that man would one day land on the Moon, but some of the earliest ideas and technologies were first developed in Africa. The following July she died, and I missed her stories. Time went by and man did land on the moon. Eventually I would land in Africa and learn more about amazing peoples, their entrepreneurial endeavours and their strategies. I spent much time in Southern Africa; my studies included research about entrepreneurship in Botswana (Dana & Ratten, 2017), Lesotho (Dana, 1997), Mozambique (1996) and Namibia (1993), revealing unique dynamics of entrepreneurship.

Hence, I was elated to learn that my respected friend Patient Rambe was involved in a book about this region that is dear to me, and I felt honoured when Robert E. Hinson invited me to write this foreword to their exciting volume that enlightens the reader about unique dynamics of entrepreneurship in Africa. Chapters emphasise the transformative power of entrepreneurial endeavours, and thus enhance our understanding of African entrepreneurship and its potential.

Richer than the sum of its parts, this book investigates the crucial interplay between technology and managerial strategies and for this I salute the contributors and the editors.

Léo-Paul Dana
Dalhousie University
Halifax, Canada

References

Dana, L-P. (1993). An analysis of strategic intervention policy in Namibia. *Journal of Small Business Management, 31*(3), 90–95.

Dana, L-P. (1996). Small business in Mozambique after the war. *Journal of Small Business Management, 34*(4), 67–71.

Dana, L-P. (1997). Voluntarily socialist culture and small business in the kingdom of Lesotho. *Journal of Small Business Management, 35*(4), 83–87.

Dana, L-P., & Vanessa Ratten, V. (2017). Characteristics and structures of informal entrepreneurship in Botswana. In C. C. Williams & A. Gurtoo (Eds.), *Routledge handbook of entrepreneurship in developing economies* (pp. 412–424). Routledge.

Preface

The research and narratives of entrepreneurship development in the African continent in general and Southern African region in particular, are both intriguing and challenging, due to their rich technology, social and cultural tapestry interfaced with policy inconsistency, legislative complexity, the high fluidity of consumer preferences and politically uncertain nature. The African entrepreneurial future is scintillating given the prevalence of relatively functional public and private institutions, youth and gender dividends, rising levels of internet penetration, the extensive use of mobile phones and digital platforms, coupled with the high level of creative ingenuity and the entrepreneurial spirit exhibited by the youthful population on the continent. Juxtaposed with this commendable narrative, are high levels of poverty, social inequality, social deprivation, underperforming and dysfunctional institutional arrangements and paucity of basic infrastructure to support entrepreneurial pursuits. The need to apply a Political, Economic, Social, Technological, Environmental and Legal (PESTEL) perspective to investigate the nature, processes and outcomes of entrepreneurship development on the African continent is, therefore, gaining currency among entrepreneurial scholars. Yet, there is limited knowledge on how technological perspectives and managerial practices interact in shaping entrepreneurship development including the mechanisms and boundary conditions through which these concepts interact and collide.

In this book, we feature various topics spanning conceptual, empirical and literature review-based studies that foreground how different digital technologies, digital innovations and managerial practices are brought to bear on entrepreneurship development in the Southern African region. We propose, a Context-Structure-Technology (CST) nexus as useful conceptual, empirical and empirical lenses for unpacking how technology, managerial practices and situated contexts collide and coalesce in shaping entrepreneurship development and digital entrepreneurship success in Southern Africa. Using an embeddedness perspective, we propose a CST lens, with which entrepreneurship and digital entrepreneurship success must be examined through the interaction and collision of human agency and institutional (cognitive, social, legal, political, economic and technological) structures in situated contexts. We argue, therefore, that while human action has the potential to facilitate, enable and nurture the nature and configurations of structures, the structure and its constitution also have a bearing on how, when, where and with whom human agency is constructed, enacted and reinforced.

The above considerations came alive in our choice of topics and their treatments in the organisation of the book. The first segment explored topics that interfaced technology, contexts and the pursuit of digital entrepreneurship to spotlight how digital technologies, digital innovations and digital transformation coalesced and interacted in the situated contexts in which entrepreneurship unfolded. The second segment explored a range of managerial practice topics spanning how ethical standards are subverted in human resource practices in entrepreneurial firms, the managerial and survival strategies that small and medium enterprises (SMEs) harnessed to remain solvent and seize hold of sustainability opportunities during and post-Covid-19. The other element was to examine the range of Covid-19-imposed restrictions that African governments imposed on entrepreneurial firms and SMEs to ascertain their extent of gender inclusivity and sensitivity. Consistent with the CST perspective, we also examined how technology orchestration and appropriation was brought to bear upon managerial practices to demonstrate the interplay between human agency and social structure in contexts plagued by institutional voids.

In January 2022, we issued an open call for academics and researchers to submit their concept and working papers with us for possible consideration and publication in a book exploring Technological and Managerial Perspectives on Entrepreneurial Development in Southern Africa. In the following three months, the concept and working paper proposals were evaluated for their scholarly relevance, rigour and significance using a double-blind peer-review process. Meanwhile, the expanded book proposal (inclusive of authors' abstracts) also underwent rigorous peer review by three anonymous reviewers appointed by the Publisher and their generous inputs were incorporated in the revised book proposal, which was resubmitted. The revised proposal also underwent a second round of reviews, and minor comments were incorporated in the final proposal. The contributors whose concept and working paper proposals were deemed to exhibit potential were invited to develop full papers for consideration for publication. Each paper was subjected to two rounds of double-blind peer review by three anonymous reviewers. The editors also assisted the individual authors in aligning their ideas and scholarly contributions with the technology and managerial theme of the book, its African contextual and entrepreneurship development thrust. Of the submissions received, we made our selection based on their contribution to the book's themes and level of scholarly rigour, and we were delighted with the nine chapters that have been included in this book. The authors were from universities in Ghana, Lesotho, South Africa and Zimbabwe.

This book on Entrepreneurial Development in Southern Africa would not have been published without the contributions of authors and the publisher. We, therefore, extend our sincere gratitude to the contributors for their diligence and keen interest in publishing their scholarly works in this book and for their willingness to productively collaborate on this most important intellectual endeavour. We also thank Palgrave Publishers for expressing interest in our entrepreneurship development topic and the unwavering support and dedication they generously provided throughout this publication journey—from the book proposal to the final publication of the book.

We sincerely hope that this book will be a valuable resource to Ph.D. students striving to deepen their understanding of entrepreneurship development in Africa. Moreover, academics, researchers, practitioners and policymakers will also find this book thought-provoking, instructive and illuminating as they navigate the complex terrain of the technological and managerial implications of entrepreneurship and digital entrepreneurship on the continent. Undoubtedly, this intellectual piece will be a valuable addition to their scholarly collection.

The Editors

Bloemfontein, South Africa — Patient Rambe
Accra, Ghana — Robert Ebo Hinson

Contents

Notes on Contributors

Emem O. Anwana is Associate Professor in the Department of Applied Law in the Faculty of Management Sciences at Durban University of Technology. She holds a Ph.D. in Business Law. Her research interest is in business law, entrepreneurship, corporate governance and CSR. She has published in *IEEE, Social Science* (MDPI) and *Springer International Publishing*.

Willie Chinyamurindi is Professor at the University of Fort Hare. He holds a Ph.D. specialising in Organisational Behaviour. His areas of interest are within areas of human and organisational capability development. Willie has published in leading journals such as *Employee Relations, Journal of Workplace Learning* and *Education + Training*.

Samuel John Chiromo holds a Ph.D. from the University of South Africa (UNISA), Pretoria, South Africa. He is Senior Lecturer in the Department of Applied Management at the same university. His research interests include entrepreneurship, economic development and taxation. His scholarly work has been published in the following academic journals: *Journal of Contemporary Management* and *Journal of Education*.

Robert Ebo Hinson is current Pro-Vice-Chancellor of the Ghana Communication Technology University, having served as Deputy Vice Chancellor-Academic and Acting Vice Chancellor of the University of Kigali. He has also acted as Rector of the Perez University College and Director of Institutional Advancement at the University of Ghana.

Professor Hinson is Distinguished Visiting Professor at the University of Johannesburg. He is also Chartered Marketer and Visiting Professor of Marketing at Lincoln University in the UK. He is Member of Africa Edifund Board in Ghana, Advisory Board Member of the CAS Group under the Jospong Group of Companies and Chair of the Telemedia Communications Board. In a 26-year marketing career, he has provided marketing, brand, customer experience, and sales advice to over 100 local and international brands and has served on many local and international boards. He has won several awards in his professional and academic marketing career. He is a Christian and has, for the last thirty years, been Member of the United Denominations originating from the Lighthouse Group of Churches. He is a married family man and a holder of two doctorate degrees, one in Marketing and the other in International Business Economics.

Mildred Mahapa is Senior Lecturer in the Department of Business Administration at the National University of Lesotho. She holds a Ph.D. in Human Resource Management and has written several articles in the field of Human Resource Management.

Nhamo Mashavira is Associate Professor in the Department of Human Resource Management (HRM) at Great Zimbabwe University. He holds a doctorate in HRM from the Central University of Technology, Free State, in South Africa. His research interests are in the interface of HRM practices with entrepreneurial venture performance, decent work and the sustainability of contemporary organisations. He has published extensively in journals under the auspices of AOSIS, the *Journal of Risk and Financial Management* and *MDPI*.

Lekhooa Matela is Lecturer in the Department of Business Administration at the National University of Lesotho. He holds a Master's degree in Management specialising in Entrepreneurship and New Venture Creation.

Gwendoline Vusumuzi Nani holds a Ph.D. from the University of the Free State (UFS) Bloemfontein, South Africa. She is Director of the Graduate School of Business at National University of Science and Technology (NUST), Zimbabwe and experienced University Lecturer. Her research interest is different types of entrepreneurship spanning general entrepreneurship, rural entrepreneurship, women entrepreneurship, youth entrepreneurship, corporate entrepreneurship, family entrepreneurship, university entrepreneurship, intrapreneurship and small enterprise research. Her publications appear in the following journals: *Journal of Contemporary Management*, *Acta Commercii* and *Academic Journal of Interdisciplinary Studies*.

Patient Rambe is Research Professor in the Office of the Dean in the Faculty of Management Sciences at the Central University of Technology, Free State in South Africa. He is Director of the Centre for Enterprise and Entrepreneurship Studies in the same faculty and established Research Scientist (C2) of the National Research Foundation. He holds a Ph.D. in Educational Technology from the University of Cape Town and another Ph.D. in Business Management from the University of the Free State. His most recent co-edited book is: *The Future of Entrepreneurship in Africa: Cross-Sectoral Perspectives Post-COVID-19* (CRC Press and Taylor and Francis). He currently serves as Associate Editor of the African Journal of Information Systems. His scholarly works are published in *International Entrepreneurship and Management Journal* (Springer), *International Journal of Management Education* (Elsevier), *Journal of Social Entrepreneurship* (Taylor & Francis), *Journal of Innovation and Entrepreneurship* (Springer), *European Journal of Innovation Management* (Emerald), *Journal of Foodservice Business Research* (Taylor & Francis), *Management Research Review* (Emerald), *Internet and Higher Education* (Elsevier) and the *British Journal of Educational Technology* (Wiley).

List of Tables

Introduction to the Edited Volume

Robert Ebo Hinson and Patient Rambe

1 Introduction

Entrepreneurship has become a very significant and influential force that is driving economic growth, innovation, and social transformation in an ever-evolving world that constantly presents both challenges and opportunities (Maniam et al., 2018). The African continent, including Southern Africa, with its diverse cultures, abundant resources, and untapped entrepreneurial talent, presents a promising potential for entrepreneurial development. Despite this potential, the continent is often ranked high among the regions with inequalities, mainly due to soaring levels of poverty, the gap between the rich and poor, and unemployment levels

R. E. Hinson (✉)
Ghana Communication Technology University, Accra, Ghana
e-mail: rehinson@gctu.edu.gh

Department of Marketing and Entrepreneurship, University of Ghana Business School, Accra, Ghana

P. Rambe
Faculty of Management Sciences, Central University of Technology, Free State, Bloemfontein, South Africa
e-mail: prambe@cut.ac.za

P. Rambe and R. E. Hinson (eds.), *The Future of Entrepreneurship in Southern Africa*, Palgrave Studies in Technology and Innovation in Africa, https://doi.org/10.1007/978-3-031-55935-8_1

(Adeyeye et al., 2023). To change this narrative, governments across the continent have implemented several policies and interventions to reduce unemployment and poverty in the sub-region. The South African government, for instance, has instituted supply-chain interventions such as the provision of subsidies and incentives to companies that employ the youth, availed youth training programmes, and rendered direct public sector employment opportunities (Tshishonga, 2022). In Ghana, several policies and interventions have been created and implemented by the government to reduce poverty and youth unemployment over the years. These interventions span the National Youth Employment Programme (NYEP), Youth Enterprise Development Programme (YESDEP), the Nation Builders Corps (NABCO), Youth in Agriculture Programme (YAP), and the National Entrepreneurial and Innovation Programme (NEIP) (Jumpah et al., 2022). In Nigeria, programmes such as the National Poverty Eradication Programme (SPEP), Youth Entrepreneurship Support Programme, and Startup Nigeria were efforts by the government geared at lessening the impact of poverty and unemployment, particularly among the youth.

Despite the multiple interventions implemented by the various governments within the African continent to combat unemployment and poverty levels, the national unemployment rates in these countries remain high at around 7.2% (Statista, 2023). In South Africa, for instance, the unemployment rate as of August 2023 was 33%. The current unemployment rates (second quarter, 2023) in Ghana, Nigeria, and Kenya are 4%, 4.2%, and 6%, respectively. Though some levels of advancements in economic growth and development have been recorded in these countries, the gap between education and employability, coupled with a limited range of industries, has created a situation where numerous well-educated and motivated young individuals find themselves caught in a cycle of unemployment. This is a clear indication that the governments within the sub-region are struggling to deal with the high unemployment rates, largely due to the huge number of students graduating from educational institutions annually compared to the number of jobs created and the number of people retiring each year. According to scholars (e.g. Autio et al., 2014), the surest alternative to addressing the problem is new venture creation, particularly among the youth through entrepreneurial development. The literature also highlights that governments around the world are committed to promoting and growing small businesses as a means of eradicating poverty and eliminating social deprivation and inequality. Thus, given the scarcity of opportunities in the formal sector, which leaves many young individuals with limited choices, effective entrepreneurship becomes an appealing option (Baptista et al., 2008; Decker et al., 2014). Through effective entrepreneurial development, young people can gain a diverse set of skills in areas encompassing business management, financial literacy, marketing, and customer relations from entrepreneurship programmes and projects. These acquired skills enhance their employability and empower them to initiate their own businesses (Autio et al., 2014). Notably, startups possess a unique potential to generate a substantial number of jobs in diverse sectors of the economy. Therefore, exploring factors that speed up entrepreneurial development and how to grow and sustain a business is a step in the right direction.

Globally, the contribution of small businesses to gross domestic product (GDP), employment creation, poverty reduction, and economic development is not in doubt. According to Južnik et al. (2019), SMEs account for 68% of total employment and 58% of total added value to the European economy, making them the backbone of the European economy. In Japan, for instance, 99.7% of all businesses are SMEs that employ 70% of the working population and contribute over 50% of added value to manufacturing products (Yoshino & Taghizadeh-Hesary, 2019). The story is not different from the perspective of developing countries. In South Africa, for instance, the SME sector contributes 57% to the GDP and employs 70% of the population (Ussif & Salifu, 2020). In Ghana, Nigeria, and Kenya, SMEs constitute 48%, 40%, and 80% of businesses and employ 80%, 84%, and 80%, respectively, of the employable population.

The high failure rate of SMEs poses a significant challenge to poverty reduction efforts and is a matter of great concern for both the government and the public. In Africa, the statistics are particularly alarming. Researchtec Global (2022) reveals that approximately 54% of startup businesses fail within their first three years on the continent. This means that at least half of the new businesses created in Africa do not survive beyond their initial three years of operation. The situation is even more precarious in countries like Ghana, Ethiopia, and Rwanda, where a staggering 75% of startups fail within their first year of establishment, as shown in the Researchtec Global report.

The reasons behind these failures are often attributed to poor entrepreneurial skills, inadequate marketing strategies, a lack of innovation, absence of clear growth and internationalisation strategies, and a failure to adapt to technological advancements. These factors are prevalent among SMEs across the continent. In South Africa, the situation is particularly dire, as highlighted by Bushe (2019). The country has one of the lowest established business survival rates globally, standing at a mere 2.3%. This stark reality supports the previous assertion by Ligthelm (2011) that only 12% of small businesses in South Africa manage to survive beyond their first four years. These statistics serve as compelling evidence of the unfavourable business environment that entrepreneurs face in South Africa.

The implications of these high failure rates are far-reaching. Beyond the financial losses incurred by individual entrepreneurs, business closures have a detrimental impact on employment opportunities, economic growth, and poverty alleviation efforts. The government, policymakers, and stakeholders must address the underlying challenges to create a more supportive ecosystem for SMEs. This includes initiatives to enhance entrepreneurial skills, provide access to affordable financing, foster innovation and technological adoption, and improve market access and marketing support. For instance, academic spinoffs that commercialise new to the market technologies typically have many liabilities and require financial resources, business and entrepreneurial competencies, and longer incubation times before they can gain sustainable financial returns (Novotny et al., 2020; Rasmussen et al., 2011). Efforts are already underway to tackle these issues. Governments are implementing policies and programmes to support entrepreneurship and create an enabling environment for business growth. These include creating convivial environments where new startups can develop relatively quickly, locate effective business partners, customers, and markets while steering their financial growth (Novotny et al., 2020). Collaborative efforts between public and private sectors, academia, and civil society are being forged to provide training, mentorship, and funding opportunities for aspiring and existing entrepreneurs. For instance, incubator organisations have been created to ideally shield new startups from excessive competition from incumbent firms and such supportive environmental conditions at founding have been found to imprint upon a new venture in ways that affect their growth and survival (Mathius et al., 2015). It is crucial, therefore, to address the root causes of business failure and provide the necessary support structures to enhance the survival and success rates of SMEs.

2 The Importance of Entrepreneurial Development in Southern Africa

Given the challenges enumerated above, exploring factors that speed up entrepreneurial development to encourage business creation and growth in Southern Africa and Africa is critical. For instance, apart from developing strong teams, budgets, and operations to support business activities (Borini et al., 2014), enterprising firms in emerging markets are increasingly called on to navigate complex issues of optimal pricing, infrastructural gaps (e.g. unreliable electricity supply, unnavigable roads), environmental sustainability challenges, and preference gaps (i.e. diversity of tastes, preferences, and habits) from customers (von Zedtwitz & Hadengue, 2019). In the South African context, SMEs have witnessed other environmental challenges such as stringent business operation conditions, bribery, and extortion by law enforcement agencies, burglaries, theft, thuggery, outright vandalism, and other acts of aggressive behaviours. Therefore, understanding these range of institutional, legislative, operational, civil, and societal hurdles as a whole is crucial for a number of compelling reasons. Entrepreneurial development will play a vital role in fostering economic growth, job creation, and social transformation. With its diverse economies and unique challenges, Southern Africa presents both opportunities and obstacles for entrepreneurs. Understanding the importance of entrepreneurial development in this region is crucial for unlocking its potential and driving sustainable development. Moreover, the unique demographic landscape of the sub-region provides ample opportunity for entrepreneurial growth and social development. For instance, Africa's working-age population will grow by approximately 450 million people—about 3% per annum—between 2015 and 2035 (Page, 2019). By 2050, Africa will have 362 million young people between the ages of 15 and 24 years old (Brooks et al., 2014; Page, 2019). Therefore, the continent's young population, along with the expanding middle class, is experiencing a demographic dividend that, if managed effectively, can propel economic progress and social development to new heights. For this reason, policymakers, researchers, and stakeholders must understand the challenges and opportunities faced by entrepreneurs in Africa so that an enabling environment can be created to foster entrepreneurial success.

Entrepreneurial development in the sub-region will provide economic growth and job creation:

Entrepreneurship is a key driver of economic growth in Southern Africa. By nurturing a vibrant entrepreneurial ecosystem, countries in the region can stimulate innovation, attract investments, and create new business opportunities. Entrepreneurial and startup ecosystems are credited with creating complex systems that nurture specialisation, innovation, and creative discovery and exploitation of entrepreneurial opportunities (Qian et al., 2013) through value proposition and value creating activities. Entrepreneurs contribute to expanding industries, increasing productivity, and generating income, thus fuelling economic development. Moreover, successful entrepreneurial ventures often lead to job creation, reducing unemployment rates and promoting inclusive growth.

Again, developing the entrepreneurial potentials of the region will significantly lead to poverty alleviation and social empowerment. Entrepreneurship has the potential to alleviate poverty and empower disadvantaged communities in Southern Africa. By providing opportunities for self-employment and income generation, entrepreneurship can uplift individuals and communities out of poverty. It enables marginalised groups, such as women, youth, people living with disabilities and rural populations, to participate in mainstream economic activities and access productive resources for sustainable livelihoods. By providing opportunities for innovation orchestration, for platform development and fostering ecosystems through public procurement and supporting pilots, trials, and demonstration projects (Nguyen et al., 2020), startups operating in well-supported ecosystems can bring the marginalised into mainstream economies, thereby creating a more inclusive society. Entrepreneurial development programmes that target these groups can empower them economically and contribute to reducing income inequalities.

Another key benefit for developing entrepreneurship is the innovation and technological advancement:

Entrepreneurship is closely linked to innovation and technological advancement in Southern Africa. Entrepreneurs often drive the development and adoption of new technologies, creating solutions that address local challenges and meet market demands. When entrepreneurship unfolds in ecosystems that support specialisation and healthy competition in specific industrial clusters, literature suggests that framework conditions are created, especially institutional environments for fostering generic innovation capacities and increasing innovation diversity (Nguyen et al., 2020). By fostering an entrepreneurial culture that encourages innovation, Southern Africa can enhance its competitiveness in the global economy. Though fostering digital innovation, which involves new combinations of digital and physical components to produce new market offerings (Yoo et al., 2010), small firms can significantly benefit from their efforts at internationalisation into foreign markets. Entrepreneurial ventures that leverage technology not only spur economic growth but also improve the quality of goods and services, enhancing the region's overall competitiveness.

Above all, entrepreneurial development within the sub-region will help in reaping the full benefits of the African Continental Free Trade Area (AfCFTA). By nurturing a thriving entrepreneurial ecosystem, Southern Africa can take full advantage of the AfCFTA to enhance intra-African trade, expand market access, and drive sustainable development. By expanding market access and trade opportunities, entrepreneurial development in Southern Africa will be vital for capitalising on the expanded market access and trade opportunities offered by the AfCFTA. For instance, access to African markets through the AfCFTA is expected to expand the size of Africa's economy to US$29 trillion by 2050 (Republic of South Africa, 2023). By developing and nurturing entrepreneurs, the region can foster the growth of small and medium-sized enterprises (SMEs) and startups that are well-positioned to tap into this larger continental market. Upon standards harmonisation and technical regulatory convergence for the continent, diminishing of market control and improving access to currently untapped African markets, it is estimated that the AfCFTA has a potential to boost intra-Africa trade by 52.3% by eliminating import duties and double such trade if non-tariff barriers are reduced (Republic of South Africa, 2023). Entrepreneurs, therefore, can leverage the removal of trade barriers and reduced tariffs to access new customers, explore untapped markets, and expand their businesses beyond national borders. This increased market access creates a platform for entrepreneurs to take advantage of the AfCFTA's vision of promoting intra-African trade and boosting economic integration.

Again, as the technological landscape of Africa is advancing rapidly, exploring the entrepreneurial development within the sub-region has become even more critical. The rise of digital technologies, mobile connectivity, and innovative digital platforms can overcome traditional barriers and unlock new avenues for entrepreneurial ventures. The emergence of a wide range of digital technologies and the ever-expanding digital infrastructure especially mobile and wearable computing, social media, blockchain, virtual and augmented reality, cloud computing services, data analytics and machine learning, robotics, Internet of Things, and 3D printing are shaping the nature, process, and outcomes of digital innovations (Nambisan et al., 2020) while transforming how, when, and where entrepreneurs pursue their entrepreneurship exploits. Thus, exploring the intersection of technology and entrepreneurship in Africa could harness these advancements, bridge the digital divide, and propel the continent to the forefront of global innovation. Entrepreneurial development in Africa has the potential to address pressing socio-economic challenges plaguing the continent. The issues of poverty, unemployment, and inequality can all be tackled through entrepreneurship. By nurturing and supporting African entrepreneurs, innovative solutions can be developed to address these challenges, leading to sustainable development and creating a more equitable society. Exploring and developing entrepreneurial education as well as entrepreneurship in the continent is equally important as it offers significant benefits to managers who seek to enhance their understanding of dynamic business environments and acquire practical knowledge. By examining successful entrepreneurial ventures across the continent, managers can gain valuable insights into innovation, adaptability, and resource optimisation. The book provides a rich collection of case studies, best practices, and real-world examples that can inspire managers to adopt an entrepreneurial mindset within their organisations and drive transformative change. Thus, the book sheds light on managerial strategies that are effective in navigating the unique challenges faced by entrepreneurs in Africa. These strategies encompass market entry approaches, resource allocation, talent acquisition, and building resilient supply chains. By studying the experiences of successful African entrepreneurs, managers can gain practical guidance and adapt these strategies to their own organisational contexts. This enables them to enhance their decision-making capabilities and foster sustainable growth in African markets.

3 Technological Perspectives on Entrepreneurial Development in Southern Africa

Digital technologies, digital innovation, and digital transformation have been advanced as the lifeblood of new business model development, value creation resource orchestration for firms in advanced and emerging economies (Nambisan et al., 2020). For instance, the wave and pace of digital innovation highlights the potential of digital technologies to enable, constrain, and shape the nature of innovation as collective action for modern firms and organisations (Majchrzak & Griffith, 2020). Therefore, in the digital era, venture firms and SMEs can only play a vital role in employment generation, poverty reduction, economic growth, and export earnings, particularly in developing countries (Hinson, 2010) when they can tap into digital innovations and new technology affordances to transform the configuration of their business models, be more agile in face of environmental adversities, leverage such technology to establish their value proposition and expand the market. In the digital era, it is crucial for export firms to harness the power of the internet to secure competitive advantages and maximise their impact on the export business. Technology will play a pivotal role in entrepreneurial development within the sub-region in terms of driving innovation, enhancing productivity, and enabling connectivity. Specifically, technology will enhance connectivity and access to information (Ocloo et al., 2023). For instance, technology, particularly the internet and mobile devices, has revolutionised connectivity and access to information in Southern Africa. Entrepreneurs now have the ability to access global markets, connect with suppliers and customers, and gather market intelligence with relative ease. Technology has democratised access to information, empowering entrepreneurs with the knowledge and resources necessary to make informed business decisions. By leveraging technology for research, networking, and market analysis, entrepreneurs in Southern Africa can identify opportunities and develop competitive strategies (Akpan et al., 2023).

The internet and digital technologies offer numerous benefits that can significantly enhance the capabilities of SMEs as well as their export drives. Firstly, they serve as a rich source of information that firms can leverage to fulfil their business functions effectively. Access to market research, industry trends, and customer insights empowers small businesses to make informed decisions, identify new market opportunities, and tailor their products or services to meet customer demands. Therefore, digital innovation and digital technologies are credited with facilitating, adapting and switching research strategies as institutional environments change or are shaped by these strategies (Jarvenpaa et al., 2020).

Additionally, the internet enables direct communication and connection between firms and customers, bypassing intermediaries. This direct link helps businesses establish strong customer relationships, understand their needs, and provide personalised solutions. By eliminating intermediaries, small businesses can retain greater control over their products, pricing, and customer experience, thus enhancing their competitiveness in the global market. Globally, digital platforms such as Alibaba, Amazon, Bolt (for South Africa), and Uber have created a large fortune from disintermediation as customers have unfettered direct access to their product and market offerings without the involvement of intermediaries.

Furthermore, the internet reduces communication costs for export firms. Traditional methods of communication, such as international phone calls and physical mail, can be expensive and time-consuming. However, digital communication channels, such as email, video conferencing, and instant messaging, enable cost-effective and instantaneous communication with partners, suppliers, and customers across the globe (Akpan et al., 2023; Ocloo et al., 2023). This efficiency in communication facilitates smoother business operations, faster decision-making, and quicker responses to customer inquiries, leading to improved customer satisfaction and increased competitiveness.

In the introduction chapter, Hinson and Rambe provide a comprehensive and influential review of the entrepreneurship landscape in Africa and Southern Africa and undertake a deep dive into the interface of managerial concerns and technology implications for an enterprising and entrepreneuring Africa. They pinpoint that the management-technology nexus is at the coalface of a deeper comprehension of the nature, processes, complexity, and outcomes of the entrepreneurship on the African continent in general and Southern Africa in particular.

Moreover, as noted by Friedman (1999), the advent of new information technologies has transformed the dynamics of global trade. Developing countries are no longer limited to trading raw materials and relying on the West for finished products. With the aid of technology, developing countries have the opportunity to become significant producers themselves. The internet has levelled the playing field, allowing small businesses in developing countries to access global markets, showcase their products or services, and compete on a global scale. Mashavira and Chinyamurindi's thought-provoking chapter leverages insights from Context-Structure-Technology (CST) nexus to underscore the factors needed for digital entrepreneurship success in Africa. They foreground the need to balance human and technology capabilities, to sufficiently account for the Context-Structure-Technology (CST) nexus in shaping how and when factors driving digital entrepreneurship success yield the intended results. Drawing on a systematic literature review covering the venture firms and SMEs on the entire African content, their work spotlights the valence of an ecosystem that privileges and leverages existing digital entrepreneurship business models. The study pinpoints networks unfolding at a societal and organisational level as crucial to the success of digital entrepreneurship among small firms operating in the digital sector, and these could be the avenues through which technology capabilities that align with context-specific problems emerge.

Technological advancements have largely enabled the growth of e-commerce platforms, providing entrepreneurs in Southern Africa with the means to expand their market reach beyond traditional borders. E-commerce platforms allow entrepreneurs to showcase and sell their products or services to a global customer base. This eliminates geographical constraints and enables entrepreneurs to tap into new markets, both domestically and internationally. By leveraging technology to establish online storefronts, payment gateways, and logistics solutions, entrepreneurs can overcome traditional barriers to entry and drive business growth. Consistent with this logic, Rambe's ground-breaking chapter considers the nature, structure, and future prospects of digital entrepreneurship on the Africa continent. It maps the future of digital entrepreneurship landscape by forecasting the range of technologies and phenomena that hold promise for the future of Africa's digital enterprises including how these can be exploited to promote sustainable digital entrepreneurship on the continent. Fusing Diffusion of Innovation Theory and Bottom of the Pyramid Innovation, the chapter spotlights home-grown innovation hubs (i.e. iHubs), Web 3.0 startups, platform firms ("platifirms"), touchless smart technologies, crypto hedge funds, inclusive digital economies, and green certified cities as technologies and phenomena that hold promise and will take centre stage in Africa's digital entrepreneurship landscape in the near future. The chapter postulates that leveraging sustainable digital entrepreneurship necessitates tapping into these technologies and developments including the accommodation of small digital firms at the bottom of the pyramid in these technological innovation exploits.

Technology offers tools and solutions that enhance efficiency and productivity for entrepreneurs in Southern Africa. Cloud computing, automation, and digital workflow systems streamline business processes, reducing manual tasks and improving operational efficiency. This allows entrepreneurs to allocate more time and resources to value-adding activities, such as innovation, customer engagement, and strategic planning. Additionally, technology enables entrepreneurs to leverage data analytics and business intelligence tools to gain insights into customer behaviour, market trends, and operational performance, enabling data-driven decision-making. To unravel the nexus between digitalisation, digital innovation, sustainable business model development and value creation, Rambe continues the theme of digital entrepreneurship, albeit with a different focus than the previous chapter. He reviews and appraises the research stream on the aforesaid concepts and demonstrates that digital platforms ("platfirms"), crowdfunding, cloud-based computing, social media marketing, tockenisation and securitisation of assets, big data-driven decision-making, and artificial intelligence (AI)-informed business processes are business model forms, processes, and practices that could transform the digital futures of African SMEs. The study suggests that acquiring, assembling, combining, and integrating resources that trigger digitalisation processes, digital innovation, and business model development and value creation provide one of the surest ways to digital business sustainability in Africa.

4 Managerial Perspectives for Entrepreneurial Development

Entrepreneurial development plays a crucial role in empowering managers of small and medium enterprises (SMEs) by equipping them with the necessary skills, knowledge, and mindsets to navigate challenges and seize opportunities effectively in today's competitive business landscape. Effective management practices and strategies are essential for navigating the challenges, seizing opportunities, and driving success in the dynamic and competitive business landscape. Nani and Chiromo's chapter, therefore, explores the managerial and survival strategies that SMEs in Southern Africa harnessed during and post-Covid-19 to remain operative and to wither the business operation storms brought by the pandemic. The chapter spotlights the combinatory strategies they employed spanning technology acquisition, reskilling and reconfiguration of acquired competencies, re-engineering of business operations to accommodate an online presence, and the replacement of the traditional brick-and-mortar *modus operandi*. The authors proffer a carefully crafted and detailed framework for leveraging the survival, coping, and resilience strategies of SMEs to minimise the socio-economic and health challenges during and post pandemics. They also render illuminating policy prescriptions that could support future businesses.

Some of the effective management practices that managers of SMEs could gain from entrepreneurial development are frameworks for effective strategic decision-making, operational efficiency, and human resource management. Effective managers analyse market trends, identify growth opportunities, and develop innovative strategies to capitalise on them. They assess risks, allocate resources efficiently, and make informed choices that align with the long-term vision of the venture. Strategic decision-making enables entrepreneurs to adapt to changing market dynamics, stay ahead of the competition, and achieve sustainable growth. Effective entrepreneurial development will also enable managers of small businesses to gain operational efficiency, which leads to increased productivity and cost-effectiveness. Thus, managers will be able to streamline workflows, implement performance measurement systems, and identify areas for improvement. Consistent with the aforesaid human resources management hurdles, Mahapa and Matela theorise and empirically investigate the intersection of human resources management in African SMEs and the pursuit of ethical practices. Adopting a qualitative lens to analyse this connection, the authors establish that the majority of HRM tasks and functions are executed by business founders who harbour vested interest in their ventures. This orchestrates some serious ethical dilemmas as personal idiosyncratic interests may interfere with objectivity, impartial and impersonal conduct required of venture imperatives and business operational standards. The dilemmas encountered in recruitment, rewards, training, and performance assessment of employees were highlighted as conflict of interests and dilemmas emanating from discrimination, nepotism, and favouritism. Their study proposes a comprehensive HRM practice framework that is ideally suited to address these hurdles.

Entrepreneurial development programmes provide managers of SMEs with a comprehensive understanding of various business functions, including finance, marketing, operations, and strategic management. This knowledge equips managers with the skills to analyse market trends, identify growth opportunities, and make informed decisions. Consistent with the recognition of how Covid-19 lockdown regulations in the SADC region stifled the advancement of female-owned businesses, Anwana's illuminating study explores the regulative architecture and policy regime of the countries in this regional bloc. Situated in Feminist and Capability theories, the chapter employs a gender lens to characterise and seize hold of the dynamics of female-owned/run businesses' survival strategies during and post-Covid-19 from a gendered perspective. Exploring a wide range of issues spanning access to basic infrastructure, access to markets, entrepreneurial resources, education skills, and technological knowledge, decision-making including incidences of bureaucratic interference, the chapter enumerates and critically discusses the ways in which gender roles, power dynamics, and social norms are implicated in the success of such businesses. The chapter recommends the institution of gender-sensitive legislation to emancipate and empower women and gender-focused regulatory framework to assist the SADC region in meeting the SDGs and the AU agenda 2063.

In the concluding chapter, Rambe and Hinson bring a dual pathway to grasping the delivery of entrepreneurship education and its attendant consequences. They challenge the scholarly essence of the long-held causation logic perspective (which mainly focuses on planning, control, and rational analysis to get to a predefined outcome) on teaching entrepreneurship, which tends to stifle creativity, block innovative thinking, and discourage students from starting a business venture. Appreciating the context-specific and context-informed nature of entrepreneurship and entrepreneurship education, they present the effectuation logic as a germane alternative heuristic and practical guide to teaching entrepreneurship given its capacity to embrace contextual and technological innovation. As such, they advance the notion that this logic's focus on teaching "through" entrepreneurship is better equipped to prepare future entrepreneurs to assume the challenge of creating meaningful ventures in ways that solve societal problems, create jobs, and alleviate poverty. This is particularly critical as the effectuation logic foregrounds entrepreneurs' reliance on available combinatorial resources, building opportunities for co-creation of knowledge, products, and processes rather than predefining goals in highly uncertain environments.

5 Conclusion

Exploring the potential for transformative economic growth and new business opportunities in Africa, this book delves into the key factors that contribute to successful entrepreneurial ventures. These factors include access to finance, supportive regulatory frameworks, mentorship programmes, and networking opportunities. By analysing these components, entrepreneurs and business leaders can gain a deeper understanding of what is needed for their own success and growth on the continent. Small businesses in developing countries have the potential to drive export growth, generate employment, and reduce poverty. However, in the digital age, harnessing the capabilities of the technology becomes paramount for small businesses, particularly startups, to secure competitive advantages and maximise their impact. The internet provides access to valuable information, facilitates direct connections with customers, lowers communication costs, and enables developing countries to become significant producers. By embracing technology and leveraging the internet, small businesses can unlock new opportunities, expand their global reach, and contribute to the economic development of their countries.

Additionally, the book examines the role of technological innovation in driving business growth in Africa. It highlights emerging trends such as digital platforms, e-commerce, digital marketing, showcasing how entrepreneurs can use these technologies to expand their market reach, improve operational efficiency, and gain a competitive edge. The book also features inspiring stories of successful African entrepreneurs who have leveraged technology to drive their businesses forward, providing practical insights and inspiration for those looking to follow in their footsteps.

References

Adeyeye, S. A. O., Ashaolu, T. J., Bolaji, O. T., Abegunde, T. A., & Omoyajowo, A. O. (2023). Africa and the nexus of poverty, malnutrition and diseases. *Critical Reviews in Food Science and Nutrition, 63*(5), 641–656.

Akpan, I. J., & Ibidunni, A. S. (2023). Digitization and technological transformation of small business for sustainable development in the less developed and emerging economies: A research note and call for papers. *Journal of Small Business & Entrepreneurship, 35*(5), 671–676.

Autio, E., Kenney, M., Mustar, P., Siegel, D., & Wright, M. (2014). Entrepreneurial innovation: The importance of context. *Research Policy, 43*(7), 1097–1108.

Baptista, R., Escária, V., & Madruga, P. (2008). Entrepreneurship, regional development and job creation: The case of Portugal. *Small Business Economics, 30*, 49–58.

Borini, F., Costa, S., Berezza, M., & Oliverira, M. (2014). Reverse innovation as an inducer of centres of excellence in foreign subsidiaries of emerging markets. *International Journal of Business and Emerging Markets, 6*(2), 163–182.

Brooks, K. M., Filmer, D. P., Louise, F. M., Aparajita, G., Alemu, M. T., Premand, P., Ringold, D., Sharma, S., & Zorya, S. (2014). Youth employment in Sub-Saharan Africa (Vol. 2): Full report (English). Africa development forum. World Bank Group.

Bushe, B. (2019). The causes and impact of business failure among small to micro and medium enterprises in South Africa. *Africa's Public Service Delivery and Performance Review, 7*(1), 1–26.

Decker, R., Haltiwanger, J., Jarmin, R., & Miranda, J. (2014). The role of entrepreneurship in US job creation and economic dynamism. *Journal of Economic Perspectives, 28*(3), 3–24.

Friedman, T. (1999). The lexus and the olive tree: Understanding globalization. Farrar, Straus, Giroux.

Hinson, R. (2010). The value chain and e-business in exporting: Case studies from Ghana's non-traditional export (NTE) sector. *Telematics and Informatics, 27*(3), 323–340.

Jarvenpaa, S. L., Echeverri-Carroll, E. L., & Aura Pedraza-Avella, A. (2020). Digital innovation and entrepreneurship in and around institutional voids: The case of Fundacin Cardiovascular (FCV) in Colombia. In S. Nambisan, K. Lyytinen, & Y. Yoo (Eds.), *Handbook of digital innovation* (pp. 41–63). Edward Elgar Publishing.

Jumpah, E. T., Owusu-Arthur, J., & Ampadu-Ameyaw, R. (2022). More youth employment programmes, less youth in work: A relook of youth employment initiatives in Ghana. *Cogent Social Sciences, 8*(1), 2066053.

Južnik Rotar, L., Kontošić Pamić, R., & Bojnec, Š. (2019). Contributions of small and medium enterprises to employment in the European Union countries. *Economic Research-Ekonomska Istraživanja, 32*(1), 3296–3308.

Ligthelm, A. (2011). Survival analysis of small informal businesses in South Africa, 2007–2010. *Eurasian Business Review, 1*, 160–179.

Majchrzak, A., & Griffith, T. (2020). The new wave of digital innovation: The need for a theory of sociotechnical self-orchestration. In S. Nambisan, K. Lyytinen, & Y. Yoo (Eds.), *Handbook of digital innovation* (pp. 17–40). Edward Elgar Publishing.

Maniam, B., Engel, J., & Subramaniam, G. (2018). Examining the significance and impact of social entrepreneurship. *International Journal of Engineering & Technology, 7*(4.38), 818–824.

Mathius, B., Williams, D., & Smith, A. (2015). Entrpreneurial inception: The role of imprinting in entrepreneurship action. *Journal of Business Venturing, 30*(1), 11–28.

Nambisan, S., Lyytinen, K., & Yoo, Y. (2020). Digital innovation: Towards a transdisciplinary perspective. In S. Nambisan, K. Lyytinen, & Y. Yoo (Eds.), *Handbook of digital innovation* (pp. 2–12). Edward Elgar Publishing.

Nguyen, N., Mariussen, A., & Hansen, J. O. (2020). The role of smart specialisation in providing regional strategic support for establishing sustainable start-up incubation ecosystems. In A. Novotny, E. Rasmussen, T. H. Clausen, & J. Wiklund (Eds.), *Research handbook on start-up incubation ecosystems* (pp. 19–39). Edward Elgar.

Novotny, A., Rasmussen, E., Clausen, T., & Wickland, J. (2020). Helping birds to fly: Introducing start-up incubation ecosystems. In A. Novotny, E. Rasmussen, T. H. Clausen, & J. Wiklund (Eds.), *Research handbook on start-up incubation ecosystems* (pp. 1–17). Edward Elgar Publishing.

Ocloo, E. C., Coffie, I. S., Asigbe-Tsriku, G. R. M., & Opuni, F. F. (2023). Sustaining small enterprises through digital technologies in the Post-COVID-19 Era. In *Technological Innovation Driving Sustainable Entrepreneurial Growth in Developing Nations* (pp. 305–328). IGI Global.

Page, J. (2019). *How industries without smokestacks can address Africa's youth unemployment crisis*. Global Economy and Development, Brookings Institution.

Qian, H., Acs, Z., & Stough, R. (2013). Regional systems of entrepreneurship: The nexus of human capital, knowledge and new firm formation. *Journal of Economic Geography, 13*(4), 559–587.

Rasmussen, E., Mosey, S., & Wright, M. (2011). The evolution of entrepreneurship competences: A longitudinal study of university spin-off venture emergence. *Journal of Management Studies, 48*(6), 1314–1345.

Republic of South Africa (2023). Trade, industry and competition on implementation of the African Continental Free Trade Area (AfCFTA). Department of Trade, Industry and Competition. https://www.gov.za/news/media-statements/trade-industry-and-competition-implementation-african-continental-free-trade. Posted October, 12 2023.

Researchtech Global. (2022). Top 10 reasons why businesses fail in Africa. https://www.researchtecglobal.com/blog/top-10-reasons-why-businesses-fail-in-africa#:~:text=The%20average%20start%2Dup%20failure,the%20continent%2C%20ending%20up%20failing. Accessed December 5, 2023.

Tshishonga, N. S. (2022). Uprooting poverty and unemployment through youth entrepreneurship leadership and skills development. In *Promoting Entrepreneurship to Reduce Graduate Unemployment* (pp. 63–83). IGI Global.

Statista. (2023). Unemployment rate in Africa from 2012 to 2024. https://www.statista.com/statistics/1319860/unemployment-rate-in-africa. Retrieved on December 23, 2023.

Ussif, R., & Salifu, K. (2020). Contributions of small & medium to economic developments in sub-Saharan Africa. *International Journal of Academic Accounting, Finance & Management Research, 4*(3) 63–78.

Von Zedtwitz, M., & Hadengue, M. (2019). Reverse innovation: Review of a decade. In F. Therin, F. P. Appio, & H. Yoon (Eds.), *Handbook of research on techno-entrepreneurship ecosystems, innovation, and development* (pp. 26–45). Edward Elgar.

Yoo, Y., Henfridsson, O., & Lyytinen, K. (2010). The new organising logic of digital innovation: A agenda for information systems research. *Information System Research, 21*(4), 724–735.

Yoshino, N., & Taghizadeh-Hesary, F. (2019). Role of SMEs in Asia and the financing challenges they face. In *Unlocking SME Finance in Asia* (pp. 3–22). Routledge.

Technological Perspectives

Factors for Digital Entrepreneurship Success on the African Continent: A Systematic Literature Review

Nhamo Mashavira and *Willie Chinyamurindi*

1 Introduction

There is a noted growth in the proliferation of technology within the business sector. This has led to a complete change in the business world in adopting structures that support technology usage (Schroeder, 2016). As seen by Xing and Marwala (2017), using technology might transform what we understand to be business and work. A continued need exists to find synergies that enhance competitiveness using technology (World Economic Forum, 2016). This creates an opportunity for digital technologies.

Digital technologies are potentially helpful in new business ventures and digital start-ups (von Briel et al., 2018). Such technologies can be linked to creating digital products or services (Lyytinen et al., 2016) and potentially support entrepreneurial activity (Tiwana et al., 2010).

N. Mashavira
Great Zimbabwe University, Masvingo, Zimbabwe

W. Chinyamurindi (✉)
University of Fort Hare, East London, South Africa
e-mail: wchinyamurindi@ufh.ac.za

P. Rambe and R. E. Hinson (eds.), *The Future of Entrepreneurship in Southern Africa*, Palgrave Studies in Technology and Innovation in Africa, https://doi.org/10.1007/978-3-031-55935-8_2

Despite these positive developments, there are continued calls to understand the role of technology in the business environment. In pushing for this role, there is an argument that business ventures need to develop, especially in their use of digital technologies (Niemand et al., 2020). Such technologies and tools allow for integrating applications that help improve how businesses function. Further, such tools by response have been branded as Fourth Industrial Revolution (4IR) digital technologies (Vaidyaa et al., 2018). This also includes coupling aspects such as the Internet of Things (IoT) in business and industrial processes (der Forschungsunion Wirtschaft–Wissenschaft & Acatech, 2013).

Technology usage can manifest in three expressions as roles, especially for the business environment. First, the idea of horizontal integration across the entire value creation network. Second, the focus is on end-to-end engineering in the whole product cycle. Finally, vertical integration and focus on networked manufacturing systems. This brings into focus technologies such as (a) the Internet of Things (IoT), (b) big data, (c) cloud computing, (d) blockchain, (e) additive manufacturing, (f) 3D printing, (g) Artificial Intelligence, (h) Augmented Reality, (i) autonomous robotics and, finally, (j) cobots (Vaidya et al., 2018). In countries like South Africa, 4IR is being prioritized as necessary in driving the next frontier, not only toward local and regional competitiveness but also to cement South Africa's authority on the global scale (Marwala, 2020).

There is also an acknowledgment that for technology to have wider resonance, some precursors must be in place, especially in small businesses. These include the presence of small business dynamic capabilities. The literature defines such capabilities as organizational competencies that exist in (a) routines, (b) operational processes, and (c) resources assisting a business to perform in a changing business environment (Chwilkowska-Kubala et al., 2019). Through dynamic capabilities, a distinction can be made between those firms that perform better than others (Zott, 2003). A threat that often exists to the full expression of such capabilities is change. Such change in the business environment can be attributable to the nexus of opportunity and complexity (McIntyre, 2018). A response to the opportunity and complexity nexus could be to encourage the development of action-dynamic capabilities in the form of processes. Within the literature, such capabilities have been attributed to forming alliances, product development, and strategic decision-making

(Eisenhardt & Martin, 2000). Again, these are also influenced by changes in the business environment (McIntyre, 2018).

The capacity of human capabilities to synchronize with innovation changes has a direct effect on the success of digital entrepreneurship. Nel-Sanders and Thomas (2022) admit that among the challenges currently influencing the sustainability and growth of entrepreneurship in South Africa is 4IR readiness. As rightfully observed by Muzanenhamo and Rankhumise (2022), issues within digital entrepreneurship literature space managing aspects related to managing the context. In essence, this places priority in value given to the human and organizational capabilities for digital entrepreneurship (Huggins et al., 2017). The challenge (and even opportunity) being how can these human and organizational capabilities be harnessed for success.

The focus for the South African economy and especially for the small businesses sector is a level of preparedness that is required to changes happening influenced by technological developments. This has been seen to be the desire of balancing between being reactive but also pioneering in terms of the use of technology for success (Marwala, 2020). This would entail a combination of activities of deep integration but also collaboration and embracing change (Nalubega & Uwizeyimana, 2019). Put differently, the argument here is for a nuanced response that allows for using capabilities to adapt and transform sectors such the small business sector (Groenewald & Okanga, 2019; Jere & Ngidi, 2020). Despite this noted importance, there is still a level of uncertainty about how this can happen (de Koker & du Plessis, 2020) especially within a small business context. Further, there is a need to unpack the human and organizational capabilities that are needed for success especially concerning digital entrepreneurship development.

The chapter follows a structure. First a context of the study is presented with emphasis on the digital sector and the role of technology in business development on the African continent. This is then followed by the research objective and the literature review narrowed to cover issues related to the factors needed for digital entrepreneurship success. Third, a methodology section explores the steps used for the Systematic Literature Review (SLR) that was undertaken. The chapter then concludes with the findings and the implications in how digital entrepreneurship can be development on the African continent.

2 Context of the Study

The backdrop of this study is the African small business context deemed as becoming an increasingly influential factor in quests for development (Chimucheka et al., 2019; Conradie & Lamprecht, 2018). At the core, small businesses are deemed critical in assisting human development and more comprehensive benefits at a macro-scale (Meyer & Peng, 2016; Pereira & Malik, 2017). However, Goldman and Kruger (2021) argue that such a context is grappled by challenges and pressures imposed by the 4IR. Calls exist, especially in the current era where there is the encouragement of 4IR technologies, for studies that explore how such capabilities can assist in not just the performance of firms but also how business excellence is attained (Georgiev & Ohtaki, 2019). Such calls warrant understanding best practices around how digital technologies have been incorporated for success or failure in business (Stock & Seliger, 2016). Such an empirical focus could be valuable in extending our understanding of digital technologies, especially within the contemporary business space (de Sousa Jabbour et al., 2018).

At the core, especially within an African context (following international trends), there is a need to understand how the impact of digital technologies affects development outcomes (Mayer & Oosthuizen, 2021), particularly among entrepreneurial ventures. This becomes critical for three reasons. First, the argued importance of small businesses' role relates to quests for development, especially in Africa (Jevwegaga et al., 2018). Second, the prioritization of digital technology adoption across the African continent is deemed crucial in positioning the competitiveness of Africa (Marwala, 2020). Third, given the first two arguments, there is a need to also place organizational capabilities as essential drivers for human and economic development (Bag et al., 2021). This becomes important, especially on the African continent.

Some scholars (Contractor et al., 2018) call for researchers in emerging economies and developing nations on the African continent to explore the impact of digital technology usage (Ellis-Chadwick & Doherty, 2012; Teh et al., 2014). At the core could be the need to close the gap, as Marwala (2020) argued. This is an opportunity to use a Systematic Literature Review (SLR) in response to these presented calls. In so doing, other angles of inquiry could be explored. For instance, ascertaining and understanding the role of management processes and dynamic capabilities within the digital technologies space (Melnyk et al., 2018). Such an inquiry could assist in getting a consolidated summary of all critical studies on the African continent that encourage digital technology usage experience (Buer et al., 2018; Tortorella & Fettermann, 2018). Notably, most research answering such calls is located within countries mainly in the West (Ben-Daya et al., 2019; Ivanov et al., 2016; Li et al., 2020; Oettmeier & Hofmann, 2016). There is a need to be expansive, especially on the African continent, where digital technologies are being adopted with popularity (Xu et al., 2018) and encouraged (Marwala, 2020).

An SLR to understand the factors needed for the success of digital entrepreneurship on the African continent has potential benefits. The focus on developing African economies should be on using technology to be reactive to change and pioneering (Marwala, 2020). This would entail not only a "deep integration" but also "collaboration" and "embracing change" given the proliferation of digital technologies, especially in the African context (Nalubega & Uwizeyimana, 2019, p. 1). There is also a need to channel existing capabilities to adopt digital technologies (Groenewald & Okanga, 2019; Jere & Ngidi, 2020). Such an effort is crucial, especially given the growing uncertainty about how this can happen, especially within a small business context (de Koker & du Plessis, 2020).

Finally, an SLR can assist in enhancing understanding, especially on the factors needed for digital entrepreneurship success on the African continent. Given that African research on dynamic capabilities within small businesses is receiving much interest (Chinyamurindi et al., 2021), this creates an important platform to advance this research stream by fusing aspects related to drivers that influence digital entrepreneurship. The angle of digital technology usage can assist this process. Further, the vital role of small business capabilities such as decision-making (Magoma et al., 2021), knowledge management (Labuscagne, 2020), information technology (Ako-Nai & Singh, 2019), supply chain (Loury-Okoumba & Mafini, 2021), innovation capacity (Mogashoa & Selebi, 2021), and human capital management (Chinyamurindi et al., 2021) and how these can be integrated within digital technology quests is an aspect that is gaining currency on the African continent. All these gaps answer calls, especially in Africa, to research exploring digital technology usage and its links to the business world (Bosch & Roussouw, 2021). Further, given Africa's focus on advancing digital technology development and use, this research has potential and merit (Marwala, 2020).

This research narrows the focus to the concept of digital entrepreneurship and the factors needed for its success on the African continent.

Digital entrepreneurship is viewed as using digital media and other information technology tools to assist a business (Davidson & Vaast, 2010). Using digital entrepreneurship opportunities, digital infrastructure, and entrepreneurial agents must be in place (Sussan & Acs, 2017). Such infrastructure and agents become practical conduits to the success of digital entrepreneurship efforts (Nambisan, 2017). Calls exist for continued understanding of digital entrepreneurship in pioneering future avenues through which theoretical and practitioner contributions can be made (Le Dinh et al., 2018).

3 Research Objective

Through an SLR, the research is guided by the following objective: to explore the capabilities as motivators that influence the success of digital entrepreneurship on the African continent.

4 Literature Review

Theoretical Literature

The chapter adopts the Dynamic Capabilities View (DCV) (Teece, 2012). The DCV has been argued by Chwilkowska-Kubala et al. (2019, p. 1) as "a much-debated theoretical construct or organization and management discourse." This has seen the DCV being framed as an essential contribution to contemporary management research (Schilke et al., 2018). The DCV assists in understanding usage-adoption issues related to technology. The DCV is linked to other theories, such as the Resource-Based View (Barney, 1991; Prahalad & Hamel, 1990; Wernerfelt, 1984).

Dynamic capabilities become important within digital entrepreneurship for three main reasons. First, there is a view that emerging economies and developing nations on the African continent need such capabilities to respond to challenges within the business environment (Pandit et al., 2018). This includes channeling dynamic capabilities to improve business performance and sustainability, especially within small businesses (Crane et al., 2019). Second, the role of technological capabilities is considered critical, especially for developing emerging economies (Chimucheka et al., 2019; Gwena & Chinyamurindi, 2018). This also accounts for the crucial role of digital technologies (Jere & Ngidi, 2020; Groenewald & Okanga, 2019). This also becomes important, especially within the emerging market context and on the African continent (Doh et al., 2016; Marano et al., 2017). Third, dynamic capabilities are acknowledged in business growth (Helfat et al., 2009; Teece et al., 1997; Zahra et al., 2006; Zollo & Winter, 2002). However, capabilities and the link with digital technologies still need to be explored, especially within Africa. Further, using the concept of firm-specific advantages (Rugman & Verbeke, 2001, 2003; Rugman et al., 2011), there is also a need to explore the link between dynamic capabilities and digital technologies with business performance outcomes. There is no better context to study all this than the African context, given the nuanced focus on digital technologies used within the business sector (Bosch & Roussouw, 2021) and the broader benefit to society in general (Marwala, 2020).

Empirical Literature

There is growing concern within the entrepreneurship space about the need to promote digitization (Niemand et al., 2020). In contemporary society, digitization quests attest to the transformation happening in the community (Anderson, 2014; Brynjolfsson & McAfee, 2014; World Bank, 2016). Entrepreneurs can make use of digital technologies in their work. Such technologies may include but are not limited to (a) the Internet of Things, (b) cloud computing, (c) big data, and (d) analytics (Li et al., 2020). These digital technologies are believed to improve business efficiency and factors related to connectivity, communication, and automation (Ardolino et al., 2018)—such digital technologies present opportunities for humans and economic development (Li et al., 2020). People and dynamic organizational capabilities are at the core of driving such aspects (Ivanov et al., 2019), seeking economic rent (Dubey et al., 2019). There is a need to find localized usage experiences around such digital technologies (Marwala, 2020).

Among entrepreneurs, digital entrepreneurship offers opportunities. This includes setting up their businesses and a platform to connect with the outside world (Elia et al., 2016; Hull et al., 2007). Thus, digital entrepreneurship offers the opportunity to develop the venture and broader ramifications for society (Ahmad & Hoffman, 2008). Researchers, especially in the Global North, continue to pay attention to the development of digital entrepreneurship research (Kraus et al., 2018).

In summary, digital entrepreneurs have at their disposal a range of tools. These include artificial intelligence (AI), the Internet of Things (IoT), big data, and blockchain technology (Ahlstrom et al., 2020; Nambisan et al., 2019; Si et al., 2023).

There are growing calls to also understand the field of digital entrepreneurship outside the Global North. This also includes a multidisciplinary understanding of digital entrepreneurship (Sahut et al., 2019). Another position is the need to understand digital entrepreneurship behaviors (Autio et al., 2018; Du et al., 2018), including how such behaviors influence outcomes at the firm level and beyond (Nambisan et al., 2018). The crucial aspect of the management role within digital entrepreneurship is another flagged point that needs attention (Lanzolla et al., 2018). Ultimately, others position the need to link the efficacy of digital entrepreneurship efforts to policy imperatives (Nambisan et al., 2019).

For digital entrepreneurship success, some precursors may need to be in place. Scholars argue for the necessary technology capabilities to be in place (Marion & Fixson, 2021). These can support how the technology should work and allow for connectedness within and outside the firm. Another position is the critical role of a community of innovation in aiding digital entrepreneurship efforts (Chesbrough et al., 2014; von Hippel, 2005). There is a need for continued synergy between technology and the community to allow for digital entrepreneurship success. Such synergy can help create value and benefit the organization and the entire ecosystem (Möller & Rajala, 2007). In essence, business models can potentially exist from such configuration (Tapscott, 1996, 2014) and potentially be expansive for the enterprise (Martínez-Martínez, 2022; Tapscott et al., 2000).

The literature also notes challenges that exist within the digital entrepreneurship literature stream. First, small businesses may need to gain the necessary capabilities to start and grow digital entrepreneurial pursuits. This is a pattern noted in the literature (Acs et al., 2017; Song, 2019; Eila et al., 2020). Second, despite acknowledging the importance of digital entrepreneurship, the field still needs to grow (Autio et al., 2018). Other scholars call for an integrative approach to studying digital entrepreneurship as a stream (Nambisan, 2017). Such efforts can potentially edify understanding of the digital entrepreneurship stream (Si et al., 2020; Zahra, 2022).

The presented literature presents strides, gaps, and angles of inquiry that warrant further attention. Using SLRs within digital entrepreneurship is gaining currency (Satalkina & Steiner, 2020). This chapter adds to this growing inquiry into exploring trends within digital entrepreneurship research on the African continent.

5 Methodology

Research Design

The study conducted a systematic literature review to solicit information related to digital entrepreneurship, especially on the African continent.

Research Paradigm

The paradigm utilized in the study was a qualitative research paradigm. The aim here, as Ellis (2014) argued, was to not only measure but also quantify information related to studies conducted around digital entrepreneurship on the African continent.

Ethical Consideration

In conducting the SLR, some guidelines were followed as stipulated (Caldwell, 2014; Horn-Lodewyk, 2022). The SLR is usually classified as a low-risk study as researcher information deemed personal is usually not used. Ethical clearance was obtained as part of the research process and adhering to the participating university requirements.

Data Collection Procedure

The SLR process followed a series of research design steps. These were also part of guidelines from the literature (Horn-Lodewyk, 2022). There were five in total:

Step 1: Formulate a Focused Review Objective

- The following research objective was proposed to explore the capabilities as motivators that influence the success of digital entrepreneurship on the African continent.

Step 2: Formulate a Search Strategy

- Three primary databases were used to retrieve information through consulting with the participating university library. These included: (a) ScienceDirect; (b) Google; and (c) Scielo (especially for South African research papers). Search items were used on selected electronic databases. These included words and terms such as (a) "digital entrepreneurship"; (b) "online entrepreneur"; and (c) "digital entrepreneur." All these searches were accompanied by an additional set of words: " + Africa" to narrow the review's focus to the African continent. The outcomes of these searches were then evaluated and stored as part of a more extensive repository of outcomes.

The inclusion criteria consisted of only those studies conducted on the African continent. Further, the studies must have had a focus on digital entrepreneurship. The studies must also have been in English. Finally, published theses and dissertations were also included for as long as these reported on a clear empirical focus of review being done. This also applied to the books used for this review. Our observation was that some of these books reported included an empirical review process similar to that which is done for journal manuscripts. Given this, we opted to include books that included this evidence of review especially for the individual chapters featured in such books. An exclusion criteria was followed. Only studies in English were used. Further, newspaper articles, books, and commentaries that did not state a clear empirical review process were excluded.

Step 3: Perform a Critical Appraisal

- A research assistant assisted in the process of screening the articles sourced. The process here involved using the research objective to ascertain the process of eligibility for the study. The use of inclusion and exclusion criteria assisted with this. The activity then consisted of a report with a decision after each article. Two outcomes existed. First to include, as the article fits the criteria of the SLR. Second, to exclude, as the article did not fit the criteria of the SLR. For these two, reasons were given for inclusion or exclusion.

Step 4: Summarize the Evidence Using

- 4a. Data Extraction—information guided by the research aims and objectives: (a) African country the study was conducted; (b) challenges within the confines of digital entrepreneurship; and (c) the capabilities for success concerning digital entrepreneurship.
- 4b. Data Analysis—a process of logical and analytical reasoning was used in accepting and eliminating information as per step two.

Step 5: Summarize the Findings

- Based on the presented steps, a summary table depicting trends related to digital entrepreneurship research on the African continent was created. Table 1 details the studies used for this SLR as per the outlined steps:

6 Findings

The study explored the capabilities as motivators that influence the success of digital entrepreneurship on the African continent. Table 1 summarizes the factors found as part of the African continent's SLR of digital entrepreneurship research.

Based on the findings from Table 1, inferences can be made about the factors needed for digital entrepreneurship success on the African continent. Notably, the factors needed for digital entrepreneurship success note a balance between human and technology capabilities, summarized as a Context-Structure-Technology (CST) nexus.

First, the context becomes a crucial fertile ground for digital entrepreneurship development. The findings from Table 1 show context enablers of digital entrepreneurship. For instance, the study by Nkwei et al. (2023) affirm the need to encourage those behaviors within the context that enables the development of digital entrepreneurial ventures. This is also supported by case examples from Nigeria and South Sudan,

Table 1 Summary of studies consulted (n = 20)

Author(s)	*African country*	*Source (database used)*	*Challenges*	*Capabilities*
(Nkwei et al., 2023)	South Africa	Journal	A need exists to assist young adults in keeping with changes, especially exploring opportunities related to digital technology	Encourage behaviors such as risk-taking in entrepreneurship development
(Friederici, 2017)	Multiple African Countries	Book with evidence shown of clear empirical review	Africa needs to develop technological ecosystems for competitiveness continually	A need exists for an entire context involved in the entire ecosystem through technological and infrastructure investments
(Emembolu et al., 2022)	Nigeria & and South Sudan	Journal	Lack of access to capital and environmental issues such as insecurities and political instability were identified as the two top challenges female entrepreneurs face in Nigeria and South Sudan	Improving digital literacy and competencies could help reduce inequalities and improve future business opportunities

Author(s)	*African country*	*Source (database used)*	*Challenges*	*Capabilities*
(Abubakre et al., 2021)	South Africa	Journal	Examining the influence of "Ubuntu" on digital entrepreneurship activities in South Africa	Ubuntu is the basis of a community orientation to digital entrepreneurship. Ubuntu offers an alternative to the broad spread heroic view in which digital entrepreneurship narratives are centered around the individual entrepreneur(s)
(Möbius & Wünsch, 2020)	East Africa	Book with evidence shown of clear empirical review	Exploring insights into the status quo concerning digital entrepreneurship in higher education across East Africa	Although the university forms the heart of the study and is valued, it needs reform, vigor, focus, and close direct associations with the private sector. This has the potential to educate digital entrepreneurs within a vibrant entrepreneurship ecosystem that is supported by a participatory, reciprocal mindset and spirit

(continued)

Table 1 (continued)

Author(s)	*African country*	*Source (database used)*	*Challenges*	*Capabilities*
(Friederici, 2017)	African continent	Journal	Clarifies the role of work hubs for African technology entrepreneurs and captures the viewpoints of entrepreneurs	Funders, supporters, and leaders should refrain from regarding hubs as interventions that lead to linear impact chains, since such misconceptions appear to have caused many false expectations toward African hubs
(Irene, 2019)	South Africa	Book with evidence shown of clear empirical review	A majority of women-owned businesses are not in the tech sector but are instead in the service-oriented sector. Technology, rather than being at the core of their businesses, is a tool for enhancing their businesses to make them more effective	The technology considered to be most effective for many women entrepreneurs is complicated to assess and is considered to be time-consuming. Some women entrepreneurs need to gain knowledge of what the market can do and how to assess what is best for their businesses

Author(s)	*African country*	*Source (database used)*	*Challenges*	*Capabilities*
(Acheampong, 2019)	Ghana	Book with evidence shown of clear empirical review	Power fluctuations and mobile connectivity were the significant challenges that hindered the timely and successful use of technology to improve the performance of farmers	Corporate agricultural entrepreneurs are improving farmers' productivity through technology in ways such as providing farmers with pricing data, soil preparation, crop inputs, cultivation training, crop inspection, pesticide application, techniques for crop harvesting, sale of crops through voice helplines, SMS platforms, crowdfunding, and training for farmers through technology and mobile phones

(continued)

Table 1 (continued)

Author(s)	*African country*	*Source (database used)*	*Challenges*	*Capabilities*
(Swartz et al., 2022)	South Africa	Journal	Women-owned digital platform start-ups that attract risk capital investment by university-educated and experienced corporate entrepreneurs need government support	Entrepreneurs' increased awareness of opportunities developed from factors such as impatience at the slow pace of change in post-Apartheid South Africa, personal values, and building for-profit business models driven by social purpose and corporate ennui
(Ansong & Turkson, 2022)	Ghana	Book with evidence shown of clear empirical review	An organizational culture accustomed to manual service delivery procedures by SMEs in the food sector could have improved the smooth adoption of digital strategies in the initial stages	One of the most essential success factors in adopting digital strategies was adopting less expensive or low-cost digital tools instead of expensive proprietary software

Author(s)	*African country*	*Source (database used)*	*Challenges*	*Capabilities*
(Chen & Pang, 2022)	African university students in China	Journal	To explore how the students discovered new opportunities in digital entrepreneurship as university students in China	Engagement in digital entrepreneurship led to empowerment and new forms of belongingness. The participants leveraged their social, educational, and cultural capital to establish start-ups
(Steel, 2021)	Sudan	Journal	The challenge of navigating the disruptions of going global, such as shifting geopolitical orders, fluctuations in import taxes and currencies, and changing transnational networks and shipment procedures	Digital platforms such as Facebook and WhatsApp help make the aspirations of online entrepreneurs a reality, as they provide them with a place to market their businesses and contact potential clients

(continued)

Table 1 (continued)

Author(s)	*African country*	*Source (database used)*	*Challenges*	*Capabilities*
(Jeza & Lekhanya, 2022)	South Africa	Journal	To explore the influence of digital technologies on the South African business sector, as well as examining the extent to which digital maintenance and rapid changes in technology could disrupt operations	Digital transformation significantly affects the building of customer relationships and ensures easy accessibility of the business. Digital marketing and online selling were the leading digital platforms successfully implemented by most South African SMEs
(O. C. & C Strategy Consultants, 2018)	South Africa	Consultant Report with evidence shown of clear empirical review	To identify areas for improvement in regulations and policies that affect tech entrepreneurship in South Africa	The inputs forming the pre-conditions for success and the resultant outputs feed each other in an iterative process that affects the vibrancy of a tech entrepreneurship ecosystem
(Mamabolo & Lekoko, 2021)	Botswana	Journal	To explore how female entrepreneurs in Botswana creates entrepreneurial ecosystems that support their business ventures	The entrepreneurial ecosystems created by women included digital technology, among other attributes, as part of the ecosystem

Author(s)	*African country*	*Source (database used)*	*Challenges*	*Capabilities*
(Steedman et al., 2022)	Ghana	Journal	To understand how the imaginaries of platform entrepreneurship are spatially shaped and locally defined	Instead of naïvely adhering to techno-optimist imaginaries, through their practices, filmmaking entrepreneurs in Ghana challenged the power geometry of the current platform ecosystem dominated by prominent Silicon Valley players
(Kedira & Kouame, 2022)	Bukina Faso and Cameroon	Journal	To clarify how financial technology use may translate into self-employment and possible ways through which it can improve marginalized social groups' livelihoods	The dynamics involved are much more complex as financial technology gets into and interacts with sophisticated webs of informal and formal financial institutions and transactional patterns
(Muzanenhamo & Rankhumise, 2022)	South Africa	Journal	A lack of technological know-how and few mobile social media users are the major factors affecting the development of South African digital entrepreneurs	Businesses and individuals need to embrace digital entrepreneurship and consider human capital's impact on businesses' success

(continued)

Table 1 (continued)

Author(s)	*African country*	*Source (database used)*	*Challenges*	*Capabilities*
(Gaglio et al, 2022)	South Africa	Journal	Estimating the relationships between digitalization and innovation, and between innovation and productivity	Public programs planned to foster inclusive digitalization should consider the types of digital technologies that are most beneficial and accessible to small enterprises, including those operating informally
(The World Bank Group, 2018)	South Africa	Empirical Report of studies by the World Bank Group	There is a need for more adequacy in government initiatives to the specific needs of the entrepreneurial sector to start and grow a business. Implementation and coordination are issues that lead to significant confusion among entrepreneurs, leading to a likely sub-optimal allocation of resources	There is a need to clarify policy and regulatory frameworks for digital entrepreneurship while strengthening the digital entrepreneurship ecosystem through targeted actions like improving the quality and quantity of available digital skills at all skill levels, the creation of a tech visa, and so on

Author(s)	*African country*	*Source (database used)*	*Challenges*	*Capabilities*
(Wamukoya &. Ng'weno)	Kenya	Book with evidence shown of clear empirical review	Interventions need to be put in place in order to reduce the high levels of youth unemployment in Kenya	Technological advances are creating new frontiers to deal with the problem of youth unemployment, with ICT playing a pivotal role
(GSMA Mobile for Development Report)	Kenya	GSMA Mobile for Development report with case material based on empirical review	Although many start-ups have achieved early success, the number realizing scale is still small since a myriad of financial, commercial, and technology challenges remain	With the proper support, technology-focused business angels and networks emerging in the region could create the much-needed supply of early stage capital and hands-on mentorship

placing value on a context that encourages context barriers such as lack of access to capital and environmental issues (Emembolu et al., 2022). Context issues, as shown in Table 1, affect aspects related to digital entrepreneurship development.

Second, structure emerges as an essential factor encouraging aspects related to digital entrepreneurship development. From Table 1, some pre-conditions must exist necessary to encourage digital entrepreneurship contextually. Infrastructure development to allow digital entrepreneurial ventures to exist and flourish can be flagged as salient from the context.

The third aspect concerns technology as crucial to support the context-structure arguments made. Table 1 shows that technology capabilities as factors encouraging digital entrepreneurship include encouraging an appetite for digital literacy skills and technological acumen. For small businesses, we noted the necessity for support regarding (a) decision-based technological capabilities, (b) supply-chain capabilities, and (c) marketing capabilities. These technology capabilities are the main driver, especially for digital entrepreneurial ventures.

7 Discussion

The study explores the factors needed for the success of digital entrepreneurship on the African continent. The study revealed that type of capabilities that need to be in place for digital entrepreneurship success on the African continent. These include context-specific capabilities especially the ones that encourage digital entrepreneurship business development. Saliently, these included the necessity of an ecosystem that first sees the value of the existence of digital entrepreneurship business models. For instance, policies at a national level were crucial just as an entrepreneurship ecosystem that sees value in the need to harness technology to assist in small business development. Further, the study also notes the importance of capabilities that allows for responsiveness to rapid change. The role of networks at a societal and organizational level was crucial and motivator to small businesses located in the digital sector. To this end, it was crucial that existing small businesses find links and synergies to quests on the ground for African countries to connect with 4IR ideals.

The need for capabilities that foster technological innovation also served a motivator to the emergence of digital entrepreneurship efforts. This is something that is being encouraged especially in developing nations (Vaidya et al., 2018). Further, capabilities that encourage the value creation that emerges from technological investment became a useful motivator. For instance, our findings note African country quests to develop digital skills as potential feeder to the emergence of digital entrepreneurship efforts. The role that technologies such as (a) the Internet of Things, (b) big data, (c) cloud computing, (d) blockchain, (e) additive manufacturing, (f) 3D printing, (g) artificial intelligence, (h) augmented reality, (i) autonomous robotics, and (j) cobots (Vaidya et al., 2018) served as useful motivator to translate these business efforts.

There is an acknowledgment of the need and desire for African countries to seek ways to use technology for development (World Economic Forum, 2016). The African continent's competitiveness may hinge on developing such technology capabilities (Marwala, 2020). The study's findings, as manifest through factors related to CST, emphasize the role digital technologies can play in transforming individual entrance into the digital entrepreneurship space, including the emergence of business ventures (von Briel et al., 2018). Paying attention to factors as manifest through the CST from the SLR can reveal areas of targeted intervention (Bruce et al., 2023). Addressing the factors within the CST as espoused in the SLR assists in ensuring that there is a passage on the ground that encourages digital entrepreneurship ventures (der Forschungsunion Wirtschaft–Wissenschaft & Acatech, 2013).

In summary, capabilities for digital entrepreneurship success as factors exist as CST issues. These become valuable precursors needed for success (Schroeder, 2016). In paying attention to such factors, small businesses may have opportunities to help them transform the business sector and society (Xing & Marwala, 2017). Further, this can be an avenue through which technology capabilities can emerge that align with context-specific problems (Vaidya et al., 2018). The CST nexus also illustrates those capabilities needed for the success of technology firms of the African continent. Effort here is on developing those capabilities that ensure context response, internal alignment, and the use of technology for success (Chwilkowska-Kubala et al., 2019).

Contribution

The chapter makes some critical contributions. First, given the focus on the dynamic capabilities needed for the success of digital entrepreneurship, the chapter assists in making suggestions as to how the African continent can develop this vital space. The findings of this work can help small businesses use technology to seamlessly address societal challenges while emphasizing internal alignment (Arcidiacono & Pieroni, 2018). The chapter contributes to the dynamic capabilities literature by showing those factors needed for digital entrepreneurship success, especially in Africa. This answer calls for such studies as this one (Chwilkowska-Kubala et al., 2019).

Second, through the findings, implications can be drawn in proposing digital technology usage and the success of digital entrepreneurship. Such an implication becomes important given the continued quest to pay attention to research of this kind (Kim, 2017). The implication extends not just the realm of theory but also practice. Third, the chapter and its findings also proffer attention to factors needed in the internal (organizational environment) and the external (macro environment) for digital entrepreneurship development. Paying attention to these issues can enhance organizational processes for success. Notably, this can include using digital technologies for forecasting, especially when dealing with complex processes, improving product and service quality, and reducing costs that impede business functioning (Jayaram, 2016).

Fourth, stemming from the chapter and its findings could be policy implications that can affect how small businesses develop and flourish. The chapter thus answers the call for African research with a nuanced impact on development (Liao et al., 2008; Marwala, 2020). The digital entrepreneurship space is used as a point of illustration. Potentially, this advanced understanding of an area of inquiry is essential for the success of the African continent.

Limitations and Future Research

Some limitations can be drawn from our study. First, the SLR was an attempt to bring together all the published research related to digital entrepreneurship on the African continent. Some published research may have needed to be included in our attempt to distill the published material under this theme. Hence, caution should be exercised concerning this. The sources under review and used for this analysis do not represent all published material under the digital entrepreneurship theme. Second, there also appears to be a need for more clarity of terms within the literature around the research theme depending on geographical location. For instance, in some countries, the term used is "digital entrepreneurship," yet in other contexts, usage is around terms such as "technology (online) business." This presents some challenges in conducting the SLR. It becomes difficult to come to a unified definition as far as terminology is concerned. Again, this presents a limitation to this study. We also caution and encourage future researchers to consider improving on this.

Future research could also conduct a bibliometric analysis of the identified studies against outcomes such as performance. A crucial aspect of this study pertains to the identified role of capabilities that informs not just the operation but also the performance of small businesses. In ascertaining this link with uncertainty, future research could profile the capabilities to inform digital entrepreneurship operation and performance. Further, a platform for making these links could be data used in digital entrepreneurship research to be widely available for others to download and perform analysis that informs theory and practice. Finally, future research could make an agenda also to understand the subjective experience that accompanies operating in the digital entrepreneurship space. Qualitative research can help understand aspects related to complexity within the digital entrepreneurship space. The unit of analysis can be the individual entrepreneur or the organization.

8 Conclusion

We extoll efforts being taken to understand aspects related to digital entrepreneurship on the African continent. This SLR gives a picture of not only the challenges in forming digital entrepreneurship studies but also the ensuing capabilities for this success. The African continent has the potential to be pioneering in using digital technologies for business success. This can extend to the entrepreneurship space. Small businesses could emerge as a catalyst for the transformation of the African continent by using digital technologies.

References

Abubakre, M., Faik, I., & Mkansi, M. (2021). Digital entrepreneurship and indigenous value systems: An Ubuntu perspective. *Information Systems Journal*, *31*(6), 838–862. https://doi.org/10.1111/isj.12343

Acs, Z. J., Stam, E., Audretsch, D. B., & O'Connor, A. (2017). The lineages of the entrepreneurial ecosystem approach. *Small Business Economics*, *49*, 1–10. https://link.springer.com/article/10.1007/s11187-017-9864-8

Acheampong. G. (2019). The nature of corporate digital agricultural entrepreneurship in Ghana: 175–198. In N. D. Taura (Ed.), *Digital entrepreneurship in Sub-Saharan Africa, Palgrave studies of entrepreneurship in Africa*, https://doi.org/10.1007/978-3-030-04924-9_7

Ahlstrom, D., Arregle, J. L., Hitt, M. A., Qian, G., Ma, X., & Faems, D. (2020). Managing technological, sociopolitical, and institutional change in the new normal. *Journal of Management Studies*, *57*(3), 411–437. https://doi.org/10.1111/joms.12569

Ahmad, N., & Hoffmann, A. (2008). *A Framework for Addressing and Measuring Entrepreneurship*. https://doi.org/10.2139/ssrn.1090374

Ako-Nai, A., & Singh, A. M. (2019). Information technology governance framework for improving organizational performance. *South African Journal of Information Management, 21*(1), 1–11. https://hdl.handle.net/10520/EJC-169378619a

Anderson, J. R. (2014). *Rules of the mind*. Psychology Press.

Ansong, E. & Turkson, C. (2022). COVID-19 pandemic and the small- and medium-sized enterprise: Digital strategies for surviving in a developing economy. In R. Boateng, S. L. Boateng, T. Anning-Dorson, L. Olumide Babatope (Eds.), *Digital innovations, business and society in Africa. Advances in theory and practice of emerging markets*. Springer, Cham. https://doi.org/10.1007/978-3-030-77987-0_10

Arcidiacono, G., & Pieroni, A. (2018). The revolution lean six sigma 4.0. *International Journal on Advanced Science, Engineering and Information Technology*, *8*(1), 141–149.

Ardolino, M., Rapaccini, M., Saccani, N., Gaiardelli, P., Crespi, G., & Ruggeri, C. (2018). The role of digital technologies for the service transformation of industrial companies. *International Journal of Production Research, 56*(6), 2116–2132.

Autio, E., Nambisan, S., Thomas, L. D., & Wright, M. (2018). Digital affordances, spatial affordances, and the genesis of entrepreneurial ecosystems. *Strategic Entrepreneurship Journal, 12*(1), 72–95. https://doi.org/10.1002/sej.1266

Bag, S., Telukdarie, A., Pretorius, J. C., & Gupta, S. (2021). Industry 4.0 and supply chain sustainability: Framework and future research directions. *Benchmarking: An International Journal*, *28*(5), 1410–1450.

Barney, J. (1991). Firm resources and sustained competitive advantage. *Journal of Management, 17*(1), 99–120. https://doi.org/10.1177/014920639101700108

Ben-Daya, M., Hassini, E., & Bahroun, Z. (2019). Internet of things and supply chain management: A literature review. *International Journal of Production Research, 57*(15–16), 4719–4742. https://doi.org/10.1080/00207543.2017.1402140

Bosch, Z. J., & Rossouw, D. (2021). Strategic positioning of a motorcycle manufacturer within the Fourth Industrial Revolution. *Acta Commercii, 21*(1), 1–11. https://doi.org/10.4102/ac.v21i1.907

Bruce, E., Shurong, Z., Ying, D., Yaqi, M., Amoah, J., & Egala, S. B. (2023). The effect of digital marketing adoption on SMEs Sustainable Growth: Empirical evidence from Ghana. *Sustainability, 15*(6), 4760. https://doi.org/10.3390/su15064760

Brynjolfsson, E., & McAfee, A. (2014). *The second machine age: Work, progress, and prosperity in a time of brilliant technologies*. WW Norton & Company.

Buer, S. V., Strandhagen, J. O., & Chan, F. T. (2018). The link between Industry 4.0 and lean manufacturing: Mapping current research and establishing a research agenda. *International Journal of Production Research, 56*(8), 2924–2940. https://doi.org/10.1080/00207543.2018.1442945

Caldwell, K. (2014). *By the bootstraps: Social entrepreneurs with intellectual disabilities and the reification of success* (Doctoral Dissertation). University of Chicago, Chicago.

Chesbrough, H., & Bogers, M. (2014). Explicating open innovation: Clarifying an emerging paradigm for understanding innovation. *New Frontiers in Open Innovation*. Oxford University Press, Forthcoming, 3–28.

Chen, L., & Pnag, C. L. (2022). Becoming digital entrepreneurs: African students in China Glocalism: Journal of Culture. *Politics and Innovation, 3*(8), 1–24. https://doi.org/10.12893/gjcpi.2022.3.8

Chimucheka, T., Dodd, N., & Chinyamurindi, W. T. (2019). The effect of entrepreneurial orientation on the performance of immigrant-owned SMMEs in the Eastern Cape Province of South Africa. *African Journal of Hospitality, Tourism and Leisure, 8*(1), 1–17.

Chinyamurindi, W., Kyogabiirwe, J. B., Kabagabe, J. B., Mafabi, S., & Dywili, M. (2021). Antecedents of small business financial performance: The role of human resource management practices and strategy. *Employee Relations: The International Journal*. https://doi.org/10.1108/ER-03-2020-0138

Chinyamurindi, W. T., & Gwena, C. (2018). Effects of knowledge management on innovation capabilities amongst small and medium enterprises in South Africa: The case of Buffalo City Metropolitan Municipality. *The Southern African Journal of Entrepreneurship and Small Business Management, 10*(1), 1–10. https://doi.org/10.4102/sajesbm.v10i1.177

Chwiłkowska-Kubala, A. (2021). What are the sources of regional airport economic effectiveness? The dynamic capabilities perspective with evidence from Poland. *Journal of Air Transport Management, 92*, 102024. https://doi.org/10.1016/j.jairtraman.2021.102024

Chwilkowska-Kubala, A., Malewska, K., & Mierzejewska, K. (2019). Digital transformation of energy sector enterprises in Poland. Rationale and practices. *Organization and management series*. https://doi.org/10.29119/1641-3466.2022.162.5

Conradie, S., & Lamprecht, C. (2018). What are the indicators of a successful business rescue in South Africa? Ask the business rescue practitioners. *South African Journal of Economic and Management Sciences, 21*(1), 1–12. https://hdl.handle.net/10520/EJC-e87d0dc24

Contractor, F., Foss, N. J., Kundu, S., & Lahiri, S. (2018). *Viewing global strategy through a microfoundations lens*. https://doi.org/10.2139/ssrn.3291634

Contractor, F. J., Lahiri, S., Elango, B., & Kundu, S. K. (2014). Institutional, cultural, and industry-related determinants of ownership choices in emerging market FDI acquisitions. *International Business Review, 23*(5), 931–941. https://doi.org/10.1016/j.ibusrev.2014.02.005

Cortellazzo, L., Bruni, E., & Zampieri, R. (2019). The role of leadership in a digitalized world: A review. *Frontiers in Psychology, 10*(1938). https://doi.org/10.3389/fpsyg.2019.01938

Crane, A., Matten, D., Glozer, S., & Spence, L. J. (2019). *Business ethics: Managing corporate citizenship and sustainability in the age of globalization*. Oxford University Press.

Czakon, W., Niemand, T., Gast, J., Kraus, S., & Frühstück, L. (2020). Designing coopetition for radical innovation: An experimental study of managers' preferences for developing self-driving electric cars. *Technological Forecasting and Social Change, 155*, 119992. https://doi.org/10.1016/j.techfore.2020.119992

Davidson, E., & Vaast, E. (2010, January). Digital entrepreneurship and its socio-material enactment. In *2010 43rd Hawaii International Conference on System Sciences* (pp. 1–10). IEEE. https://ieeexplore.ieee.org/abstract/document/5428439

de Koker, L. T., & du Plessis, T. (2020). Research as a service offering of knowledge management firms in the fourth industrial revolution. *South African Journal of Information Management, 22*(1), 1–8. https://doi.org/10.4102/sajim.v22i1.1178

de Sousa Jabbour, A. B. L., Jabbour, C. J. C., Foropon, C., & Godinho, M. (2018). When titans meet–Can industry 4.0 revolutionise the environmentally-sustainable manufacturing wave? The role of critical success factors. *Technological Forecasting and Social Change, 132*, 18–25. https://doi.org/10.1016/j.techfore.2018.01.017

der Forschungsunion Wirtschaft–Wissenschaft, P. K., & Acatech, F. (2013). Umsetzungsempfehlungen für das Zukunftsprojekt Industrie 4.0. *Abschlussbericht des Arbeitskreises Industrie, 4*. (Frankfurt am Main).

Doh, J., Husted, B. W., & Yang, X. (2016). Guest editors' introduction: Ethics, corporate social responsibility, and developing country multinationals. *Business Ethics Quarterly, 26*(3), 301–315. https://doi.org/10.1017/beq.2016.40

Dubey, R., Gunasekaran, A., Childe, S. J., Papadopoulos, T., Luo, Z., Wamba, S. F., & Roubaud, D. (2019). Can big data and predictive analytics improve social and environmental sustainability? *Technological Forecasting and Social Change, 144*, 534–545. https://doi.org/10.1016/j.techfore.2017.06.020

Du, W. D., Pan, S. L., Zhou, N., & Ouyang, T. (2018). From a marketplace of electronics to a digital entrepreneurial ecosystem (DEE): The emergence of a meta-organization in Zhongguancun, China. *Information Systems Journal, 28*(6),1158–1175.

Eila, B., Essi, S., Nataša, P.-B., & Stevan, T. (2020). Supporting the development of digitally competent VET teachers in Serbia and Russia. *Образование и Наука, 22*(9), 174–203.

Eisenhardt, K. M., & Martin, J. A. (2000). Dynamic capabilities: What are they? *Strategic Management Journal, 21*(10–11), 1105–1121. https://doi.org/10.1002/1097-0266(200010/11)21:10/11%3C1105::AID-SMJ133%3E3.0.CO;2-E

Eggers, F., Niemand, T., Kraus, S., & Breier, M. (2020). Developing a scale for entrepreneurial marketing: Revealing its inner frame and prediction of performance. *Journal of Business Research, 113*, 72–82. https://doi.org/10.1016/j.jbusres.2018.11.051

Elia, G. A., Marquardt, K., Hoeppner, K., Fantini, S., Lin, R., Knipping, E., Peters, W., Drillet, J. F., Passerini, S., & Hahn, R. (2016). An overview and future perspectives of aluminum batteries. *Advanced Materials, 28*(35), 7564–7579. https://doi.org/10.1002/adma.201601357

Ellis, A. K. (2014). *Research on educational innovations*. Routledge.

Ellis-Chadwick, F., & Doherty, N. F. (2012). Web advertising: The role of e-mail marketing. *Journal of Business Research, 65*(6), 843–848.

Emembolu. I., Emembolu. C, Aderinwale. O., & Lobijo. E. (2022). Digital entrepreneurship in Africa: Case studies of Nigeria and South Sudan in digital service delivery in Africa. In O. Adeola, J. N. Edeh, R. E. Hinson, F. Netswera *Platforms and Practices*. Springer International Publishing. https://doi.org/10.1007/978-3-030-83909-3_6

Friederici, N. (2017). *Innovation hubs in Africa: An entrepreneurial perspective*. https://doi.org/10.2139/ssrn.3123840

Gaglio, C., Kraemer-Mbula, E., & Lorenz, E. (2022). The effects of digital transformation on innovation and productivity: Firm-level evidence of South African manufacturing micro and small enterprises. *Technological Forecasting & Social Change, 182*, 1–12.

Georgiev, S., & Ohtaki, S. (2019). Critical success factors for TQM implementation among manufacturing SMEs: Evidence from Japan. *Benchmarking: An International Journal, 27*(2), 473–498.

Goldman, G. A., & Kruger, J. (2021). Viewing 'open strategy ' as a viable approach to the management of strategy. *Journal of Economic and Financial Sciences, 14*(1), 579. https://journals.co.za/doi/full/10.4102/jef.v14i1.579

Groenewald, D., & Okanga, B. (2019). Optimising enterprise resource planning system to leverage a firm's absorptive and adaptive capabilities. *South African Journal of Information Management, 21*(1), 1–15.

GSMA Mobile for Development report. (2014). Digital entrepreneurship in Kenya 2014. [Online]. https://www.gsma.com/mobilefordevelopment/wp-content/uploads/2014/02/Digital-Entrepreneurship-in-Kenya-2014.pdf. Accessed June 14, 2023.

Helfat, C. E., Finkelstein, S., Mitchell, W., Peteraf, M., Singh, H., Teece, D., & Winter, S. G. (2009). *Dynamic capabilities: Understanding strategic change in organizations*. John Wiley & Sons.

Hirsch-Kreinsen, H. (2015, June). Einleitung: Digitalisierung industrieller Arbeit. In *Digitalisierung industrieller Arbeit* (pp. 10–31). Nomos Verlagsgesellschaft mbH & Co. KG.

Huggins, R., Prokop, D., & Thompson, P. (2017). Entrepreneurship and the determinants of firm survival within regions: Human capital, growth motivation and locational conditions. *Entrepreneurship and Regional Development, 29*(3–4), 357–389. https://doi.org/10.1080/08985626.2016.1271830

Hull, K. L., & Sanford, M. S. (2007). Catalytic and highly regioselective cross-coupling of aromatic C–H substrates. *Journal of the American Chemical Society, 129*(39), 11904–11905. https://pubs.acs.org/doi/full/10.1021/ja074395z

Horn-Lodewyk, J. N., Merwe, B. V. D., Kali, G. M., & Munro, L. (2022). Evaluating the knowledge and training of forensic pathologists and registrars performing forensic radiography at a forensic pathology mortuary in the Free State province, South Africa. *Health SA Gesondheid (online), 27*, 1–10. https://doi.org/10.4102/hsag.v27i0.2014

Irene, B. N. O. (2019). Technopreneurship: A discursive analysis of the impact of technology on the success of women entrepreneurs in South Africa. In N. D. Taura et al. (Eds.), *Digital Entrepreneurship in Sub-Saharan Africa, Palgrave Studies of Entrepreneurship in Africa*, (pp. 147–174). https://doi.org/10.1007/978-3-030-04924-9_7

Ivanov, D., Dolgui, A., & Sokolov, B. (2019). The impact of digital technology and Industry 4.0 on the ripple effect and supply chain risk analytics. *International Journal of Production Research, 57*(3), 829–846. https://doi.org/10.1080/00207543.2018.1488086

Ivanov, D., Sokolov, B., Dolgui, A., Solovyeva, I., & Jie, F. (2016). Dynamic recovery policies for time-critical supply chains under conditions of ripple effect. *International Journal of Production Research, 54*(23), 3397–3413.

Jayaram, A. (2016, December). Lean six sigma approach for global supply chain management using industry 4.0 and IIoT. In *2016 2nd international conference on contemporary computing and informatics (IC3I)* (pp. 89–94). IEEE.

Jere, J. N., & Ngidi, N. (2020). A technology, organisation and environment framework analysis of information and communication technology adoption by small and medium enterprises in Pietermaritzburg. *South African Journal of Information Management, 22*(1), 1–9. https://doi.org/10.4102/sajim.v22i1.1166

Jevwegaga, H., Ade-adeniji, O., Ibidunni, A. S., Olokundun, M. A., Borishade, T. T., Falola, H. O., Obaoye, D., & Ogunniyi, A. (2018). Role of SMEs' entrepreneurial activities and industrial clustering on SMEs' performance. *Academy of Entrepreneurship Journal, 24*(1), 1–7.

Jeza, S., & Lekhanya, L. M. (2022). The influence of digital transformation on the growth of small and medium enterprises in South Africa. *Problems and Perspectives in Management, 20*(3), 297–309. https://doi.org/10.21511/ppm.20(3).2022.24

Johnson, C., Bester, H., Van Vuuren, P. J., & Dunn, M. (undated), Africa's digital platforms: Overview of emerging trends in the market, Available online on 26 September,2023 at https://cenfri.org/wp-content/uploads/Africas-digital-platforms-trends-report.pdf

Katsuda, A., Naito, Y., & Ishihara, T. (2022). Value co-creation in the health-care ecosystem for sustained excellence: realization of patient-centered medicine through task shifting of nurses. *The TQM Journal*, (ahead-of-print). https://doi.org/10.1108/TQM-01-2022-0027

Kedir, A., & Kouame, E. (2022). FinTech and women's entrepreneurship in Africa: The case of Burkina Faso and Cameroon. *Journal of Cultural Economy, 15*(4), 452–467. https://doi.org/10.1080/17530350.2022.2041463

Kraus, S., Ribeiro-Soriano, D., & Schüssler, M. (2018). Fuzzy-set qualitative comparative analysis (fsQCA) in entrepreneurship and innovation research–the rise of a method. *International Entrepreneurship and Management Journal, 14*, 15–33.

Kim, K. H., & bok. (2017). A study on the development of the key promoting talent in the 4th industrial revolution-utilizing six sigma MBB competency.

Journal of Korean Society for Quality Management, 45(4), 677–695. https://doi.org/10.7469/JKSQM.2017.45.4.677

Labuscagne, C. W. (2020). Knowledge forms in the project lifecycle: A blueprint for knowledge management in small creative agencies in Johannesburg. *South African Journal of Information Management, 22*(1), 1–9. https://doi.org/10.4102/sajim.v22i1.1138

Lanzolla, G., Sabini, E., Profilo, M. A., Mazzi, B., Sframeli, A., Rocchi, R., Menconi, F., Leo, M., Nardi, M., P., Vitti, & Marinò, M. (2018). Relationship between serum cholesterol and Graves' orbitopathy (G.O.): A confirmatory study. *Journal of Endocrinological Investigation, 41*, 1417–1423. https://doi.org/10.1007/s40618-018-0915-z

Le Dinh, T., Vu, M. C., & Ayayi, A. (2018). Towards a living lab for promoting the digital entrepreneurship process. *International Journal of Entrepreneurship, 22*(1), 1–17.

Li, C., Murad, M., Shahzad, F., Khan, M. A. S., Ashraf, S. F., & Dogbe, C. S. K. (2020). Entrepreneurial passion to entrepreneurial behavior: Role of entrepreneurial alertness, entrepreneurial self-efficacy and proactive personality. *Frontiers in Psychology, 11*, 1–19.

Li, Y., Dai, J., & Cui, L. (2020). The impact of digital technologies on economic and environmental performance in the context of industry 4.0: A moderated mediation model. *International Journal of Production Economics, 229*, 107777. https://doi.org/10.1016/j.ijpe.2020.107777

Liao, S., Fei, W. C., & Liu, C. T. (2008). Relationships between knowledge inertia, organizational learning and organizational innovation. *Technovation, 28*(4), 183–195.

Loury-Okoumba, W. V., & Mafini, C. (2021). Supply chain management antecedents of performance in small to medium scale enterprises. *South African Journal of Economic and Management Sciences, 24*(1), 1–13. https://doi.org/10.4102/sajems.v24i1.3661

Lyytinen, K., Yoo, Y., & Boland, R. J., Jr. (2016). Digital product innovation within four classes of innovation networks. *Information Systems Journal, 26*(1), 47–75. https://doi.org/10.1111/isj.12093

Magoma, T., Khumalo, S., & Du Plessis, T. (2021). Affordability of IBM Cognos business intelligence tool features suitable for small-and medium-sized enterprises' decision-making. *South African Journal of Information Management, 23*(1), 1–9. https://doi.org/10.4102/sajim.v23i1.1291

Mamabolo, A., & Lekoko, R. (2021). Entrepreneurial ecosystems created by woman entrepreneurs in Botswana. *South African Journal of Business Management, 52*(1), a2228. https://doi.org/10.4102/sajbm.v52i1.2228

Marano, V., Tashman, P., & Kostova, T. (2017). Escaping the iron cage: Liabilities of origin and CSR reporting of emerging market multinational enterprises. *Journal of International Business Studies, 48*(3), 386–408.

Marion, T. J., & Fixson, S. K. (2021). The transformation of the innovation process: How digital tools are changing work, collaboration, and organizations in new product development. *Journal of Product Innovation Management, 38*(1), 192–215. https://doi.org/10.1111/jpim.12547

Martínez-Martínez, S. L. (2022). Entrepreneurship as a multidisciplinary phenomenon: Culture and individual perceptions in business creation. *Academia Revista Latinoamericana de Administración, 35*(4), 537–565.

Marwala, T. (2020). *Closing the gap: The fourth industrial revolution in Africa*. Pan Macmillan.

Mayer, C. H., & Oosthuizen, R. M. (2021). Anxiety and excitement in the fourth industrial revolution: A systems-psychodynamic perspective. *South African Journal of Industrial Psychology, 47*, 1813. https://doi.org/10.4102/sajip.v47i0.1813

McIntyre, O. (2018). Transnational environmental regulation and the normativisation of global environmental governance standards: The promise of order from chaos. *Journal of Property Planning and Environmental Law, 10*(2), 92–112.

Melnyk, S. A., Flynn, B. B., & Awaysheh, A. (2018). The best of times and the worst of times: Empirical operations and supply chain management research. *International Journal of Production Research, 56*(1–2), 164–192. https://doi.org/10.1080/00207543.2017.1391423

Meyer, K. E., & Peng, M. W. (2016). Theoretical foundations of emerging economy business research. *Journal of International Business Studies, 47*, 3–22.

Möbius, M., & Wünsch, U. (2020). *East Africa digital entrepreneurship ecosystem in higher education*. [Online]. https://www.giz.de/en/downloads/giz2021-en-entrepreneurship-higher-education.pdf. Accessed June 13, 2023.

Möller, K., & Rajala, A. (2007). Rise of strategic nets—New modes of value creation. *Industrial Marketing Management, 36*(7), 895–908. https://doi.org/10.1016/j.indmarman.2007.05.016

Mogashoa, M. M., & Selebi, O. (2021). Innovation capacity: A perspective on innovation capabilities of consulting engineering firms. *The Southern African Journal of Entrepreneurship and Small Business Management, 13*(1), 372.

Muzanenhamo, A., & Rankhumise, E. (2022). Literature Review on Digital Entrepreneurship in South Africa: A Human Capital Perspective. *Entrepreneurship and Sustainability Issues, 10*(2), 464–472. https://doi.org/10.9770/jesi.2022.10.2(29)

Myers, M. D. (2019). Qualitative research in business and management. *Qualitative research in business and management*, 1–364.

Nalubega, T., & Uwizeyimana, D. E. (2019). Public sector monitoring and evaluation in the Fourth Industrial Revolution: Implications for Africa. *Africa's*

Public Service Delivery and Performance Review, 7(1), 1–12. https://hdl.handle.net/10520/EJC-1974c48914
Nambisan, S. (2017). Digital entrepreneurship: Toward a digital technology perspective of entrepreneurship. *Entrepreneurship Theory and Practice, 41*(6), 1029–1055. https://journals.sagepub.com/doi/pdf/10.1111/etap.12254
Nambisan, S., Wright, M., & Feldman, M. (2019). The digital transformation of innovation and entrepreneurship: Progress, challenges and key themes. *Research Policy, 48*(8). https://doi.org/10.1016/j.respol.2019.03.018
Nel-Sanders, D., & Thomas, P. (2022). The role of government in promoting innovation-led entrepreneurial ecosystems. *Africa's Public Service Delivery and Performance Review, 10*(1), a640. https://doi.org/10.4102/apsdpr.v10i1.640
Niemand, T., Rigtering, J. P. C., Kallmünzer, A., Kraus, S., & Maalaoui, A. (2020). Digitalization in the financial industry: A contingency approach of entrepreneurial orientation and strategic vision on digitalization. *European Management Journal, 39*(3), 317–326.
Nkwei, E. S., Rambe, P., & Simba, A. (2023). Entrepreneurial intention: The role of the perceived benefits of digital technology. *South African Journal of Economic and Management Sciences, 26*(1), a4936. https://doi.org/10.4102/sajems.v26i1.4936
O. C. & C Strategy Consultants. (2018). Tech entrepreneurship ecosystem in South Africa .[Online]. https://www.occstrategy.com/media/1295/tech-entrepreneurship-ecosystem-in-south-africa.pdf. Accessed June 14, 2023.
Oettmeier, K., & Hofmann, E. (2016). Impact of additive manufacturing technology adoption on supply chain management processes and components. *Journal of Manufacturing Technology Management, 27*, 944–968.
Pandit, D., Joshi, M. P., Sahay, A., & Gupta, R. K. (2018). Disruptive innovation and dynamic capabilities in emerging economies: Evidence from the Indian automotive sector. *Technological Forecasting and Social Change, 129*, 323–329.https://doi.org/10.1016/j.techfore.2017.09.035
Pereira, V., & Malik, A. (2017). Identities in transition: The case of emerging market multinational corporations and its response to glocalisation. *Social Identities, 24*(4), 1–15.
Prahalad, C. K., & Hamel, G. (1990). The core competence of the corporation. *The University of Illinois at Urbana-Champaign's Academy for Entrepreneurial Leadership Historical Research Reference in Entrepreneurship*, Available at SSRN: https://ssrn.com/abstract=1505251
Rugman, A. M., & Verbeke, A. (2001). Subsidiary-specific advantages in multinational enterprises. *Strategic Management Journal, 22*(3), 237–250. https://doi.org/10.1002/smj.153

Rugman, A. M., & Verbeke, A. (2003). Extending the theory of the multinational enterprise: Internalization and strategic management perspectives. *Journal of International Business Studies, 34*(2), 125–137.

Rugman, A. M., Verbeke, A., & Nguyen, Q. T. K. (2011). Fifty years of international business theory and beyond. *Management International Review, 51*(6), 755–786.

Sahut, J. M., Peris-Ortiz, M., & Teulon, F. (2019). Corporate social responsibility and governance. *Journal of Management and Governance, 23*, 901–912. https://doi.org/10.1007/s10997-019-09472-2

Satalkina, L., & Steiner, G. (2020). Digital entrepreneurship and its role in innovation systems: A systematic literature review as a basis for future research avenues for sustainable transitions. *Sustainability, 12*(7), 2764. https://doi.org/10.3390/su12072764

Schilke, O., Hu, S., & Helfat, C. E. (2018). Quo Vadis, dynamic capabilities? A content-analytic review of the current state of knowledge and recommendations for future research. *Academy of Management Annals, 12*(1), 390–439. https://doi.org/10.5465/annals.2016.0014

Schroeder, W. (2016). Germany's Industry 4.0 strategy. *London: Friedrich Ebert Stiftung*. https://www.fes-london.org/fileadmin/user_upload/publications/files/FES-London_Schroeder_Germanys-Industrie-40-Strategy.pdf. Accessed April 29, 2020.

Si, S., Hall, J., Suddaby, R., Ahlstrom, D., & Wei, J., et al. (2023). Technology, entrepreneurship, innovation and social change in digital economics. *Technovation*. https://doi.org/10.1016/j.technovation.2022.102484

Si, S., Zahra, S. A., Wu, X., & Jyh-Fu, J. D. (2020). Disruptive innovation and entrepreneurship in emerging economics. *Journal of Engineering and Technology Management, 58*, 1–12.

Sussan, F., & Acs, Z. J. (2017). The digital entrepreneurial ecosystem. *Small Business Economics, 49*, 55–73.

Steedman, R., Alacovska, A., Langevang, T., & Resario, R. (2022). Imaginaries of platform entrepreneurship in the creative industries: Techno-optimism and subversion in Ghanaian filmmaking. *Information, Communication & Society,*. https://doi.org/10.1080/1369118X.2022.2062252

Steel, G. (2021). Going global—going digital. *Diaspora Networks and Female Online Entrepreneurship in Khartoum, Sudan, Geoforum, 120*, 22–29. https://doi.org/10.1016/j.geoforum.2021.01.003

Stock, T., & Seliger, G. (2016). Opportunities of sustainable manufacturing in industry 4.0. *procedia CIRP*, *40*, 536–541. https://doi.org/10.1016/j.procir.2016.01.129

Song, A. K. (2019). The Digital Entrepreneurial Ecosystem—a critique and reconfiguration. *Small Business Economics, 53*(3), 569–590. https://doi.org/10.1007/s11187-019-00232-y

Swartz, E. M., Scheepers, C. B., & Toefy, T. (2022). Women entrepreneurs' opportunity identification of digital platform start-ups: Emerging evidence from South Africa. *International Journal of Gender and Entrepreneurship, 14*(3), 352–374. https://doi.org/10.1108/IJGE-06-2021-0096

Tapscott, D. (1996). *The digital economy: Promise and peril in the age of networked intelligence*. McGraw-Hill.

Tapscott, D. (2014). *The digital economy anniversary edition: Rethinking promise and peril in the age of networked intelligence*. McGraw-Hill.

Tapscott, D., Ticoll, D., & Lowy, A. (2000, May). Digital capital: Harnessing the power of business webs. *Ubiquity*, *2000*, 3-es. https://dl.acm.org/doi/fullHtml/doi.org/10.1145/336228.336231

Teh, P. L., Yong, C. C., & Lin, B. (2014). Multidimensional and mediating relationships between TQM, role conflict and role ambiguity: A role theory perspective. *Total Quality Management & Business Excellence, 25*(11–12), 1365–1381. https://doi.org/10.1080/14783363.2012.733266

Teece, D. J., Pisano, G., & Shuen, A. (1997). Dynamic capabilities and strategic management. *Strategic Management Journal, 18*(7), 509–533. https://doi.org/10.1002/(SICI)1097-0266(199708)18:7%3C509::AID-SMJ882%3E3.0.CO;2-Z

Teece, D. J. (2012). Dynamic capabilities: Routines versus entrepreneurial action. *Journal of Management Studies, 49*(8), 1395–1401. https://doi.org/10.1111/j.1467-6486.2012.01080.x

Tiwani, S. V. (2010). *Managing learner behaviour: a collective case study of three effective secondary schools* (Doctoral dissertation). http://hdl.handle.net/10500/4814

Tortorella, G. L., & Fettermann, D. (2018). Implementation of Industry 4.0 and lean production in Brazilian manufacturing companies. *International Journal of Production Research, 56*(8), 2975–2987. https://doi.org/10.1080/00207543.2017.1391420

The World Bank Group. (2018). South Africa Digital Economy Assessment. [Online]. https://app.box.com/s/p17i7zpatr265tywoad3ooqcsgutzr3w/file/1237486567609. Accessed June 14, 2023.

Vaidya, S., Ambad, P., & Bhosle, S. (2018). Industry 4.0–a glimpse. *Design Engineering*, 2351, 9789.

von Briel, F., Recker, J., & Davidsson, P. (2018). Not all digital venture ideas are created equal: Implications for venture creation processes. *The Journal of Strategic Information Systems, 27*(4), 278–295. https://doi.org/10.1016/j.jsis.2018.06.002

Von Hippel, E. (2005). Democratizing innovation: The evolving phenomenon of user innovation. *Journal Für Betriebswirtschaft, 55*, 63–78. https://doi.org/10.1007/s11301-004-0002-8

Wamukoya, C. M. &. Ng'weno. A (2017). I-Entrepreneurship: Changing lives through technology. In B. Ndem & T. Weiss (Eds.), Digital Kenya, Springer. https://doi.org/10.1057/978-1-137-57878-5_6

Wernerfelt, B. (1984). A resource-based view of the firm. *Strategic Management Journal, 5*(2), 171–180. https://doi.org/10.1002/smj.4250050207

World Bank Group. (2016). *World development report 2016: Digital dividends*. World Bank Publications.

World Economic Forum. (2016). The future of jobs: Employment, skills and workforce strategy for the fourth industrial revolution. *Global Challenge Insight Report*. http://www3.weforum.org/docs/WEF_Future_of_Jobs.pdf

Xing, B., & Marwala, T. (2017). Implications of the fourth industrial age on higher education. *arXiv preprint* arXiv:1703.09643.https://arxiv.org/ftp/arxiv/papers/1703/1703.09643.pdf

Xu, M., David, J. M., & Kim, S. H. (2018). The fourth industrial revolution: Opportunities and challenges. *International Journal of Financial Research, 9*(2), 90–95. https://doi.org/10.5430/ijfr.v9n2p90

Zahra, S. A. (2022). Institutional change and international entrepreneurship after the war in Ukraine. *British Journal of Management, 33*, 1689–1693.

Zahra, S. A., Sapienza, H. J., & Davidsson, P. (2006). Entrepreneurship and dynamic capabilities: A review, model and research agenda. *Journal of Management Studies, 43*(4), 917–955. https://doi.org/10.1111/j.1467-6486.2006.00616.x

Zollo, M., & Winter, S. G. (2002). Deliberate learning and the evolution of dynamic capabilities. *Organization Science, 13*(3), 339–351. https://doi.org/10.1287/orsc.13.3.339.2780

Zott, C. (2003). Dynamic capabilities and the emergence of interindustry differential firm performance: Insights from a simulation study. *Strategic Management Journal, 24*(2), 97–125. https://doi.org/10.1002/smj.288

Digital Entrepreneurship in Africa: New Frontiers, Prospects, Opportunities and Challenges for Small Digital Enterprises

Patient Rambe

1 Introduction

This chapter was precipitated by Friedereci et al.'s (2020) scintillating and provocative multi-case study-based book titled "*Digital Entrepreneurship in Africa: How a continent is escaping Silicon Valley's long Shadow*." In essence, the book documents multiple cases of the development of African digital enterprises. Specifically, it acknowledges the ability of African digital entrepreneurs to apply and adapt digital technologies to their local economic, social and political contexts creatively and productively. Further, the book documents the blending of digital technologies with analogue outreach infrastructure and highlights the primacy of protracted entrepreneurial learning and ecosystem development among entrepreneurs before demonstrable outcomes materialise. Paradoxically, the authors contour the skewed concentration of digital products in urban

P. Rambe (✉)
Faculty of Management Sciences, Central University of Technology, Free State, Bloemfontein, South Africa
e-mail: prambe@cut.ac.za

P. Rambe and R. E. Hinson (eds.), *The Future of Entrepreneurship in Southern Africa*, Palgrave Studies in Technology and Innovation in Africa, https://doi.org/10.1007/978-3-031-55935-8_3

and regional markets to the exclusion of the hinterlands (Friedereci et al., 2020).

While the book acknowledges the emergence of new entrepreneurial identities in Africa, it equally critiques the feasibility of replicating the Silicon Valley digital entrepreneurship success stories on the continent by emphasising the sharp cultural and racial contradictions between Silicon Valley's ideals and local realities founded on reproduced postcolonial dependencies on the West. Lastly, the informative book also alludes to the high exhibition of the entrepreneurial spirit among digital entrepreneurs coinciding with the inability of average African digital enterprises to grow exponentially and scale internationally, their inability to produce digital infrastructure, attract venture capital (VC) and incapability to disrupt traditional industries (Friedereci et al., 2020). Collectively, these institutional, operational and technological hurdles severely undermine the pursuit and realisation of sustainable digital entrepreneurship on the African continent. This overarching picture of structural, operational and managerial bottlenecks among African digital enterprises spurred three pertinent questions namely:

1. Drawing on the current state of digital entrepreneurship on the African continent, what digital technologies (e.g., tools, artefacts) and digital phenomena (e.g., platforms, infrastructure and practices) can be forecasted to sustain digital entrepreneurship into the future?
2. What new frontiers (i.e., developments) and prospects (i.e., outlook and forecasts) can this sustainable digital entrepreneurship take?
3. What opportunities and challenges do these new frontiers present to digital entrepreneurs and policymakers on the African continent?

Mapping the digital technologies and digital phenomena that can activate and actuate the horizon of future digital entrepreneurship in Africa is critical for several reasons. First, although internationalisation of digital enterprises is the surest way of sustaining exponential growth of such firms (Awuah et al., 2007; Thai et al., 2022), digitalisation is often presented as an effective way of supporting business development for SMEs by diversifying their offerings to fit global markets (Reim et al., 2022). Moreover, despite the prominent use of digital technologies for business scaling and business model innovations, small firms especially those that domicile in African countries are yet to fully exploit the affordances of digital technologies to develop integrated formal business models (Panda et al., 2017) that spur their growth and sustainability. To the extent that digital platforms are open, affordable and widespread (McIntyre & Srinivasan, 2017), digital entrepreneurship and innovations could flourish in SMEs largely due to their more flexible strategies and relatively shorter decision-making times compared to large enterprises (Cenamor & Frishammar, 2021). As such, there has been growing calls for researchers and practitioners to explore the business innovations and entrepreneurship enabled by digital technologies and platforms (Xie et al., 2022).

An exploration of the new frontiers and prospects of future digital entrepreneurship is fundamental to the rapid growth of the African digital enterprises and by extension the economic growth of the continent. Yet to remedy the skewed geographical distribution of digital entrepreneurship (largely concentrated in metropolitan cities and industrial regions) and the stunted and linear growth of such a phenomenon (Friedereci et al., 2020), research needs to investigate the role of digital technologies and platforms in leapfrogging under-served rural areas and hinterlands. Moreover, how digital technologies can be appropriated as vehicles for technology-based industrialisation and infrastructure development should also be a subject of critical inquiry. Therefore, developing a kaleidoscope of prospects and the future of digital entrepreneurship is critical as digital technologies are often hailed for their capacity to integrate products and services across functional, organisational and geographic boundaries (Sebastian et al., 2017), accelerating the pace of industrial agglomeration including their ability to usher in significant transformation in different industries (Ghezzi et al., 2015).

An exploration of the opportunities and challenges the new frontiers present to digital entrepreneurs and policymakers on the African continent has the potential to increase the digital entrepreneurial capabilities of African entrepreneurs and the digital enterprise footprint of the continent. Although it has been assumed that the extensive adoption of digital technologies during the Covid-19 pandemic increased the digital competencies of entrepreneurs in first world economies to compete in the global marketplace (Ratten, 2022), African entrepreneurs were found under-capacitated and reactive to the exigencies and contingencies imposed by Covid-19. The extensive closures of small businesses, their inability to respond effectively to the uncertainty imposed by social distancing and travel restrictions and their inability to craft flexible and agile business innovation models that accommodate the new realities of the pandemic environment, bear testimony to SME limitations. Essentially, business closures, contraction of SME operations during the Covid-19 pandemic weakened SME financial positions and exposed them to greater financial risk (Omar et al., 2020). Evidence of worker and production inputs shortages due to distortions of supply chains, also negatively affected SME sales during the pandemic (Adam & Alarifi, 2021; Gurría, 2020).

Consistent with these situated conditions, we argue that if African entrepreneurs anticipated such pandemic-based disruptions, they could have exploited the affordances of digital platforms to avail products and services, to create a new audience focused on obtaining reliable and real-time information (Nelson & Lei, 2018; Ratten, 2022) in ways that augment digital entrepreneurship. Therefore, the capacity of African entrepreneurs to proactively respond to growing pandemic-imposed inequalities, future crises and their associated resilience in such contexts calls for greater scenario planning, futurist thinking and proactivity in anticipation of future adversities. This is because post-pandemic times such as those of Covid-19 exposed the significant inequality between developed and developing countries, imposed significant changes in lifestyles and access to basic infrastructure and compelled entrepreneurs to engage in greater collaboration and engagement with government, organisations, institutions and communities (Gozgor & Lau, 2023). These conditions further necessitate tapping into digital technologies and infrastructure.

The rest of the chapter is organised as follows: First the Diffusion of Innovation Theory and Bottom of the pyramid innovations are presented as germane theoretical and conceptual lenses for explaining the architecture of digital technologies and infrastructure on the African continent. Second, related studies on digital entrepreneurship are discussed to provide a panoramic perspective of the state of architecture of this phenomenon on the continent. Third, the related studies cover the range of technologies and phenomena on the African horizon that could drive digital entrepreneurship into the future. Fourth, the opportunities and challenges presented by these technologies and phenomena for small business are presented. Fifth, the implications of the study for theory, policy and practice are presented. Lastly, the limitations of the study and the conclusion are given.

2 Theoretical Development

Diffusion of Innovation Theory

To develop an integrated account of future technologies that will fuel the maturity of digital entrepreneurship on the African continent, the Diffusion of Innovation Theory (DOI) together with the Bottom of the Pyramid Innovations are employed as theoretical and conceptual lenses. The Diffusion of Innovation Theory captures *how*, *why* and *at what rate* new ideas, technology and process innovations spread through an organisation, a society or a country (Rogers, 2003). For Cua (2012), the *how* captures the innovation process while the *why* represents the justification for appropriating the innovation or rejecting it, signifying the perceived attributes of the innovation. In the African context, for example, the extent to which innovation hubs are adopted could be a consequence of a combination of personal, organisational and socio-cultural factors. These factors range from the hubs' perceived economic value, the extent to which they embrace home-grown indigenous innovations emanating from grassroots indigene entrepreneurs and organisational mechanisms through which such innovations are created, sanctioned and diffused into communities and societies. While the direction of causality pertaining to whether individual interactions and their networks drive societal adoption of innovations (Tarde, 1903) or whether societal perceptions drive individuals' appropriation of innovations (Gidden, 1990) remains an open conversation, the ambivalent view is that there is a bi-directional relationship between individuals, organisations and societies with regard to technology and innovation adoption. For instance, while the preference for direct personal engagement with customers may compel some indigene entrepreneurs to maintain and prefer brick-and-mortar enterprises over digital platforms, the migration of customers into online spaces (societal pressures) may compel some entrepreneurs to also incubate digital start-ups.

Typically, individual perceptions of specific innovations may drive the rate of adoption, shape the context of adoption and the scale at which such innovations are adopted. For instance, relative advantage (*perceived usefulness*), compatibility, ease of use, complexity, ability to be tested (*trialability*), demonstrability (*observability*) and voluntariness (Cua, 2012) all drive the rate and scale of innovation adoptions. In the African contexts, digital entrepreneurs may only adopt new innovations if they perceive some technical, economic, social and cultural value in their adoption (relative advantage). They may also be keen to apply new technologies and innovations if these align with their intended entrepreneurial goals and strategies. Similarly, the capacity of innovation hubs, Web 3.0 start-ups and platifirms to be adopted is a function of how users, consumers and communities perceive the efficacy and valence of these institutions and technologies as much as it is a function of the context of their usage. Therefore, in highly dynamic and volatile markets characterised by ambiguous industry structures, blurred market boundaries, fluid business models, ambiguous and shifting players and unpredictable change (Menon, 2008), it may be unclear what these technologies and institutions' roles are in facilitating access to capital, IT capabilities and managerial skills (Mata et al., 1995; Nambisan, 2023). This uncertainty is particularly acute for people at the bottom of the pyramid, who despite their entrepreneurial ingenuity, may lack proprietary knowledge and intellectual expertise to deploy digital technologies and innovations in ways that support digital entrepreneurship in emerging contexts. Despite its inherent promise to explain the innovation, the innovation process, diffusion process and the perceived attributes of the innovation (Cua, 2012), the theory may not sufficiently account for how innovations are adopted by marginalised communities, where innovation adopters and opinion leaders are few. This necessitates the use of a complementary theory to address this shortcoming.

Despite the shortcomings, DOI theory addresses the critical questions relating to the people's awareness and ascertaining of the value of business innovations, the process of its exploitation to facilitate its acceptance and wider adoption and the evaluative decisions to facilitate its implementation (Cua, 2012). The theory explains successful diffusion of innovation as a function of the innovation's affordances (i.e., its capabilities and drawbacks), the traits of innovation adopters (especially potential adopters' perceptions of opinion leaders' reactions) or social influence; and the larger social and political context, including the salience of issues related to the innovation (especially how its proponents and opponents frame the meaning of the innovation, and the timing of its introduction) (Dearing & Cox, 2018). Therefore, despite its limitations in accounting for endogenous innovations, the theory provides a useful interpretive lens for understanding the complex conditions under which business innovations and digital entrepreneurship unfold especially in contexts marked by institutional voids.

Bottom of the Pyramid Innovations

The terms "bottom of the pyramid" (BOP) denotes the largest and poorest socio-economic group in the economic value chain (Perez et al., 2013). Essentially, the concept captures the 2.5 billion people in the world who live on less than US$2.5 per day (Shah, 2008). These are largely the populations that live in Africa, Southeast Asia, Eastern Asia, Latin America and the Caribbean (Subrahmanyan & Gomez-Arias, 2008) that are largely plagued by poverty, social inequality, disease and high crime rates. In these deprived contexts, the foreign or indigenous innovations that unfold must be affordable, easy to employ and customisable to meet the complex material needs of these communities. Ironically, consisting of more than 4 billion of the world population, this group accounts for five trillion dollars in purchasing power, which implies a lucrative market emerges from serving the world's poorest (Lehikoinen et al., 2018).

In these contexts punctuated by marginalised and erratic access to modernity, globalisation, latest technologies and electronic media, the belief systems, cultural practices and norms of the populations are often rigid and inflexible. Therefore, the uptake, commodification and domestication of latest technology innovations become a momentous and unsurmountable enterprise. Consequently, companies that penetrate bottom of the pyramid markets (i.e., low-income markets) may struggle to change consumers' behaviour and therefore, must transform the way products are made and delivered. As such, firms that underestimate these hurdles miscalculate the resources, innovation capabilities and time involved, and their project teams end up poorly equipped to accomplish their tasks (Simanis & Duke, 2014). Closely linked to this complexity are the largely untapped business opportunities that could arise from introducing new frugal innovations in these under-explored, economic and cultural contexts. As research suggests, the BOP market presents a large opportunity for large businesses emanating from the conversion of such a market into a profitable venture capitalising on billions of potential customers accessing products and services for the first time (Prahalad & Hart, 2002). Paradoxically, in these markets the proclivity to resist new products is high due to deeply ingrained mind-sets and routines because such novelty presents unanticipated disruptions among people with limited financial means and limited product experience (Simanis & Duke, 2014).

The BOP market often comprises unorganised and fragmented multiple markets, which complicate companies' penetration into these markets and culminates in their negation by large companies (Lehikoinen et al., 2018). These complexities present opportunities for local start-ups and indigene entrepreneurs to create frugal innovations and creative inventions that meet the social needs of these under-served populations. Therefore, how latest and future innovations can infiltrate BOP markets and the extent to which such innovation can be legitimised in these contexts constitute useful subjects of inquiry. These conditions create huge debates on whether sustaining innovations or disruptive innovations would be the most deal for such under-served markets.

Overall, DOI provides a coherent approach to the technological choices that innovation adopters in the digital ecosystem consider before and when adopting innovations (e.g., its perceived cost, or the perceived monetary cost compared to alternative innovations, expense of adopting and implementing an innovation; innovation effectiveness, innovation simplicity and innovation compatibility) (Dearing & Cox, 2018). However, the theory does not sufficiently account for the circumstances of digital entrepreneurs who (1) do not rely on external innovations (2) draw on their local innovation and entrepreneurial ingenuity and agency in assessing innovation rather than that of opinion leaders. This shortcoming makes the BOP innovation approach a germane complement of DOI. Conversely, while the BOP innovation approach accounts for the reconfiguration of resources and expertise, continual learning by entrepreneurs and coordination/integration of resources needed to learn about new innovations in context (El Malouf & Bahemia, 2023; Menon, 2008), it may not account for decisions that are made with the direct involvement of opinion leaders in resource-poor contexts. This is where DOI becomes quite useful. Even though DOI is useful for explaining collective innovation-decisions (i.e., building consensus among individuals in innovation adoption or rejection), authority innovation-decisions (i.e., adoption or rejection of innovation being shaped by powerful individuals and contingent innovation-decisions (i.e., choices to adopt or reject innovations made only after a previous innovation-decision) (El Malouf & Bahemia, 2023; Rogers, 2003), the theory does not sufficiently speak to endogenously developed innovations as the concepts of diffusion suggest the assimilation of innovation from outside a community or society. The BOP innovations, therefore, account for the limitations of DOI theory.

3 Research Method

Given the multiple voices and fragmentation of literature surrounding the concepts of digital entrepreneurship, digital technologies and digital platforms with reference to emerging markets, a conceptual paper approach was deemed most ideal for mapping these contending views on these issues. To prevent conceptual clutter in the absence of empirical data, Gilson and Goldberg (2015) define a conceptual paper as one that transcends summarising recent research, by seeking to provide an integration of literature, add value to existing literature and highlight directions for future inquiry. While conceptual papers may not necessarily propose new theories at the construct level, they underscore some commonalities that build coherence in literature (Cropanzano, 2009). Therefore, the study employed the current state of literature on digital entrepreneurship in Africa to make sense of how digital technologies, digital platforms, digital artefacts and digital infrastructure could usher in digital entrepreneurship that leapfrogs Africa into the future. In the absence of testable empirical evidence, conceptual papers, therefore, seek to bridge existing theories by linking literature across disciplines to provide multi-level insights, and broaden the scope of our thinking. For this study, we sought to connect the aforesaid theories (DOI and BOP innovations), with digital entrepreneurship, digital technologies (i.e., digital tools and digital artefacts), digital phenomena (e.g., digital platforms, digital ventures) and practices (e.g., business model innovation, venture creation, venture capital) to leverage the pursuit and prospects of entrepreneurship in Africa in the future. Lastly, apart from providing a retrospective review, conceptual pieces must offer future directions oriented towards where the literature ought to be going based on where it has been (Gilson & Goldberg, 2015).

4 Related Studies

Digital Entrepreneurship: An Overview

Despite the prominence of digital entrepreneurship (DE) in the last decade (Ratten, 2022), the crafting of a precise definition remains a mirage. Essentially, the popular conception of DE emphasises the migration of components of or all business processes and activities from brick-and-mortar contexts to digital environments (Esmaeeli, 2011; Hull et al., 2007; Nambisan, 2016). In recent years, a more comprehensive definition of DE has flourished. For instance, the concept is defined as the process of entrepreneurial creation of digital value using various socio-technical digital enablers to support effective acquisition, processing, distribution and consumption of digital information (Sahut et al., 2019). At the vortex of DE is the appropriation of digital technologies such as digital artefacts, platforms, networks, digital infrastructure and practices to facilitate direct or computer-mediated interactions, competition and collaboration between service providers, entrepreneurs and innovators and customers. The popularity of DE manifests in the prevalence of do-it-yourself (DIY) digital platforms such Amazon, Facebook, Air BnB, Bolt, Uber and Alibaba, whose value creation and capture unfold through the interaction between suppliers and consumers in the digitally embedded ecosystem. The underpinning driver of DE is platiformisation, that is, a shift from individual products/services to platforms as intermediaries for transactions and for organising value-creation processes (e.g., Hagiu & Altman, 2017; Parker et al., 2016). The goal of platform owners is to encourage the formation of ecosystems of complementors that build their businesses on the platform and, thereby, create value for users (Jacobides et al., 2018; Nambisan et al., 2018).

- ***Home-Grown Innovation Hubs (ihubs)***

In the past years, there has been an exponential growth of innovation hubs (henceforth called ihubs or tech hubs) on the African continent. The World Bank estimated that there were 117 technology hubs on the continent in September 2015. Boasting of 618 active ihubs spanning Nigeria (85), South Africa (80), Egypt (56), Kenya (48) and Morocco (31) and Tunisia (Briterbridges, 2023), the development of ihubs is forecast to curve new technology-based industrialisation and growth trajectories for Africa going forward. Kelly (2014) documents that government-sponsored initiatives such as the Botswana Innovation Hub is an example of a public initiative emphasising a more sustainable model for advancing economic diversity and enhancing economic competitiveness of the nation with the assistance of World Bank reimbursable advisory services. He elaborates on the innovation hubs that facilitate entrepreneurial venture development and economic growth on the continent. For instance, while Smart Xchange in South Africa provides full-fledged ICT business incubators that avail office space for the growth of new start-ups, Hive

CoLab in Uganda, represents a pre-incubator that provides co-working spaces where entrepreneurs interact in shaping and refining their business ideas. While Jokkolabs, is another example of an innovation hub that adopted a franchise model, others have sourced external seed funding from commercial partners such as the Nokia Greenhouse Nairobi or from not-for-profit organisations such as infoDev's mobile applications labs (mLabs) in Nairobi and Pretoria (Kelly, 2014).

Prather and Akeledo (2020) highlights how LaStartup Factory, a digital hub in Morocco, exploited its networked connections with StartupSquare to establish the resilience of start-ups during Covid-19 period. Working with Maghreb Start-up Network, IncubMe (Algeria), EY Tunisia and LaStartup Factory sought to support start-ups that were rendering viable Covid-19 solutions and align them to potential investment opportunities. Through the Covid-19 Maghreb Bootcamp, 20 start-up projects were identified across the different economic sectors from Algeria, Libya, Morocco and Tunisia. This innovation hub supported businesses operating in health, food waste management and provided them with expertise. Through this hub's engagements with the finance ministry, some businesses were also matched and linked with angel investors in the country (Prather & Akeledo, 2020).

De Morais (2016) contends that by creating makerspaces for individual entrepreneurs to deploy their local expertise in devising solutions to global problems encountered in their own communities, ihubs in Africa are creating technologies, goods and services that have an indigene character. He elaborates that such hubs are the critical driving forces for import-substitution as they entice Africans to "buy African" products and services. Therefore, ihubs are envisaged to stimulate sustainable digital entrepreneurship in Africa by driving innovation inclusivity, facilitating investments in research and development, creating a single common market as envisioned by African Continental Free Trade Area (AfCFTA), leading to the realisation of the UN Sustainable Development Goals (SDGs) and the African Union Agenda 2063 (Ekeledo, 2020). While there is a heavy concentration of innovation hubs in South Africa, Nigeria, Egypt, Morocco and Kenya (Friedereci et al., 2020), the limited engagement of entrepreneurs at the BOP due to accessibility challenges and suboptimal relevance of their offerings presents opportunities for future digital entrepreneurship. The critical question is how these frugal innovations of indigene entrepreneurs can be elevated and harnessed to become mainstream and disruptive technologies of the future.

While many African governments have provided some limited relief to innovators and entrepreneurs to prevent the collapse of start-ups and ventures during Covid-19 (AfriLabs, 2021), the capacity of ihubs to provide tailored financial, technical and logistical support to African innovators and entrepreneurs to scale regionally and internationally remains an under-explored area. The ihubs in Africa have demonstrated some under-preparedness for internationalisation as they have not sufficiently tackled the structural bottlenecks of weak cross-border logistics, underdeveloped transport infrastructure, high tariffs, multiple language barriers and limited access to investment capital on the continent (AfriLabs, 2021).

- ***Web 3.0 Start-ups Including Platform Firms*** ("platifirms")

Another variant of forecasted digital technologies envisaged to propel sustainable digital entrepreneurship in Africa is Web 3.0 start-ups. These digital firms are web-enabled entities that facilitate the co-creation of materials (e.g., goods, products and services) with their partners and have disrupted the way transactions previously took place by supporting a coordination mechanism using digital technology (Ratten, 2022). They describe platforms that develop information technology infrastructure and include social media, mobile computing and e-commerce platforms (Ahmed et al., 2022). Web 3.0 platforms, therefore, are those self-generated digital spaces that allow web-based businesses to connect with one another and customers through communal interactions (Baig et al., 2022). In fact, there are three types of platforms. First, there are *innovation platforms* offered by Apple or Google, where entrepreneurs offer complementary goods or services within a digital ecosystem. Second, are *digital ecosystems* through which application developers such as Google Android or Apple iOS use to develop new products. Third, are those firms employing the *platform strategy* where third-party developers may work as competitors in digital ecosystems, emphasising the production of digital products (Baig et al., 2022).

Collectively, these platform types represent a self-regulated digital enterprise system in which relevant innovations are available to the ecosystem players, allowing indigene innovators and entrepreneurs an opportunity to construct their pathways socially and culturally to technology industrialisation. Therefore, the defining characteristics of digital platforms are the facilitation of interaction, including the opportunities for users to perform technologically mediated and technology-defined tasks (Cusumano et al., 2019; Dicuonzo et al., 2022). It is not surprising that platifirms such as Microsoft, Apple, Amazon and Alphabet were reported as the highly capitalised companies in 2018 (Cusumano et al., 2019), even though such potential is yet to materialise among African digital platifirms.

The prevalence of digital platforms has facilitated the scaling of agricultural and agro-processing activities in selected African countries. For instance, Ghana-based companies, Farmerline and Agrocenta, have exploited mobile and web technologies to facilitate provision of agricultural advice, weather information and financial tips to farmers (Ndung'u & Signé, 2020). In the same vein, their research elaborates that Zenvus, a Nigerian start-up, has employed digital platforms to avail information on the measurement and analysis of soil data to inform farmers on the right fertilizers to use and correct water amounts to apply for optimally irrigating their farms (Ndung'u & Signé, 2020).

Exploring the architecture of science, technology and innovation on the African continent, Mavhunga (2017) presents an impressive and comprehensive dashboard on indigenous and home-grown platforms that are addressing a plethora of issues from sale of agriculture commodities, market trading strategies for correct pricing of products and services. For instance, Ghanaian software developers in Accra have created "eSoko" (electronic market), an ICT platform that addresses various farming-related services ranging from prevailing market prices for agricultural products, weather forecasts and crop growing tips and business strategies relating to product marketing, market monitoring, supplying and sourcing. The Madagascar variant of this platform is Rural eMarket, a multilingual app that communicates market and pricing information and enhances access to markets for rural communities. Similarly, while the interactive platform, M-Shamba, renders production, harvesting, marketing, credit, weather and climate information to rice farmers using mobile devices in Kenya, the Nigerian-based Hello Tractor is a social enterprise that supplies rural draft power and addresses labour shortages among rural farmers by creating a network of "smart tractor" owners from which farmers obtain tillage or tractors via short message services (SMS) (Mavhunga, 2017).

The most prominent appropriations of Web 3.0-related technologies manifested in disaster management and control measures that were applied during the Covid-19 pandemic. For instance, Internet-based payment systems and electronic pass management were harnessed to enforce social distancing among travellers and limit the public's contact with essential workers during national lockdowns in Ethiopia and Sierra Leone (Further Africa, 2020; The Directorate of Science, Technology and Innovation, 2020). Similarly, drones connected to computer-based information management systems were employed to issue warnings and announcements and to question people loitering on the streets about their reasons for being out during lockdowns in South Africa, Morocco, Sierra Leone and Tunisia (AFP News Agency, 2020; BBC News, 2020; Directorate of Science, Technology and Innovation, 2020, Jordan, 2020). In Rwanda, a GIS system was used to track Covid-19 cases at the household levels, to assess the need for lockdown measures and other public-health interventions (International Monetary Fund, 2020). While these technology-mediated interventions demonstrate the capacity of technology in disease control and disaster management, the use of similar technologies can be extended to business development and expansion.

The popularity of Web 3.0 firms and platforms derive from entrepreneurs' ability to use them for all services from the generation of products to the selling and marketing them online (Chandna, 2022). Apart from enhancing a participatory culture among entrepreneurs and affording them opportunities for collaboration, Web 3.0 firms are also occupying a unique space in the co-creation of value and services. Ratten (2022) distinguishes between transactional digital platforms and innovation-based platforms and argues that each operate in a particular niche in the digital infrastructure. While transactional digital platforms emphasise connecting buyers with sellers in an online format (that is internet-based communication that benefits from online interaction) (De Reuver et al., 2018), innovative digital platforms include Airbnb and Amazon that started selling products to one main market then branched out to other endeavours (Ratten, 2022). Entrepreneurs specialising in software development, digital engineering and web designing capitalise on the wisdom of the crowds and participatory culture of the internet (e.g., their own expertise and those within their embedded networks) to develop solutions for their proprietary firms and consumers. In the same vein, creative platforms especially, self-publishing and video-sharing platforms, are hailed as an antidote to the exclusionary nature of creative industries (Gillespie, 2010; Steedman et al., 2022) and are creating new digital imaginaries in a techno-social world.

- ***Touchless Smart Technologies***

Vivid manifestations of touchless technologies found expression and were domesticated during the Covid-19 pandemic. Some examples of locally designed technology interventions for combating the spread of Covid-19 included contactless soap dispensers and solar-powered hand washing sinks that were utilised to promote hygiene in Senegal, Ethiopia, Ghana and Uganda (Maharana et al., 2021). Other technologies for delivering goods and products remotely included the full steam click-and-collect programmes run via customers' mobile applications adopted by Shoprite, Woolworths and Pick n Pay in South Africa (Dakora & Rambe, 2022). These innovations involved customers paying for their selected items electronically in parking bays and retail staff delivering such items in customers' car boots instantly. In this recent study, we also report on multiple digital merchandising and sales adopted by retail shops such as South Africa's retail giant, Shoprite's virtual grocery voucher, the launch of the digital business unit (ShopriteX) by Shoprite, Checkers Rush, a cashless and checkout-free store concept introduced in their retail stores (Dakora & Rambe, 2022).

Another variant of smart touchless technologies manifest in drones connected to sensors and other autonomous objects (e.g., driverless cars, chatbots, robots and GIS-based information) and face-recognition technologies. For instance, Ethiopia developed mobile phone applications for recording personal identification information and temperature at ports of entry, and Covid-19 surveillance systems harnessed this information for contact tracing activities (Wild, 2020). In South Africa, a technology used for identifying rhinoceros poaching hotspots was repurposed for capturing health and location data to spot new Covid-19 case clusters in communities (JSI, 2020; Maharana et al., 2021). One would assume that the affordances of smart touchless technologies can be repurposed by indigene entrepreneurs and innovators to create new business innovation models that generate and capture value for small digital businesses. In the digital space, therefore, while top-down digital approaches can be harnessed to provide high-level direction to digital enterprise development and value creation, bottom-up approaches can enable the adaptation of digital initiatives to local settings while providing feedback to policymakers to improve national digital policies (Mamphiswana & Bekele, 2020). For instance, how indigene entrepreneurs can harness the possibilities of a just energy transition by using renewable energy sources to power their innovations and facilitate value capture, is the open-ended question that demands deeper scrutiny in digital entrepreneurship literature.

- *Crypto Hedge Funds for Digital Asset Management*

Having articulated technologies and platforms on the horizon in Africa that are yet to enjoy ubiquitous access and universal application, this chapter turns its attention to digital phenomena that are likely to take the African continent by storm. For instance, blockchain technologies especially cryptocurrencies and distributed ledgers, are expected to be the next big frontier on the African digital entrepreneurship space. For instance, as a major innovation in decentralised finance (DeFi), cryptocurrencies' total market capitalisation stood at $2.2 trillion while the total locked value in DeFi protocols grew by over 1000% year over year in December 2021 (Aggarwal & Salangsang, 2022).

One of the key aspects of DeFi is hedge funds. Bajulaiye et al. (2020) define hedge funds as entities managed by a team of skilled professional advisers, experts in company analysis and portfolio management, offering investors a range of investment opportunities. They elaborate that such fund managers employ multiple strategies and trading instruments such as debt, equity, options, futures, foreign currencies including high-risk investment strategies, restructurings, credit derivatives and currency trading, to obtain superior returns for their funds (Bajulaiye et al., 2020). In recent years, trading in crypto assets, originally dominated by private investors, has been overtaken by hedge fund managers (Bernegger, 2020). Evidence suggests that of the 150 largest global crypto hedge funds, the most popular crypto hedge fund strategy is quantitative (48% of funds), followed by discretionary long-only (19%), discretionary long/short (17%) and multi-strategy (17%) (Annual PwC–Elwood Crypto Hedge Fund Report, 2020). The report demonstrates that pertaining to crypto fund performance, systematic crypto funds have been outperforming passive strategies (investing long-only), discretionary long/short and multi-strategies significantly.

The Capital Law Fund Group blog highlights that digital asset hedge fund managers are using a complex amalgam of fundamental and quantitative strategies to manage funds, which range from index and token-specific funds, long-only funds, algorithmic quant funds and node funds.

It elaborates that apart from investing directly in crypto asset tokens, funds can invest indirectly, using options and futures, as well as through income-generating assets inherent in technology and in liquid securities issued by public companies that hold crypto assets (https://www.capitalfundlaw.com/blog/crypto-funds-strategy). In short, the future of African digital entrepreneurship lies in hedge asset fund managers that are investing in crypto assets and the capacity of African entrepreneurs to invest into this space persistently will change the complexity of digital entrepreneurship. This is critical to developing digital enterprises because crypto currencies emphasise data ownership and control, allowing users (entrepreneurs) to discern and evaluate information using AI and contextualised analysis to bring more entrepreneurially relevant results and better decision-making (Aggarwal & Salangsang, 2022).

In the South African context, one of the innovative approaches to growing digital assets is using cryptocurrency as a hedge against inflation. In such a volatile emerging market, crypto currency has been employed not only as a panacea to addressing bottom-line challenges but also resolving complex business challenges (e.g., business liquidity, credibility, paying for alternative energy sources) that the South Africa businesses are confronted with (Panchia, 2023). In view of the volatility of the South African rand, cryptocurrency especially stablecoins (backed by the US dollar) has kept finances protected from devaluation (e.g., by storing funds in USDT or earning in other stable tokens like USDC). Moreover, cryptocurrencies are now serving as potent tools for socio-economic development by facilitating low-cost remittances and microloans (Panchia, 2023).

5 New Frontiers and Prospects

Although decentralised finance, central bank digital currencies, global supply chain configurations and green certified cities are established technologies and concepts in the developed world, they are only beginning to take root in developing countries. For instance, research suggests that although there has been a surging interest by African central banks in central bank decentralised currencies (CBDCs) in recent times, many such CBDCs are only at trial stages and few projects of this nature are at advanced stages (Alberola & Mattei, 2022). For this purpose, these technologies and concepts are discussed under new frontiers and prospects for the digitalised entrepreneurship on the African continent.

- **Decentralised Finance**

Decentralised finance (DeFi) constitutes a different financial architecture in which financial record keeping is centralised but access to the system is anonymous and unrestricted and any form of intermediation could be premised on it (Makarov & Schoar, 2022). They elaborate that DeFi such as blockchain architecture are credited with eliminating unnecessary intermediaries, improving efficiencies of financial systems and stimulating competition among players within the financial system. As a form of decentralised ledger technology, blockchain constitutes a secure data system for storing data, in which all peers share the same copy of a database called the ledger, without the intervention of any central authority (Nair et al., 2022). As a service that operates on blockchain technology, DeFi is credited with eliminating delays and failure of intermediaries, diminishing the cost of transactions and reducing credit risk when used in lending (Atlam et al., 2018; Garg et al., 2021; Ozili, 2022c). By availing different lending options to entrepreneurs at the bottom of the pyramid, DeFi presents a germane strategy for mainstreaming such entrepreneurs into financial ecosystems, especially those entrepreneurs excluded from traditional banking systems.

By providing a decentralised information-sharing system in which there are specific audit trails of downloaded files within the DeFi ecosystem, it is envisaged that such technology will allow digital entrepreneurs to resort to such evidence in dispute resolution and forensics (Baygin & Karakose, 2021). Moreover, for digital health entrepreneurs availing services through online platforms, the use of DeFi presents a reconfigured business model that increases the participation and engagement of participants in their health well-being. As a centralised information-sharing initiative, DeFi allows patients to regulate the authorised sharing of their health data by employing an attribute-based encryption scheme in a distributed file system (Nair et al., 2022).

Yet the appropriation and deployment of DeFi in the financial and entrepreneurial ecosystem is not foolproof. For instance, DeFi such as blockchain technologies are not insulated from malware, is susceptible to volatility of currencies, money laundering and financial fraud. The collapse of the cryptocurrency exchange firm FTX following the withdrawal of investor funds and the subsequent incarceration of its founder Sam Bankman-Fried, is another typical example of the damaged credibility and loss of trust in DeFi such as cryptocurrencies.

- **Central Bank Digital Currencies**

As literature suggests, a central bank digital currency (CBDC) is digital money denominated in the national unit of account and a liability of the central bank (BIS, 2021). Bitter (2020) defines it as a potentially interest bearing, centrally issued, account-based, digital type of central bank liability that is accessible to the public. The motivations for introducing central bank decentralised currencies are bolstering the public good nature of the monetary system through enhancing safe, low-cost and inclusive payments, while simultaneously promoting innovation (Alberola & Mattei, 2022). Given the high costs of using cash by entrepreneurs, the use of digital currencies not only diminish the transactional costs of using hard cash, but also reduce the risk of carrying cash in emerging markets where armed robberies and cash heists are rampant. Digital currencies do not only augment access to financial systems for entrepreneurs located at the bottom of the pyramid but also reduce the astronomical cost of accessing hard cash.

The use of digital currencies has contributed to greater financial inclusion though digital payments innovation (Ozili, 2022a), preserving financial stability and increasing the contestability of payments (Engert & Fung, 2017) and the need to curb illicit cryptocurrency-induced criminal activities (Ozili, 2022b). The CBDC has also been advanced as a rival currency to privately operating cryptocurrencies such as Bitcoin and Lira. Other benefits of CBDC for those at the bottom of the pyramid are the accommodation of poor people through e-wallets issued by financial agents, reduction of demands for cash through interest-bearing CBDC (Andolfatto, 2021) and the elimination of the need for a digital account (Ozili, 2022b).

In terms of national participation, Nigeria has issued a retail CBDC, the eNaira, and Ghana and South Africa are running retail and wholesale pilot projects respectively (Alberola & Mattei, 2022). Therefore, evidence suggests an incipient adoption of CBDC on the African continent, which demonstrates that this phenomenon is envisaged to take the continent by storm in the coming years. For instance, Ozili (2022a, 2022b, 2022c) reports that by 2021, while 4 African countries had reached the pilot test stage of central bank digital currency adoption, 3 African countries had a robust payment system infrastructure that could support central bank digital currency. This demonstrates that although adoption has been sluggish, some traction is on the horizon.

Yet the use of CBDC is not without its shortcomings as there are still many grey areas. For instance, apart from developing coherent policies and procedures on the management of CBDC, banks still must invest in developing cybersecurity skills and integrate cyber risk protection in their decision-making processes (Ndung'u & Signé, 2020). Evidence of the lack of clarity and uncertainty around such currencies manifests in some countries re-introducing such currencies after some unilateral bans. For instance, Onyango (2021) animates that after a four-year ban, the Moroccan Central Bank established an exploratory committee to determine the benefits and drawbacks of a regulated digital currency ecosystem to its economy. Moreover, Tunisia is exploring ways to advance its e-dinar, a blockchain-based digital version of the Tunisian dinar that has been on issuance through the government's post office over the last five years (Onyango, 2021).

- **Global Supply Chain Reconfigurations**

The advent of Covid-19 exposed the under-preparedness of African countries to handle crises of greater magnitude, the fragility of their health supply infrastructure and unreliability of global supply chains. To compound this challenge, the war in Ukraine and the blockage of the Black Sea and Egyptian Suez Canal that served as a grain, oil and iron vessels gateway from Europe to other parts of the world further exposed the food insecurity of the African continent, necessitating a rethinking of the global supply and value chains of basic cereals and other health necessities. A value chain denotes a constellation of organisational arrangements and firms that are interconnected through a global network (De Marchi et al., 2014). As a derivation of value chains, global value chain is defined as "the full range of activities that firms and workers perform to bring a product from its conception to end use and beyond," that are executed on a global scale and that can be undertaken by one or more firms (Gereffi & Fernandez-Stark, 2011, p. 4; Hernández & Pedersen, 2017).

While global value chains have been discussed from the perspective of governance types (Buckley & Strange, 2015), business strategy and upgrading (especially the performance of high value added activities) (Armando et al., 2016), role of digitisation in participation in global value chains (Gopalan et al., 2022), a comprehensive review of the literature dealing with the state of the art of the global value chain configuration is yet to emerge (Hernández & Pedersen, 2017). Therefore, there is a compelling need to explore the extent to which a reconfiguration of global supply chains could increase the availability of global supply of raw materials, commodities and products, especially for under-served communities lying at the bottom of the pyramid. As such, digital entrepreneurs must explore pathways for the enhancement of entire value chains, identify value chain activities causing slack in resources and unwarranted costs, as well as those that optimise value generation, delivery and capture.

Following the reasoning that developing countries are entrapped in low living standards, embedded in lower radar technologies and are lagging in terms of productivity (Jurowetzki et al., 2018), the reconfiguration of global chains is likely to increase technology-based industrialisation by promoting ethical sourcing of raw materials, fair labour practices and eliminating waste by adopting efficiency enhancement strategies. By augmenting the potential for entrepreneurial learning by embracing opportunities for experimentation and trial and error from sourcing to delivery of commodities, products and services, the reconfiguration of global chains is forecasted to leapfrog African digital entrepreneurs in their innovation and creativity trajectories. Since entrepreneurship and venture development may not exhibit any fixed directionality in their development trajectories, there will be limited scope to transplant successful development strategies from advanced countries contexts to emerging economies (Lundvall & Lema, 2014). As such, Africa's new entrepreneurial development trajectory needs to account for and accommodate disruptions and improvements in global supply chains.

Yet evidence of inquiry into the configuration of global chains is an oxymoron. For instance, the upgrading of products and processes has often co-existed with downgrading, exposure to greater risks and diminished returns on capital in traditional export markets (Ponte & Ewert, 2009). Moreover, evidence suggests that the upgrading of value chains is often restricted to activities that have low value add, especially those in manufacturing (Armando et al., 2016; Navas-Alemán, 2011) and exclude high value addition in other sectors.

- **Green Certified Cities**

The building of inclusive digital economies does not only require Africa to address its energy and digital poverty but build more resilient and sustainable cities by allowing digital entrepreneurs to partner with various stakeholders such urban city planners, government policymakers, local authorities, venture capitalists and communities in building resilient and inclusive cities. Apart from advancing a just energy transition through developing sustainable energy combinations that infuse renewable energy sources into the grid, the phasing out of dated energy sources such as coal, is a critical long-term imperative for realising green certified cities. Since the centralisation of energy solutions has crippled Africa from delivering reliable and affordable energy supply and access to all, digital entrepreneurs are compelled to devise decentralised renewable and low-carbon energy solutions that accommodate and connect communities under-served or excluded from energy supply by national governments (South African Institute of International Affairs (SAIIA), 2014). Therefore, the realisation of green energy cities necessitates the equalisation of access to reliable and affordable energy services to create an inclusive digital economy, the subsidization of high-speed internet services and increased broadband and incentivisation of cost reductions through scalable corporate partnerships (SAIIA, 2014). The creation of sustainable smart cities calls into question the appropriation and domestication of technologies that employ deep learning, face-recognition, biometric data-based and touchless smart technologies to create a digital footprint in which air quality, temperature, humidity, sunshine and rainfall distribution and intensity in buildings are centrally controlled by these agile and flexible modernised technologies.

6 Opportunities

Transparent and Cost-Effective Financial Transactions

Although academic literature on DeFi remains very scant, less rigorous and fails to provide significant analysis that facilitates future forecasting activities in decentralised finance markets (Ozili, 2022a), the use of smart contracts creates protocols that replicate existing financial services in a more open, interoperable and transparent way (Schar, 2021). Resonating with this notion of decentralising access to meaningful financial products and services is the argument that nascent digital entrepreneurs especially those at the bottom of the pyramid without physical assets can exploit such DeFi transactions at minimum transactional costs. Moreover, the risk of financial loss (e.g., robberies) through carrying cash is eliminated and the opportunities of increasing financial liquidity of cash-strapped entrepreneurs are augmented. Decentralised financial products such as crypto-backed loans, interest-paying crypto savings accounts, smart contracts, staking and stablecoins (Ozili, 2022a, 2022b, 2022c) are typical examples of strategies for availing financial opportunities with implications for increasing liquidity and the scale of business operations of digital entrepreneurs.

Business Model Innovation

The use of digitalisation processes such as CBDC is envisaged to enable entrepreneurs and businesses to rethink business models that are more impactful, sustainable and connected to other sectors of the economy (Ndung'u & Signé, 2020). Therefore, the benefits of digitalisation have been extended beyond the financial sector to include real estate sector and households, transforming product designs and business models across market segments (Ndung'u, 2018) while widening opportunities for savings for African entrepreneurs. For digital entrepreneurs, the exploitation of such opportunities is envisaged to increase value creation and capture for their start-ups by widening the payment options for those struggling to pay through hard cash.

The opportunities of CBDC are rooted in digital inclusion of the financially excluded entrepreneurs and communities. With reference to Ghana's retail CBDC, the e-Cedi, Fuje et al. (2022) highlight that it avails financial services to people without bank accounts (e.g., if designed for offline use) who have a digital wallet app or a contactless smart card that can be used offline. Using this payment method, CBDCs could bring financial services to people who previously did not have bank accounts, especially if designed for offline use. As such, CBDCs democratise access to digital transactions at little or no cost and can be harnessed for distributing targeted welfare payments among citizens (including entrepreneurs) located in remote areas without internet access but who use simple feature phones (Fuje et al., 2022). In the African context where international transactions are quite costly, CBDC can be exploited to facilitate cross-border transactions and facilitate fast clearance of payments at relatively low cost. These efficiencies can also directly contribute to refinements in business model innovation through improvements in value generation, capture and delivery.

Building Digital Entrepreneurship Around Climate-Resilient Infrastructure

Since buildings especially those located in urban areas account for 30% of global energy consumption and 28% of energy-related carbon emissions, city planners and entrepreneurs are compelled to provide resilient urban infrastructure that not only reduce carbon emissions, respond to extreme weather events, reduce waste but also preserve natural resources while still providing critical infrastructure and resources (Straton, 2022). Therefore, digital entrepreneurs operating in the architectural, urban planning and sustainable city spaces must strive to contribute to green-citied cities, that draw on smart energy and digital solutions that provide smart parking, water, light and air quality supply and broadband internet connections, while avoiding space wastage, water leakages, air pollution drawing on smart technology data. Those in logistics businesses can build electronic logistics and tracking systems and smart business solutions that provide more resilient infrastructure and services with a lower-carbon footprint. As digital technologies present opportunities for smart cities to develop systems that mitigate or positively respond to chronic stresses (e.g., global pandemics, flooding, hurricanes, wildfires, disruptions to essential services), entrepreneurs' digital transformation initiatives must open opportunities for sustainable cities and green infrastructure such as green spaces, energy-efficient buildings and greater investments in more sustainable energy sources (Straton, 2022).

7 Challenges

Power Differentials in Value Chain Stakeholders

The intersection between digital entrepreneurship and facilitation of global value chains seems contradictory at first glance as these concepts are informed by different premises and assumptions. For instance, while entrepreneurial learning, which is the force driving innovation ecosystems (Lundvall, 2010) upon which digital entrepreneurship is premised tends to require stakeholders' engagement on an equal footing with government creating conditions for business to thrive, the execution of global value chains involve asymmetrical relations of power between large corporations with weakly capacitated developing countries' governments playing an insignificant role (Gereffi, 2014). Therefore, reconciling the assumptions of democratic participation and agency in innovation ecosystems (as a driver of digital entrepreneurship) with the complex reproduction of asymmetrical power inherent in global value chains remains a challenge for digital entrepreneurs as they strive to deploy digital technology to augment value creation, generation and capture.

Suboptimal Operational Agility and Resilience

Despite the capacity of digital enterprises to cope with environmental stresses, their success in realising long-term sustainability is tied to the operational agility and resilience of their context of operation. Straton (2022) observes that sustainability in delivering digital entrepreneurship is not a given as it is dependent on the capacity of individuals to share critical data across different service platforms such as city management, emergency services, utilities and residents using industrial information management. The use of smart intelligent tools and technologies that avail information in real time could promote the resilience of such cities and improve service provision in such contexts.

8 Implications for Theory

Ambivalent View of Technology

Following the Diffusion of Innovation Theory, we established two contending views of technology adoption that support digital entrepreneurship, namely determinist view and the instrumentalist view. From a determinist view of technology, technology assets, infrastructure, artefacts and networks are projected as a force triggering social progress and a stimulant for disruptive innovations (Cua, 2012). In our case, we demonstrated tech hubs as vehicles for triggering the transformation of economies through their support for import-substitution, the incubation of new ventures and the stimulation of indigenous innovations coming from entrepreneurs located at the bottom of the pyramid. Simultaneously, the Diffusion of Innovation Theory presented an instrumentalist view of technology, in which technology is projected as a tool that can be harnessed in line with organisational vision to realise predetermined ends (Rambe & Nel, 2014; Tonnies, 2001). Consistent with this argument, technologies such as those emanating from innovation hubs are conceived by firms, international organisations, governments and regional bodies as African Continental Free Trade Area (AfCFTA), East African Community and Southern African Development Community as conduits for economic transformation of economies, facilitating international free trade and the realisation of Sustainable Development Goals (SDGs such as regional industrialisation), inter-country investments and trans-frontier migrations. Our evidence provides theoretical backing for ambivalent views of technology in which socio-technical artefacts, networks and practices are conceived as an amalgam of facilitators and disruptors of economic processes and activities. The Diffusion of Innovation Theory provided evidence for both technology as a driver (or complementor) of digital entrepreneurship and social progress (e.g., employment creation, economic development, foreign direct investment and poverty reduction) while pointing to the limitations of technology in advancing cross-border logistics and inability to address international trade barriers were also acknowledged. While the instrumentalist view emphasises the capacity of technology to facilitate the "rationalisation" of capitalist social formations to improve instrumental efficiency in modern institutional forms and capitalist economies (e.g., improve productivity, drive social change), the dystopian view emphasises technologies and machines that stir innovations as extensions of new levels of productive power and sources of physical suffering (e.g., deskilling, reduction of workers' control over production process and their subordination to a new source of authority and domination and exploitation) (Feenberg, 2002; Kirkpatrick, 2020).

As a middle-ground approach between instrumental and dystopian views, the ambivalent view of platifirms demonstrated that while digital technologies (e.g., platifirms) facilitated the production of digital goods, development of digital innovation ecosystems that intensify interaction between customers and platform owners and the marketing of agricultural commodities, the same technologies also constrain human agency and consequences. For instance, as technological artefacts and digital technologies, platifirms are vehicles that undermine workers' agency (e.g., capacity for self-determination and to unionise) and compromise workers at the point of production as they foster job insecurity by reducing the cost of production (i.e., reducing the wage bill by shedding employees and getting machinery to do the work instead) of firms (Kirkpatrick,

2020). Moreover, the asymmetrical relations of power that global supply chains create between global conglomerates and customers facilitated by digital technologies point to the reality that the infusion of technologies in digital entrepreneurship does not only advance operational efficiencies and access to global markets but also undermine egalitarian relations between stakeholders in global value chains.

Implications for Policy

In view of the concerns about ihubs' inability to address identified structural bottlenecks of weak cross-border logistics, underdeveloped transport infrastructure, high tariffs, multiple language barriers and limited access to investment capital, policy interventions that address these key issues would be necessary to facilitate the advancement of digital entrepreneurship on the African continent. The stimulating role of digital technologies and innovations in facilitating faster clearances of cross-border goods and raw materials, African states' greater investment in digital infrastructure that expedites the processing of goods and commodities at national borders including the elimination of bureaucracy would be critical to addressing these hurdles. Atiase et al. (2020) emphasise the need for African governments to invest heavily in innovation hubs to increase their efficiency in generating economic and social value particularly, creating new jobs through venture creation, stimulating entrepreneurial ecosystems and developing new solutions to supply and value chains.

Given the severity of institutional voids such as unreliable electricity supply, unstable internet connectivity, poor road infrastructure, stifling bureaucracy and incoherent policies, a broader cross-national institutional framework that address these social vices must be established to create a germane environment in which digital entrepreneurship can thrive in the future. Multi-sectoral and multi-regional investments in just energy transition to the exploitation of renewables, rehabilitation of dilapidated road infrastructure through establishing integrated trans-frontier corridors, creating one-stop shops for investment promotion and policy consistency on protection of private property would be non-negotiables to creating sustainable digital entrepreneurship on the continent.

In view of the controversy surrounding the crypto assets including the money laundering and fraud that surrounds this unregulated space, there has been growing calls for national governments to rethink how to rein in such activities unfolding in the cryptocurrency terrain. Since the popularity of cryptocurrencies lie in their unregulated nature, a middle-of-the-road approach that sustains such unfettered access to wealth creation while protecting the privacy and security of personal information including the use of collectively generated information would be necessary. Policies that emphasise information security, sanctioned and responsible use of collectively generated personal information would be critical to the success of digital entrepreneurship.

Implications for Practice

Although digital platforms as expressions of digital entrepreneurship have taken root in Africa especially in agricultural value chains (e.g., input production, manufacturing, marketing and value addition), the magnitude of their impact in other sectors is still to be felt. Therefore, African digital platifirms especially those that use indigenous knowledge and expertise must strive for the commercialisation of such knowledge, the beneficiation and value addition of commodities and products made from such knowledge and the creation of global value chains from such knowledge. African firms that draw on indigenous knowledge from surrounding communities must strive to create some value proposition and business models drawing on local and practical knowledge, which meet their needs and add value to their business operations (Coetzee et al., 2012; Khane et al., 2011).

Even though most touchless technologies developed during and post-Covid-19 were framed around remote contact, face recognition, biometric data monitoring across different sectors (e.g., agriculture, health, retail and banking), these innovations were too fragmented and uncoordinated to stimulate global impact across regions and nations. National government, private sector, NGOs, academic institutions and research councils are exhorted to conduct some situational and impact analysis to identify those trialled technologies that are scalable, traceable, replicable and interoperable across platforms to determine those that can be rollout at larger scale at regional and national levels. Some collaborations in which government think tanks advise on scalable technologies with demonstrable impact, industrialists and venture capitalists sponsor such innovations, while the private sector facilitates the implementation of such technologies would be imperative. As Atiase et al. (2020) rightly observe, sustainable productive partnerships require industry to produce products for experimentation, while communities avail local knowledge about themselves and the market in which they operate to support the design of technologies that meet their needs.

Implications for Future Research

In view of the popularity of DeFi, especially central bank digital currencies at national level, the possibility of implementing a continent digital currency needs to be explored. Given the complexity of trading on the African continent due to multiple currencies, the development of a common digital currency would ease the complexities of cross-border trade and minimise transactional costs across borders. Therefore, future research needs to explore the feasibility of establishing such currency, the legal and administrative constraints and the economic possibilities to be ushered in by such innovations.

9 Research Limitations

The application of conceptual papers is not without its constraints. While we devoted effort to authenticating our sources by relying on mainstream peer-reviewed published literature, we were conscious that sometimes we drew on a limited range of grey literature such as blog posts from experts in innovation and entrepreneurship. While one would question the credibility and authority of such grey literature, we would assume that since such experts have a moral duty to protect their reputation through the appropriateness of the scholarly literature they generate, they are compelled to reflect on the impact of their writing.

10 Conclusion

The study drew on Diffusion of Innovation Theory and Bottom of the Pyramid Innovation as theoretical and conceptual lenses for exploring the range of technologies that would drive digital entrepreneurship in the future including phenomenon that hold promise for sustainable digital entrepreneurship on the continent. The study postulated that the future of digital entrepreneurship in Africa is fuelled by home-grown ihubs that commercialise digital innovations, the vitality of Web 3.0 start-ups, prevalence of touchless smart technologies and crypto hedge funds. In terms of phenomena that would dominate the future of digital entrepreneurship, DeFi, CBDC and global supply chain configurations, were identified as mega trends to anticipate on the sustainable digital entrepreneurship horizon. The study proposed future research to zoom into the commercialisation of indigenous innovations and the creation of innovation and entrepreneurship ecosystems that facilitate, monitor and track trialled technologies to establish those that can be rollout at larger scale at regional and national levels.

References

Adam, N. A., & Alarifi, G. (2021). Innovation practices for survival of small and medium enterprises (SMEs) in the COVID-19 times: The role of external support. *Journal of Innovation and Entrepreneurship, 10*, 15. https://doi.org/10.1186/s13731-021-00156-6

AFP News Agency. (2020). *Morocco launches fleet of drones to tackle virus from the sky*. AFP—YouTube. https://www.youtube.com/watch?v=Sz5bOnEP8Vk&ab_channel=AFPNewsAgency. May 6, 2020.

AfriLabs. (2021). *Building a resilient innovative Africa*. Djembe Consultants.

Aggarwal, N., & Salangsang, D. (2022). *How DeFi and Web 3.0 will shape the future of finance*. https://www.theasianbanker.com/updates-and-articles/decentralised-finance-and-web-3.0-shaping-the-future-of-financial-services. Posted January 12, 2022.

Ahmed, A., Bhatti, S. H., G¨olgeci, I., & Arslan, A. (2022). Digital platform capability and organizational agility of emerging market manufacturing SMEs: The mediating role of intellectual capital and the moderating role of environmental dynamism. *Technological Forecasting and Social Change, 177*, Article 121513.

Alberola, E., & Mattei, I. (2022, November). *Central bank digital currencies in Africa* (BIS Papers No 128). Monetary and Economic Department. Bank for International Settlements.

Andolfatto, D. (2021). Assessing the impact of central bank digital currency on private banks. *The Economic Journal, 131*(634), 525–540.

Armando, E., Azevedo, A. C., Fischmann, A. A., & Pereira, C. E. (2016). Business strategy and upgrading in global value chains: A multiple case study in information technology firms of Brazilian origin. *RAI Revista De Administração e Inovação, 13*(1), 39–47.

Atiase, V., Kolade, O., & Liedong, T. (2020). The emergence and strategy of tech hubs in Africa: Implications for knowledge production and value creation. *Technological Forecasting and Social Change, 161*. https://doi.org/10.1016/j.techfore.2020.120307

Atlam, H. F., Alenezi, A., Alassafi, M. O., & Wills, G. (2018). Blockchain with internet of things: Benefits, challenges, and future directions. *International Journal of Intelligent Systems, 10*(6), 40–48.

Annual PwC–Elwood Crypto Hedge Fund Report. (2020). *2020 Crypto hedge fund report*. https://www.pwc.com/gx/en/financial-services/pdf/pwc-elwood-annual-crypto-hedge-fund-report-may-2020.pdf

Awuah, G., Gebrekidan, D., & Osarenkhoe, A. (2007). *Interactive internationalization—The case of Swedish firms*. University of Gävle.

Baig, U., Hussain, B., Meidute-Kavaliauskiene, L., & Davidavicius, S. (2022). Digital entrepreneurship: Future research directions and opportunities for new business model. *Sustainability, 14*(9), 5004. https://doi.org/10.3390/su14095004

Bajulaiye, O., Fenwick, M., Skultetyova, I., & Vermeulen, E. (2020). Digital transformation in the hedge fund and private equity industry. *European Corporate Governance Institute (ECGI) Working Paper Series in Law N°504/2020 March 2020*. https://ssrn.com/abstract=3528068

Baygin, N., & Karakose, M. (2021). Copyright chain: Permissioned blockchain-based collaboration and design right using hyperledger composer and IPFS. *International Journal of Computer Application, 183*(2), 19–26.

BBC News. (2020). Coronavirus: Tunisia deploys police robot on lockdown patrol. *BBC News*. https://www.bbc.com/news/world-africa-52148639. Posted April 3, 2020.

Bernegger, M. P. (2020). *The emergence of cryptocurrency hedge funds*. https://cfc-stmoritz.com/blog/the-emergence-of-cryptocurrency-hedge-funds. Posted September 20, 2020.

BIS. (2021, June). *BIS Papers No 116 CBDCs beyond borders: Results from a survey of central banks*.

Bitter, L. (2020). *Banking crises under a central bank digital currency (CBDC)*. VfS Annual Conference 2020 (Virtual conference): Gender economics 224600, Verein für Socialpolitik / German Economic Association.

Briterbridges. (2023). *618 active tech hubs in Africa*. The Backbone of Africa's Tech Ecosystem. https://briterbridges.com/618-active-tech-hubs

Buckley, P. J., & Strange, R. (2015). The governance of the global factory: Location and control of world economic activity. *Academy of Management Perspectives, 29*(2), 237–249.

Capital Law Fund Group: Crypto-Asset Hedge Fund Investment Strategies. https://www.capitalfundlaw.com/blog/crypto-funds-strategy

Cenamor, C., & Frishammar, J. (2021). Openness in platform ecosystems: Innovation strategies for complementary products. *Research Policy, 50*(1). https://doi.org/10.1016/j.respol.2020.104148

Chandna, V. (2022). Social entrepreneurship and digital platforms: Crowdfunding in the sharing-economy era. *Business Horizons, 65*(1), 21–31.

Coetzee, H., Toit, I.-M., & Herselman, M. (2012). Living labs in South Africa: An analysis based on five case studies. *The Electronic Journal for Virtual Organizations and Networks, 14*, 1–29. http://hdl.handle.net/10204/6082
Cropanzano, R. (2009). Writing nonempirical articles for journal of management: General thoughts and suggestions. *Journal of Management, 35*, 1304–1311.
Cua, F. C. (2012). Applying 'business case' construct using the diffusion of innovations theory framework: Empirical case study in higher education. In Y. K. Dwivedi, M. Wade, & S. Schneberger (Eds.), *Information systems theory: Explaining and predicting our digital society Vol 1 Integrated series in information systems* (pp. 303–333). Springer.
Cusumano, M. A., Gawer, A., & Yoffie, D. B. (2019). *The business of platforms: Strategy in the age of digital competition, innovation, and power.* Harper Business.
Dakora, E., & Rambe, P. (2022). The digital transformation of food and grocery retailing under the Covid-19 pandemic: A case of major South African retailers. *The Retail and Marketing Review, 18*(1), 59–75.
Dearing, J., & Cox, J. (2018). Diffusion of innovations theory, principles, and practice. *Health Affairs, 37*(2), 183–190.
De Marchi, V., Di Maria, E., & Ponte, S. (2014). Multinational firms and the management of international networks: The contribution of studies on global value chains. In T. Pedersen, M. Venzin, T. M. Devinney, & L. Tihanyi (Eds.), *Orchestration of the global network organization: Advances in international management* (Vol. 27, pp. 463–486). Emerald Group Publishing Limited.
De Morais, J-C. B. (2016). *Are Africa's innovation hubs helping innovators realise their full potential?* Ventureburn. https://ventureburn.com/2016/11/are-africas-innovation-hubs-helping-innovators-realise-their-full-potential/. Accessed March 15, 2023.
De Reuver, M., Sørensen, C., & Basole, R. C. (2018). The digital platform: A research agenda. *Journal of Information Technology, 33*, 124–135.
Dicuonzo, G., Donofrio, F., Antonio Fusco, A., & Ranaldo, S. (2022). The role of transformational entrepreneurship in managing a digital platform: The case of Yamamay. *Journal of Strategy and Management, 15*(3), 434–449.
Directorate of Science, Technology and Innovation. (2020). *Sierra Leone joins Africa's tech nations to deploy drones for COVID-19 Response—DSTI*. https://www.dsti.gov.sl/sierra-leone-joins-africas-tech-nations-to-deploy-drones-for-covid-19-response/. Posted April 16, 2020.
Ekeledo, A. (2020). *Introduction: Building a resilient innovative Africa*. Djembe Consultants and AfriLabs.
El Malouf, N., & Bahemia, H. (2023). Diffusion of innovations: A review. In S. Papagiannidis (Ed.), *Theory hub book.* http://open.ncl.ac.uk/ISBN: 9781739604400

Engert, W., & Fung, B. S. C. (2017). *Central bank digital currency: Motivations and implications* (Bank of Canada Staff Discussion Paper, No. 16).

Esmaeeli, H. (2011). The study of effecting factors on digital entrepreneurship. *Journal of Contemporary Research in Business, 2*(12), 163–172.

Feenberg, A. (2002). *Transforming technology a critical theory revisited*. Oxford University Press.

Friedereci, N., Wahome, M., & Graham, M. (2020). *Digital entrepreneurship in Africa: How a continent is escaping Silicon Valley's long shadow*. The MIT Press.

Fuje, H., Quayyum, S., & Ouattara, F. (2022). *More African central banks are exploring digital currencies IMF blog*. Posted June 24, 2022.

Further Africa. (2020). *Ethiopia announces internet-based transportation payment service—Further Africa*. https://furtherafrica.com/2020/06/23/ethiopia-announces-internet-based-transportation-payment-service. Posted June 23, 2020.

Garg, P., Gupta, B., Chauhan, A. K., Sivarajah, U., Gupta, S., & Modgil, S. (2021). Measuring the perceived benefits of implementing blockchain technology in the banking sector. *Technology Forecasting and Social Change, 163*, 120407. https://doi.org/10.1016/j.techfore.2020.120407

Gereffi, G. (2014). Global value chains in a post-Washington consensus world. *Review of International Political Economy, 21*(1), 9–37.

Gereffi, G., & Fernandez-Stark, K. (2011). *Global value chain analysis: A primer.* Centre on Globalization, Governance & Competitive-ness (CGGC), Duke University, North Carolina, USA.

Ghezzi, A., Cortimiglia, M. N., & Frank, A. G. (2015). Strategy and business model design in dynamic telecommunications industries: A study on Italian mobile network operators. *Technological Forecasting and Social Change, 90*, 346–354.

Gidden, A. (1990). *The consequences of modern society*. Polity Press.

Gillespie, T. (2010). The politics of 'platforms.' *New Media and Society, 12*(3), 347–364. https://doi.org/10.1177/1461444809342738

Gilson, L., & Goldberg, C. (2015). Editors' Comment: So, What Is a Conceptual Paper? *Group and Organization Management, 40*(2), 127–130.

Gopalan, S., Reddy, K., & Sasidharan, S. (2022). Does digitalization spur global value chain participation? Firm-level evidence from emerging markets. *Information Economics and Policy, 59*, 1–13.

Gozgor, G., & Lau, C. K. M. (2023). Editorial: Economic and financial issues in the post-COVID-19 world: Implications and role of public health. *Frontiers in Public Health, 11*(10), 1126501. https://doi.org/10.3389/fpubh.2022.1126501

Gurría, A. (2020). Tackling coronavirus (COVID-19) contributing to a global effort. Organisation for Economic Co-operation and Development (OECD).

Hagiu, A., & Altman, E. J. (2017). Finding the platform in your product: Four strategies that can reveal hidden value. *Harvard Business Review, 95*(4), 94–100.
Hernández, V., & Pedersen, T. (2017). Global value chain configuration: A review and research agenda. *Business Research Quarterly, 20*(2), 137–150. https://doi.org/10.1016/j.brq.2016.11.001
Hull, C. E., Hung, Y.-T.C., Hair, N., Perotti, V., & DeMartino, R. (2007). Taking advantage of digital opportunities: A typology of digital entrepreneurship. *International Journal of Networking and Virtual Organisations, 4*(3), 290–303.
International Monetary Fund (IMF). (2020). *Country focus: Rwanda harnesses technology to fight COVID-19.* Drive recovery. https://www.imf.org/en/News/Articles/2020/08/06/na080620-rwanda-harnesses-technology-to-fight-covid-19-drive-recovery#:~:text=The%20Fund%20will%20support%20the,up%20an%20SME%20guarantee%20scheme. Posted August 6, 2020.
Jacobides, M. G, Cennamo, C., & Gawer, A. (2018). Toward a theory of ecosystems. *Strategic Management Journal, 39*(8), 2255–2276.
Jordan, B. (2020). *Limpopo mayor becomes Big Brother, thanks to a drone.* https://www.sowetanlive.co.za/news/south-africa/2020-04-12-watch--limpopo-mayor-becomes-big-brother-thanks-to-a-drone/. Posted April 12, 2020.
JSI. (2020). *Ethiopia's digital health response to COVID-19.* https://www.jsi.com/ethiopias-digital-health-response-to-covid-19. Posted May 14, 2020.
Jurowetzki, R., Lema, R., & Lundvall, B. -Å. (2018). Combining innovation systems and global value chains for development: Towards a research agenda. *European Journal of Development Research, 30*(3), 364–388.
Kelly, T. (2014). *Tech hubs across Africa: Which will be the legacy-makers?* https://blogs.worldbank.org/digital-development/tech-hubs-across-africa-which-will-be-legacy-makers
Khane, C. P., Siebörger, I., Thinyane, H., & Dalvit, L. (2011). The Siyakhula living lab: A holistic approach to rural development through ICT in rural South Africa. In J. V. J. Steyn (Ed.), *ICTs for global development and sustainability* (pp. 42–77). IGI-Global.
Kirkpatrick, G. (2020). *Critical theory and technology* (pp. 21–45). https://www.researchgate.net/publication/341139204_Critical_theory_and_technology/link/5eb0e00ca6fdcc7050a98549/download
Lehikoinen, L. E., Lundh, A., Meert, L., Waeingier, K., Bentsen, N., et al. (2018). Innovation and creativity at the bottom of the pyramid. *International Journal of Business and Economic Sciences Applied Research, 11*(1), 13–25.
Lundvall, B. (2010). *National systems of innovation: Towards a theory of national systems of innovation: Towards a theory of innovation and interactive learning.* Pinter.

Lundvall, B. -Å., & Lema, R. (2014). Growth and structural change in Africa: Development strategies for the learning economy. *African Journal of Science, Technology, Innovation and Development, 6*(5), 455–466.

Maharana, A., Amutorine, M., Sengeh, M., Elaine, O., & Nsoesie, E. (2021). COVID-19 and beyond: Use of digital technology for pandemic response in Africa. *Scientific African, 14*, e01041. https://doi.org/10.1016/j.sciaf.2021.e01041

Makarov, I., & Schoar, A. (2022, December). *Cryptocurrencies and decentralized finance* (BIS Working Papers No 1061). Monetary and Economic Department, Bank for International Settlements.

Mamphiswana, R., & Bekele, M. (2020). The fourth industrial revolution: Prospects and challenges for Africa. *International Association for Management of Technology* (IAMOT) *2020 Conference Proceedings* (pp. 1–12).

Mata, F., Fuerst, W., & Barney, J. (1995). Informational technology and sustained competitive advantage: A resource-based analysis. *Management Information System Quarterly, 19*(4), 487–505.

Mavhunga, C. C. (2017). Introduction: What do science, technology, and innovation mean from Africa? In *What do science, technology, and innovation mean from Africa*? MIT Press.

Mcintyre, D. P., & Srinivasan, A. (2017). Networks, platforms, and strategy: Emerging views and next steps. *Strategic Management Journal, 38*(1), 141–160.

Menon, A. (2008). Revisiting dynamic capability. *IIMB Management Review, 20*(1), 22–33.

Nair, R., Zafrullah, S., Vinayasree, P., Singh, P., Zahra, M., Sharma, T., & Ahmadi, F. (2022). *Blockchain-based decentralized cloud solutions for data transfer*. Hindawi Computational Intelligence and Neuroscience. https://doi.org/10.1155/2022/8209854

Nambisan, S. (2016). Digital entrepreneurship: Toward a digital technology perspective of entrepreneurship. *Entrepreneurship: Theory and Practice, 41*(6), 1029–1055.

Nambisan, S. (2023, August 17–18). Sustainopreneurship: The role of digitalization in a post-pandemic South Africa. *Fourth Biennial International Conference on Entrepreneurship Development*, Held at the Central University of Technology, Free State.

Nambisan, S., Siegel, D., & Kenney, M. (2018). On open innovation, platforms, and entrepreneurship. *Strategic Entrepreneurship Journal, 12*, 354–368.

Navas-Alemán, L. (2011). The impact of operating in multiple value chains for upgrading: The case of the Brazilian furniture and footwear industries. *World Development, 39*(8), 1386–1397.

Ndung'u, N. (2018). *Next steps for the digital revolution in Africa: Inclusive growth and job creation lessons from Kenya* (Brookings Institution Working Paper 2018).

Ndung'u, N., & Signé, L. (2020, January 8). *The fourth industrial revolution and digitization will transform Africa into a global powerhouse*. Foresight Africa 2020 report.

Nelson, J. L., & Lei, R. F. (2018). The effect of digital platforms on news audience behavior. *Digital Journalism, 6*(5), 619–633.

Omar, A. R. C., Ishak, S., & Jusoh, M. A. (2020). The impact of Covid-19 movement control order on SMEs' businesses and survival strategies. *Geografia-Malaysian Journal of Society and Space, 16*(2), 90–103.

Onyango, C. (2021). *Africa's appetite for digital currencies is growing*. https://qz.com/africa/2043041/the-rise-of-central-bank-and-private-digital-currencies-in-africa. Published August 5, 2021.

Ozili, P. K. (2022a). Decentralized finance research and developments around the world. *Journal of Banking and Financial Technology, 6*, 117–133.

Ozili, P. K. (2022b). Central bank digital currency research around the world: A review of literature. *Journal of Money Laundering Control*. https://doi.org/10.1108/JMLC-11-2021-0126

Ozili, P. K. (2022c, September). *Central Bank digital currency in Nigeria: Opportunities and risks*. https://doi.org/10.1108/S1569-37592022000109A008

Panchia, Y. (2023). Crypto as inflation hedge: South Africa's innovative approach to digital assets. *Forbes Africa*. https://www.forbesafrica.com/crypto/2023/08/15/crypto-as-inflation-hedge-south-africas-innovative-approach-to-digital-assets/

Panda, R., Mehta, B., & Karani, A. (2017). Business models on social media. *International Journal of Marketing and Financial Management, 5*(2), 34–42.

Parker, G., Van Alstyne, M., & Choudary, S. (2016). *Platform revolution: How networked markets are transforming the economy and how to make them work for you*. Norton.

Perez, T., Maritz, A., & de Waal, A. (2013). Innovation and social entrepreneurship at the bottom of the pyramid -A conceptual framework. *South African Journal Economic and Management Sciences, 16*, 54–66.

Ponte, S., & Ewert, J. (2009). Which way is "up" in upgrading? Trajectories of change in the value chain for South African wine. *World Development, 37*(10), 1637–1650.

Prahalad, C. K., & Hart, S. L. (2002). *The fortune at the bottom of the pyramid: Strategy and business. 26*. https://www.strategy-business.com/article/11518

Prather and Akeledo. (2020). *Building a resilient innovative Africa report*. AfriLabs in Conjunction with Djembe Consultants.

Rambe, P., & Nel, L. (2014). Technological utopia, dystopia and ambivalence: Teaching with social media at a South African university. *British Journal of Educational Technology, 45*(3), 1–20.

Ratten, V. (2022). Digital platforms and transformational entrepreneurship during the COVID-19 crisis. *International Journal of Information Management*. https://doi.org/10.1016/j.ijinfomgt.2022.102534

Reim, W., Yli-Viitala, P., Arrasvuori, J., & Parida, V. (2022). Tackling business model challenges in SME internationalization through digitalisation. *Journal of Innovation and Knowledge, 7*(3), 1–9.

Rogers, E. M. (2003). *Diffusion of innovations* (5th ed.). Free Press.

Sahut, J. M., Iandoli, L., & Teulon, F. (2019). The age of digital entrepreneurship. *Small Business Economics, 56*, 1159–1169.

Schär, F. (2021). Decentralized finance: On blockchain-and smart contract-based financial markets. *FRB of St Louis Review Federal Reserve Bank of St Louis Review, 103*(2), 153–174.

Sebastian, I. M., Ross, J. W., Beath, C., Mocker, M., Moloney, K. G., & Fonstad, N. O. (2017). How big old companies navigate digital transformation. *MIS Quarterly Executive, 16*, 197–213.

Shah, A. (2008). *Poverty facts and stats*. Global Issues: 1–7. http://www.bunburycatholic.wa.edu.au/home/sdrive/Religious_Education/TEE_Prep/Resources/Poverty_Facts_and_Stats.docx

Simanis, E., & Duke, D. (2014). Profits at the bottom of the pyramid. *Harvard Business Review, 92*(10), 87–93.

South African Institute of International Affairs (SAIIA). (2014). *Building resilience in Africa: Enabling an inclusive digital economy and energy access for all*. https://saiia.org.za/research/building-resilience-in-africa-enabling-an-inclusive-digital-economy-and-energy-access-for-all/. Accessed May 26, 2023.

Steedman, R., Alacovska, A., Langevang, T., & Resario, R. (2022). Imaginaries of platform entrepreneurship in the creative industries: Techno-optimism and subversion. *Ghanaian Filmmaking, Information, Communication & Society*. https://doi.org/10.1080/1369118X.2022.2062252

Straton, F. (2022). *Transforming cities and infrastructure for a sustainable future*. AVEVA Group.

Subrahmanyan, S., & Gomez-Arias, J. T. (2008). Integrated approach to understanding consumer behaviour at bottom of pyramid. *Journal of Consumer Marketing, 25*(7), 402–412.

Tarde, G. (1903). *The laws of imitation*. University of Chicago Press.

Thai, M. T., Turkina, E., & Simba, A. (2022). The impact of internationalisation on product innovation in emerging market firms. *International Journal of Entrepreneurship and Small Business, 46*(2), 226–243.

The Directorate of Science, Technology, and Innovation (DSTI). (2020). *Sierra Leone's COVID-19 lock down and curfew E-Pass for essential travel is here.* https://www.dsti.gov.sl/sierra-leones-covid-19-lock-down-and-curfew-e-pass-for-essential-travel-is-here/. Posted April 26, 2020.

Tonnies, E. (2001). *Tonnies: Community and civil society.* The Press Syndicate of the University of Cambridge.

Wild, S. (2020). *Antipoaching tech tracks COVID-19 flare-ups in South Africa.* Scientific American. https://www.scientificamerican.com/article/antipoaching-tech-tracks-covid-19-flare-ups-in-south-africa/. Posted May 12, 2020.

Xie, X., Han, Y., Anderson, A., & Ribeiro-Navarrete, S. (2022). Digital platforms and SMEs' business model innovation: Exploring the mediating mechanisms of capability reconfiguration. *International Journal of Information Management, 65*. https://doi.org/10.1016/j.ijinfomgt.2022.102513

Digitalisation and Digital Innovation for Sustainable Business Model Development and Value Creation: Implications for Policy and Practice for African SMMEs

Patient Rambe

1 Introduction

Despite the prominence of research investigating how large corporations have transformed their business models through the adoption of digital platforms (e.g., Khanagha et al., 2018; Klein et al., 2020), nascent evidence exists that draws special attention to the dynamics of digital innovation (e.g., digital platforms) for business model development among small and medium enterprises (SMEs) in Africa. As such, the extent to which SMEs in emerging markets can benefit from adopting digital platforms including the ways in which they deploy digital innovations to foster new value and revitalise their business models (Xie et al., 2022) remains unclear. Yet, there is compelling evidence that, in disruptive environments characteristic of those experienced during Covid-19, entrepreneurs could no longer conceive digital technologies as

P. Rambe (✉)
Faculty of Management Sciences, Central University of Technology, Bloemfontein, South Africa
e-mail: prambe@cut.ac.za

P. Rambe and R. E. Hinson (eds.), *The Future of Entrepreneurship in Southern Africa*, Palgrave Studies in Technology and Innovation in Africa, https://doi.org/10.1007/978-3-031-55935-8_4

appendages of their business models but rather as integral to their business development strategies and the development of their business models (Priyono et al., 2020). The harnessing of digital technology to support business model development has been hailed as a germane strategy for addressing disruptive environmental changes, especially where technology affordances are instrumental in the identification and exploitation of new business practices (Richter, 2020). This is particularly key in hostile environmental scenarios where fundamental changes are different from those stimulated by human innovations (Gupta & Bose, 2019).

Recent literature suggests that despite the ubiquity and extensive adoption of digital technologies, productivity growth especially in advanced economies (and lately in emerging economies) has stagnated (Velu, 2020). Moreover, it is ironic that industries that are intensive users of digital and information and communication technologies (ICTs) appear to have contributed most to the decline in productivity (Van Ark, 2016). Such a decline in productivity has been attributed to inter alia, the skills mismatches arising from product market structure changes fuelled by digitalisation, the slowdown in technological diffusion among firms at the technology frontier, aftermath of the financial crises of 2008 and mismeasurement of productivity effects arising from the digital economy propositions about "free" goods and services (Velu, 2020). For small firms, competency gaps, inability to effectively integrate digital technologies into business processes and the sporadic and fragmented adoption of technologies in the business value chain further compound the problem. Literature advances the thesis that this productivity paradox might be a consequence of the paucity of business model innovation due to ineffective management of information on the effectiveness of the business model and the poor adoption of digital technologies and ICTs (Velu, 2020). As such, a concerted effort must be taken to consider the different business model innovation permutations arising from SMME management decisions pertaining to the deployment of digitalisation and digital innovation in supporting business process models. This is particularly key, especially in resource constrained and highly volatile emerging markets such as those in Africa.

First, the paper contributes to a deeper understanding of digital innovation in the context of emerging economies. This is critical given the less coherent narrative of what digital innovation is, how it differs from earlier industrial age innovations and how it can be conceptualised from a functional and discipline perspective (Nambisan et al., 2020). Undoubtedly, despite the growing confusion regarding the dizzying variety of emerging questions and interests in digital innovation, there is scope for researchers to establish a more nuanced yet coherent understanding of this concept as a unique, coherent and dynamic phenomenon (Nambisan et al., 2020). The growing family of concepts related to digital innovation, such as digitalisation, digitisation, industry 4.0 including their relationships with business models call for a more incisive and targeted approach to unpacking the concept. This will be fundamental to distinguishing its unique qualities from other related concepts as well as frame this complex pervasive phenomenon.

Second, the chapter calls for a reassessment and development of new line of inquiry on the ways digitalisation and digital innovation contribute to specific business models particularly in an era characterised by the burgeoning growth of emerging technologies supporting the formation of digital business models. For instance, given the nascency of crowdfunding as alternative model to established traditional models of funding for SMEs, Mawson and Ball's (2020) research has demonstrated that the lack of sectorally focused studies on crowd funding has constrained our understanding of the transferability of this funding mechanism and its benefits across different types of firms and industries.

Third, although there is compelling evidence to suggest that SMMEs deploy digital technologies (e.g., social media platforms) to maintain the social presence of their brands and activities, there is scant evidence to demonstrate that they are effectively engaging their clients and their brand via digital platforms. Despite the avalanche of research that demonstrates the contribution of digital technologies to creating enterprising business opportunities for maximising revenue, increase their direct contact with consumers worldwide and reduce promotion and advertising expenditure (Abuhashesh, 2014), most SMMEs are yet to develop a customer-centric integrated formal business model via digital platforms (Panda et al., 2017). It is not surprising that there is scant literature that has explored effectiveness of social media in innovation from an organisational strategic perspective (Barlatier & Josserand, 2018; Zhang & Zhu, 2021). Therefore, there is a persistent lack of knowledge on the best or most effective ways to manage social media platforms use in business processes (Bashir et al., 2017). The study, therefore, contributes to the broader literature on business model innovation by demonstrating the range of models that can be developed to support SMEs drawing on digital technologies and digital platforms to market and merchandise their products and services.

The paper is structured as follows: first, the theoretical development section discusses the theory of disruptive technology and related literature on digitalisation, digital innovation and business model development and value creation. Second, the research method including how literature was selected is discussed. Third, the findings are presented and discussed. Fourth, the implications of the findings for theory, policy and practice are deliberated on. Fifth, the limitations of the study are documented and the lastly, the conclusion is granted.

2 Theory Development

Theory of Disruptive Technology

Clayton M. Christensen, a Harvard Professor, propounded the theory of Disruptive Technology in his Harvard Business Review article titled "*Disruptive Technologies: Catching the Wave*" to characterise innovations that significantly alter the way consumers, businesses or industries operate (Thunderbird School of Global Management, 2022). At the core of his argument in *The Innovator's dilemma* was that incumbent established companies fail due to their continual reliance on antiquated technologies and that these companies are compelled to innovate or go bankrupt. In *The Innovator's Solution*, they coined disruptive innovation to characterise any innovation that creates a new market by providing a different set of values, which ultimately and unexpectedly overtakes an existing market (Christensen & Raynor, 2013). Their argument is that a disruptive entrant in the market may introduce an inferior yet inexpensive and accessible product or service to the market, which large corporations may ignore as a competitive rival because they provide superior offering. The further enhancement of efficiency in production processes may contribute to an increase in product value while simultaneously maintaining low cost and convenience (Thunderbird School of Global Management, 2022). This combination of strategies will consequently push the incumbent dominant firms out of the market as the rival firms take their share of the market due to the relevance and credibility of their new business idea.

Disruption describes a process whereby a smaller company with fewer resources is able to successfully challenge established incumbent businesses (Christensen et al., 2015). The innovations that disruptive technologies render would culminate in the low cost of production leading to more affordable and accessible products and services to more customers and greater opportunities for improved value addition (Hwang & Christensen, 2008). Consistent with this logic, Christensen (1997) distinguishes sustaining innovations from disruptive innovations with the former representing innovations that are created by large incumbent firms to sustain the existing market and to retain their advantage over rival firms. Hwang and Christensen (2008) elaborate that the ever-improving features (e.g., for smartphones, several cameras, battery performance and displays quality) created by manufacturers help to maintain their share of the market, serve traditional customers and generate higher sales figures. This can be contrasted with disruptive innovation designed to create a new market by addressing customers not previously served by incumbents (Christensen, 1997). Alternatively, disruptive innovations target less sophisticated customer groups that account for a small portion of the market leaders' sales (Christensen et al., 2015; Schaefer, 2022).

Examples of disruptive innovations are in flux. For example, the use of digital platforms for crowdfunding has contributed to the disruption of traditional forms of financing through retail banks, state financial institutions and micro-credit schemes. Such innovations specifically target small entrepreneurs who these institutions do not accommodate or are reluctant to consider due to the lack of collateral and lack of a solid financial management history. Similarly, the use of bitcoin and blockchain-backed technology has created new forms of collateral assets, in ways deemed not historically envisaged. Similarly new business models such as charges imposed on livestreaming (YouTube), social influencing through social media marketing (e.g., Facebook) and digital platforms such as Airbnb and Uber have created digital business models that disrupted the concepts of music, social interacting, hospitality and accommodation and transport systems, respectively.

3 Institutional Voids

Contemporary literature presents institutional voids as a productive concept for understanding firm strategies in emerging economies (Jarvenpaa et al., 2020) as they direct attention to the characteristics of institutions that matter most to how firms function" (Doh et al., 2017, p. 295). Unlike developed economies, participation in economic activities in emerging economies is riddled with complex legislation, strict bylaws, unclear rules of engagement that impose uncertainty, obscure open, transparent communications, which escalate business operation risks and complicate contract enforcement during economic transactions. In this institutionally complex and volatile climate, in which plurality, uncertainty, conflict and contradiction persist regarding rule of engagement (Ahlstrom et al., 2008; Jayanti & Raghunath, 2018), bribery and corruption prevail which complicate transparent economic activities, undermine firms' autonomy and efficiency (Jarvenpaa et al., 2020). Despite these uncertainties relating electricity supply, weak and currency fluctuations, economic policy uncertainty and graft, firms can develop new pathways to ensuring competitiveness and survival. Firms can thrive from building trust networks, coalitions and partnering with other institutions to borrow from foreign countries, drawing on their collective capabilities (Jarvenpaa et al., 2020).

Digital Innovations in the Context of Institutional Voids

Evidence suggests that despite the presence of institutional voids, entrepreneurs in emerging economies have thrived on sustained growth through compositional resources and capabilities (Jarvenpaa et al., 2020). Compositional resources entail the creative assembling and integrating of open and generic resources that firms in emerging economies possess or acquire (Luo & Child, 2020). For instance, entrepreneurial firms have deployed a combination of bricolage, strategic deployment of scarce resources and the exploitation of under-appreciated or discarded resources as levers for accentuating their competitive advantage over larger firms. Apart from drawing on emerging digital technologies, entrepreneurial firms are reported to combine standardisation and modularisation to enhance compositional capabilities (Jarvenpaa et al., 2020).

4 Related Literature

Business Model and Digitalisation

Business models are complex activity systems that summarise the architecture and logic of a business and define the organisation's value proposition and its approach to value creation and capture (Velu, 2017). In their entirety, business models are activity ecosystems that connect the internal operations of the firm (e.g., resources and routines) with external stakeholders (e.g., suppliers and customers) and therefore, serve as firms' articulation of how they assert activities on the market drawing on their strategies (Baden-Fuller & Haefliger, 2013). Essentially, business models must entail three aspects, content, structure and governance—with content placing emphasis on which activities are components of the business model. Structure concentrates on the interlinkages between these activities while governance deals with which stakeholders hold the legitimate claim to make decisions about these activities (Velu, 2020). In its entirety, therefore, a business model is not only about how the business delivers value to the customer while creating some profit margins for itself but also about processes that facilitate efficiency enhancements and strategies that are effective in delivering intended outcomes and consequences for the firm.

Business models also describe how a company creates, delivers and captures value (Teece, 2010). Put differently, it denotes the way a business or business networks collaborate and cooperate at strategic and operational levels to render a range of products and/or services (bundles) to the market (Bouwman et al., 2018). As such, a firm acting as an independent legal entity or in collaboration with other firms can develop and adopt technical platforms and architectures to create and capture value for both the (networked) organisation and the customer (Bouwman et al., 2018). Therefore, drawing on their own internal capabilities and externally sourced digital technologies, firms can orchestrate technological capabilities and technical strengths to create, capture and deliver value to their partners and customers. To the extent that digitalisation can facilitate efficiency enhancements and business process improvements, Guo and Xu (2021) argue that digitalisation does not only optimise operations but also facilitates business growth through value creation, which in turn improves profits. Following this logic, digitalisation does not only focus on the capabilities of technology but also the rebuilding of vision, processes, capabilities, organisational structure and culture (Teng et al., 2022; Warner & Wäger, 2019), which impact the business model of firms.

Digitalisation involves the adoption of digital technologies to innovate a business model and provide new value-generating opportunities in the business ecosystems (Parida et al., 2019; Rajapathirana & Hui, 2018). A careful consideration of the entire business model is critical to a deeper appreciation of the role of digitalisation in the development of a business innovation model. The process of business innovation model development covers how the firm creates, delivers and captures value. Value creation refers to the offers that a company makes to a customer (Lafont et al., 2020). In the context of SMMEs, it entails grasping the value proposition and realising the customers' needs (Parida et al., 2019) through the provision of products, services or a combination of both (Burström et al., 2021). From a business model perspective value can be created through the ways the firm bundles heterogenous offerings and how it co-creates content with its customers. The process of digital model innovation can involve the creation of digital services through greater diversification of a firm's portfolio, bundling various offers and providing personalised communication to fulfil customer needs and create long-lasting competitive advantage (Endres et al., 2019).

For Reim et al. (2022), the second aspect of developing a business model, is value delivery, which encompasses all dimensions and operations pertaining to providing value to the customer. The embrace and integration of new technologies into the business are expected to accelerate the ideation, development and evolution of radical products and services while accommodating innovation spanning traditional industry/sectoral boundaries and stimulating dynamic value propositions that reshape business and industry structures (Nambisan et al., 2020). Moreover, the accommodation of digitisation (e.g., the adoption of digital platforms) can also fuel new capability reconfiguration mechanisms (Hilmersson & Hilmersson, 2020; Mei et al., 2019), which can create a renewed interest and expectation of customers in product and service offerings. The delivery of value can also necessitate SMMEs to develop firm connections with platform owners who are connected to a wide range of customers that consume the product or service and deliver value. As a form of digitalisation, the adoption of software as a service (e.g., Google Docs by Google) avails a diverse range of applications from different client devices (e.g., smartphone, tablets, laptops, desktops) through web browsers and cloud-based platforms for accessing services (Sabwa, 2013).

The last component, value capture, describes the way a company makes money (Reim et al., 2022). This necessitates the business to increase its liquidity by maximising productivity, revenue streams and minimise the cost of production and delivery of products and services. For instance, by diminishing investment in on-site infrastructure through building and managing applications, cloud-based services (as a form of digitalisation) assist SMEs to develop affordable solutions that save costs by reducing dependence on dedicated hardware and networking equipment

(Donnery, 2022). Given the portability of online data, employees may remain engaged on tasks anywhere anytime, and this creates opportunities for heightened productivity when available time is committed to on-task activities.

Business Model and Digital Innovation

Digital innovation can be defined as the creation of (and consequent change in) market offerings, business processes or business models that result from the use of digital technology (Nambisan et al., 2017). It is enabled by attempts at implementing new combinations of digital and physical components to produce new market offerings (Yoo et al., 2010). From a systems perspective, digital models constitute the "architecture" that provides a bridge between value created for customers and value captured by the business in terms of the profit (Velu, 2020). Digital innovations can allow the servitisation of artefacts into radically new products and services. They also permit the introduction of digital technologies and the combining of artefacts with other offerings to create new value propositions. For instance, a tractor connected to sensors (Porter & Heppelmann, 2014) becomes a smart tractor that is linked to other farm equipment, weather data, irrigation systems and seed optimisation systems—a new interconnection of systems that trigger radically new value propositions, which contribute to improvements in farm productivity (Velu, 2020).

The connection between digital technologies, business model and digital innovation is that, when digital technologies are adopted by a firm to adjust its business model and strategy, they have the potential to cause reverse salience (situation where business organisations' components fail to align with and be consistent with each other), which provides the stimulus for business model innovation (Velu, 2020). Therefore, business model innovation can be an outcome of changes to the interdependences between technological components, changes in components themselves, to provide a value proposition to an existing or new market (Amit & Zott, 2012).

Three aspects of digital innovation that characterise its logic as an impetus for innovation are its (1) agential core, (2) semiotic binding and (3) ontological reversal (Nambisan et al., 2020). From an agential core perspective, the embrace of digital innovation necessitates one to consider the multiple expanding and changing properties of digital technologies, which change the role and relationships of technology in social and business settings, transforming the agency that social and technical elements jointly exhibit in sociotechnical systems (Tilson et al., 2010). In digital innovation, social actors are constantly engaging with ubiquitously present technologies (e.g., mobiles and wearables, web services powered by broadband and APIs, sensors embedded in objects and environment, algorithms), which offer a range of capabilities (e.g., sensibility, addressability, editability, communicability, memorizability and associability) (Yoo, 2010). These capabilities and their uses transform business logic, behaviours and outcomes and the very meaning of products and services (Nambisan, 2017).

For Nambisan et al. (2020), semiotic binding means that all digital innovations are founded on digital representations in behaviour or data contextualised to a situated context or machine. Semiotic bindings are institutionally and socially mediated processes and therefore, while bindings change, they will also expand related institutions and innovations (Oshri et al., 2018). Ontological reversal deals with digital representations being the reflection of physical reality that already exists but with advancements in digital innovations, digital technologies are beginning to shape reality (Nambisan et al., 2020).

Following the foregoing discussion, business model innovations arising from digital technologies, therefore, may take inter alia, the following changes: *reactivating*—changing the set of activities, *relinking*—changing the linkages between activities, or *repartitioning*—changing the boundaries of the focal firm or *relocating*—or changing the location in which activities are performed (Santos et al., 2015, Velu, 2020). This is particularly key in digital platforms where new resource combinations (e.g., reskilling, repurposing activities, and service provision) may need to meet the needs of online market as well as physical markets.

5 Methodology

This chapter adopted a conceptual paper approach. Hamilton (2021) suggests that a conceptual paper succinctly reviews recent progress in a particular topic and summarises the current state of knowledge using published and existing articles. Conceptual papers often strive to bridge the gaps in theories and to develop links across disciplines by creating a sound framework, which presents a convenient means of understanding the concepts including a clear depiction of how existing constructs are interconnected (Hamilton, 2021). Although a conceptual paper often contributes to the development of a conceptual framework, it is not always a requirement as authors and scholars contribute to the body of knowledge in a variety of ways. For this study, some contributions are made to theory by employing the typology design of a conceptual paper (Miller & Salkind, 2002) to demonstrate the different elements that contribute to digital innovations and digitalisation for business model development and value creation. As literature aptly observes, the purpose of a typology design of conceptual paper is to explain differences between variants of a concept(s) (Miller & Salkind, 2002) and their relationships.

At the heart of a conceptual paper is the need to address and provide clear answers to several questions or criteria, namely (1) what's new, (2) so what? (3) why so?, (4) well done?, (5) done well?, (6) why now? and (7) who cares? (Whetten, 1989), with the most challenging being to demonstrate what is new and who will care, drawing on compelling arguments. The need to address what is new is critical as it serves as a pathway to the development of a new body of knowledge. As literature suggests, conceptual papers are credited with contributing to the understanding of a concept and providing extant knowledge in big leaps if taken seriously and grounded in thorough justification (Hamilton, 2021). Apart from bringing deeper conceptual understanding of concepts, the current study also strives to make connections between concepts and how they link with each other.

A conceptual approach was the ideal approach as it aligns with and was widely adopted by several studies on digitalisation and digital innovations (Carillo-Hermosilla et al., 2019; Godin & Gaglio, 2019; Nambisan et al., 2020). For instance, Carillo-Hermosilla et al. (2019) explored the concepts of eco-innovation' internal determinants from the perspective of resources, competences and dynamic capabilities and focused on the effect of eco-innovation of the companies on different aspects of their operations.

6 Research Procedure

Search Strategy

A Google Scholar search was conducted to establish the state of architecture of existing literature on digitalisation and digital innovation first using the keywords "digitalisation/digital technologies/digital applications", "digital innovation/technology innovation/disruptive innovations" and "Africa firms". As the search yielded multiple sources (approximately 17,000 records) covering books, journals and conference articles. After the search was narrowed to "digitalisation" and "digital innovations" and "African SMEs", and it yielded 16,900 entries. The study also examined the presence of some existing systematic review on these constructs to avoid duplication (Wang & Chebo, 2021).

The search was further narrowed to target only contemporary peer-reviewed journal articles written covering African SMEs, and this process eliminated books, conferences and other lay literature covering the concepts. Although the Web of Science and Scopus were included in the databases searched, their coverage is deemed not ideal in social sciences and humanities (Mahdi et al., 2008) compared to Google Scholar which tends to search all citations from several sources (Wang & Chebo, 2021).

To further limit the parameters and scope of the search (Jesson, 2011), the coverage was also narrowed to a 20-year period spanning 2002–2022. This was deemed to be sufficient to cover a wide range of relevant publications on the concepts in question. The number of articles was drastically reduced to about 751 articles. The further refinement of key search terms and the inclusion of a clear abstract (with research gap, context, method, key findings, recommendations) and key sections in the article (covering introduction and background, theoretical development, method, data analysis, and findings, discussion recommendations, theory, policy or practical implications) generated 323 articles. After eliminating articles with different and unconventional meanings of concepts of digitalisation and digital innovation, business model development and value creation, 271 articles remained. Following the exclusion of unclear titles, incomplete abstracts, irrelevant articles and those lacking a clear conceptual framework, only 37 remained.

Data Analysis

The synthesis sought to locate the relevant findings and summarised essential knowledge of the research domain, to develop a bigger picture of a particular domain by reducing irrelevant ideas (Wang & Chebo, 2021). Severely underdeveloped papers that lacked rigorous qualitative or quantitative analysis and clear discussion of fundings were further eliminated. Gleaning and reading of sources helped to identify, evaluate and synthesise the available literature drawing on a comprehensive, explicit and reproducible approach (Fink, 2005). The reading, extraction of concepts, arguments and ideas was meant to provide a clear and coherent searching strategy intended to lessen bias by finding, scrutinising and synthesising the relevant studies (Uman, 2011; Wang & Chebo, 2021).

7 Findings

Digital Platforms ("platifirms") and Associated Ecosystems

Of the top ten most valuable companies in the world, seven derive their value from digital platforms (Pomykalski, 2019). Such evidence demonstrates the positive connection between the extent of capitalisation and revenue generation by companies and their investment in digital platform business models (Pomykalski, 2019). The availability and deployment of platform firms have facilitated and enabled co-innovation processes. Co-innovation is deemed possible when SMEs interact and co-create artefacts, products and services with platform owners who are connected and interact with clients who interact with service or product providers (Mostaghel et al., 2022).

Digital platforms are those businesses that rely predominantly on online-based activities that integrate producers and consumers in high-value exchanges (Harvard Business Review, 2016). These platform firms (abridged as "platifirms") are also called vertical search engines (Chau & Chen, 2003), multi-sided platforms (Evans, 2003) or two-sided markets (Evans, 2002; Ruggieri et al., 2018). As "intermediaries that connect two or more distinct groups of users and enable their direct interaction" (Zhu & Furr, 2016, p. 4), platform-based business models have transitioned from transacting in market-mediated digitally encoded information (e.g., software, music and banking services) (Tasca, 2018) to a wider range of utility goods such as accommodation, transport and online retail. These "platifirms" have transitioned from fully online to bridging online with offline facilities. Most Internet-based businesses, such as Uber, Airbnb and Alibaba, are "online to offline" platforms that have harnessed the platform business model to link people, organisations and resources in an interactive ecosystem in which value can be created and exchanged (Tasca, 2018). Rather than depend on accumulating inventories, platifirms increase their scale by building on their networks of users (Parker et al., 2016). For instance, marketers just like social influencers build on the traction of traffic on their webpages (e.g., Facebook or Instagram) to create value for the platfirm, influencers, marketers and users. The success of platfirms in facilitating and generating business model innovation depends on their ability to develop from successful patterns for linking key activities, key resources, channel mix strategy, costs management, value proposition, customer segmentation and key partners in ways that generate revenues (Ruggieri et al., 2018).

One of the important areas where digital platforms and ecosystems have improved entrepreneurial development in Africa is in agropreneurship. Aguera et al. (2020) discuss how agricultural technology firms in South Africa are deploying latest technologies to unlock and optimise the agricultural supply chains; facilitate automation; agricultural data collection; processing of data; aggregation and distribution of information; and unlocking opportunities to finance. Another example is a South African-based platform-based agricultural company, AgriTechnovation, which is using platform-based technologies to develop plant nutrition products and precision farming advisory services in horticulture, social science, biology and agronomy (https://agritechnovation.co.za/). The company employs Internet of Thing-based technologies and tracking technologies to address soil chemical composition and classification, plant leaf, root and food nutrition composition, water, irrigation and weather management. Drawing on such technologies, the company's staff (i.e. agronomists, horticulturalists, field technicians, soil scientists, irrigation specialists, microbiologists, entomologists, geographical information system specialists, formulation chemists, software engineers, data scientists, satellite specialists) (https://agritechnovation.co.za/about-us-2/) employ their specialised knowledge areas and expertise and modern technology to conduct "soil moisture probes, tracking devices to track micro weather conditions (https://agritechnovation.co.za/services/). In short, many South African-based companies such as Pannar and AgriTechnovation are using precision farming particularly site-specific data to manage nutrients, pests, water, seeding rates, and other resources in a more efficient manner" (de Carbon, 2016). Moreover, blockchain technology is being employed to track agricultural produce sales, providing contracted farmers with access to essential accounting information in return for greater transparency and accountability (Olago, 2019). Other innovation platform-based services include using livestock sensors to measure vital signs in animal activity, monitor reproductive cycles or detect health problems (Aguera et al., 2020) and unmanned aerial vehicles (UAVs), such as drones, and geographic information systems (GISs) to collect aerial imagery for mapping and monitoring damage on crops, crop yield or livestock location (Nel, 2016).

Another critical area where digital platforms have been deployed to support startup firms especially those operating in the circular economy is in sustainopreneurship. Another South African startup, Kudoti, is a comprehensive digital platform that works across the entire supply chain to collect real-time data on waste material flows, teams activity, and then generates instant reports which can be shared with funders, partners and sustainability teams to enable material and products circularity (https://kudoti.com/). The digital-based firm facilitates waste recycling operations, circular economy initiatives, reductions in companies' waste footprint or enhance the circularity of their production, by providing digital solutions that can efficiently optimise outcomes and impact. The company facilitates streamlined data collection for all types of waste materials, processes and outcomes, efficient data capture and task assignment based on user roles and offers flexibility to customise data fields and inputs based in its clients' specific needs (https://kudoti.com/). A platform-based firm relies on the adoption of more sustainable and resource-efficient business models. It does so using: (a) *environmental sustainability reporting* through real-time and automated data capturing for environmental metric reports, *reverse supply chain management and optimisation* (i.e., planning and optimising logistics for end of life waste products and materials), *ensuring regulatory and certification compliance* (through customised data inputs & process flows to meet regulatory or compliance requirements), recycled materials sourcing (through onboarding and managing recycled materials suppliers for manufacturing) and product reuse and remanufacturing systems (i.e. track and manage reusable products while engaging with clients to direct used products towards manufacturing sites) (https://kudoti.com/).

Another prominent area where digital platforms have been extensively deployed in Southern Africa is financial technology (fintech) especially mobile money platforms. In Zimbabwe, one of the most successful mobile money-based platforms is Ecocash. As a mobile payment service that Econet clients use to access and make financial transactions (i.e., sending and receiving money, paying for goods and services, purchasing airtime and data, sending money to your bank account), Ecocash also allows clients to save money and access loans (Monkey Pesa: https://www.monkeypesa.com/post/top-fintech-companies-in-zimbabwe). Upon registration with an authorised money transfer agent, Ecocash clients can access multiple products and services ranging from scan and pay, Ecocash Diaspora, Ecocash express debit card, Ecocash debit card, Ecocash save, Ecocash Ta among others (https://www.monkeypesa.com/post/top-fintech-companies-in-zimbabwe).

The main advantage of platifirms is that they allow producers (e.g., developers of applications and search engines) and consumers to co-create content and interact in ways that generate and capture value for both. For instance, Apple conceived iPhone as more than a conduit of services by bringing application developers and application users together, and through their intensified participation in applications over time, the value of the company increased as "network effects" were integral to the platform strategy (Ruggieri et al., 2018). Booking.com that connects hotels to accommodation seekers and Uber that employs platform-based channels to connect riders and taxis have developed an extremely successful value creation and value capture by linking supply and demand for accommodation and transport services. The multiple technological affordances afforded by digital platforms are making the scaling up of online businesses simpler and cheaper, stimulate frictionless participation that strengthens network effects, and increase opportunities for firms to capture, analyse and exchange huge amounts of data, thereby increasing platifirms' value for all (Van Alstyne et al., 2016).

Notwithstanding the benefits of scaling and low investment in technology infrastructure, the platform-based business models are also fraughted with multiple challenges such as digital security risks, data breaches, phishing and internet fraud. For instance, while platifirms such as Alibaba had to deal with fraudulent activities, Facebook struggles with hate speech, while Twitter has trolls as their unfinished business to deal with (Parker et al., 2019). They elaborate that although platifirms traditionally thrived on unfettered data acquisition, antitrust concerns, rise in fake news and breakdown in compliance relating to personal data, the cost of collecting compliant data is expected to increase as many rules and regulations around data security and data protection are implemented (Parker et al., 2019).

Crowdfunding

Since crowdfunding is a relatively new concept, little is understood about why and how entrepreneurs strive to raise funding through this mechanism, especially whether this alternative funding is employed to fill existing funding gaps in traditional sources of entrepreneurial finance (Bruton et al., 2015) or whether it is complementary to other funding sources (Mawson & Ball, 2020). Despite the persistence of this grey area, in the technology saturated digital era where brick-and-mortar businesses and digital businesses can be financed through inexpensive calls for donations, crowdfunding has become the most popular way of raising equity or financing a global cause. Crowdfunding describes an open invitation over the Internet for financial resources through a financial donation, sometimes in exchange for a future product, service or reward (Kleemann et al., 2008). It constitutes a peer-to-peer lending model where a group of people exchange information, products and services of value to them and their networked community to realise greater social good or public cause.

Although there are many causes and different ways of crowdfunding, the most common ones are lending-based, equity-based, reward-based and donation-based. Lending-based crowdfunding involves (1) dispensing loans that can re-imbursed with interest, (2) equity based crowdfunding which allows investors to earn shares in the startup company, (3) reward based crowdfunding which involves rewarding funders with a product that has actual monetary value, often an early version of the product or service being funded and (4) donation based crowd funding which involves backers donating funds because they believe in the public cause to which money is committed (Pelizzon et al., 2016). Crowdfunding, therefore, constitutes a disruptive funding model where small firms with poor signalling pertaining to their liquidity and where information asymmetries persist between traditional banks and entrepreneurs create alternative and innovative pathways to generate funds to meet their commitments and objectives.

Founded by Desmond Koney and Zoussi Ley in Accra, Ghana in 2017, *Complete Farmer* is an Agritech startup that functions as a crowd-farming platform that offers an opportunity to invest in building sustainable farms. Its customers can become "crowd farmers" by investing in farms of Africa and remotely monitor them. The company offers data and information regarding how to produce healthy yields and best practices by offering a data-driven way to scientifically improve farming (Singh, 2021). Similarly, Livestock Wealth, a company started by Ntuthuko Shezi in 2014, is a company that focuses on crowdfunding for cattle. It connects the investors with farmers who require fundraising for cattle and the company's platform recently extended its services to include a shared farming project that sells and buys grass-fed and free-range beef (Singh, 2021).

Cloud-Based Computing

In its basic form, cloud computing denotes the availing of personal and business applications through the Internet with centralised servers, which assume the role of sharing the underlying computing resources (Klems, 2008). Essentially, it is an IT framework based on virtualisation, distributed computing, utility computing, networks, websites and software services that render clients with a service-oriented architecture (SOA) and an opportunity to reduce operating cost (Vouk, 2008). Because cloud-based computing allows SMMEs to only pay for the services they consume, literature highlights that the main benefits of such a service for small firms are affordances for rapid growth without large investments in technological equipment, software or additional personnel (Zabalza et al., 2012). By allowing for virtualisation (the separation of the operating system and application programmes of physical systems or hardware), SMEs can benefit from the deployment of IT services, without managing the hardware associated with these services (Zabalza et al., 2012). Such separation of hardware from software also facilitates the scaling of organisational effectiveness, efficiency and usability of company knowledge management systems (Antonova et al., 2009).

The four main configurations in the provision of cloud-based services which could transform the business model of SMEs are *infrastructure as a service* (IaaS), *platform as a service* (PaaS), *software as a service* (SaaS) and *function as a service* (Faas). IaaS involves service providers hosting some main infrastructure as a business would typically house in their on-site IT data centres particularly storage, servers and networking resources, and delivers them as virtual services (Augustine, 2022). PaaS is a serverless option for businesses that eliminates the need for building, housing and maintaining complex infrastructure by availing a platform for developing, running and managing applications via the cloud. SaaS is a virtual method of delivering applications with no requirements for hardware or software installations or maintenance as this service is entirely web-based and permits the service provider to manage the complete application (Augustine, 2022). With FaaS, a service provider manages the hardware and operating systems associated with hosting a software application while the user concentrates on scripting and executing codes for the applications (Augustine, 2022).

SMEs' deployment of the pay-as-you-use model allows them to make justifications for their operational expenditure and capital flows, while the scalability of IT services permits them to customise their different IT needs to specific projects during the firm's life cycle (Modisane & Jokonya, 2021). "The opportunity for SMEs to deploy requisite user applications at any place and at any time increases scalability and flexibility, and allows for more efficient use of technology" (Yaseen et al., 2022).

An example of a cloud-based service is Hello Tractor. Founded by Jehiel Oliver and Van Jones on 16 June 2014 and headquarters in Abuja, Nigeria, Hello Tractor is described as "Uber for Tractor" and its app matches farmers who are looking for tractors with owners who are looking for farmers to lend their tractors. Considered to be one of the most successful startups that join MasterCard's Start Path engagement programme, a programme that avails startups with access to industry experts and infrastructure, helping them diversify and grow their operations and build the business (Singh, 2021). Another example of a cloud computing-based firm is iProcure, a company based in Nairobi, Kenya that was founded by Nicole Galletta and Stefano Carcoforo in 2012. The company's platform connects small-scale farmers to the manufacturers of agricultural inputs used such as fertilisers, animal feed and products for plant protection for organic farming. Farmers can buy all the supplies they need through mobile vouchers availed via the platform (Singh, 2021).

Social Media Marketing

Evidence suggests that social media enhances the co-creation of content between firms and customers and affords the development of tailor-made solutions for such firms (Lorenzo-Romero et al., 2019). Compared to traditional forms of media advertising (e.g., TV, radio, newspapers), social media is generally conceived as innovative and cost-effective, and attracts substantial attention and many users (Leeflang et al., 2014). While there are different business models that are supported by social media ranging from brokerage model, merchant model, advertising model, manufacturer model and subscription model to the affiliate model (Rappa, 2001), the use of social media and digital platforms enables SMEs to expand their target market, monitor market trends and track the behaviours of customers (Pousttchi & Hufenbach, 2014).

Although the 2021 Sprout Social Index™ study revealed increasing brand awareness (58%) and increasing community engagement (41%) as the most popular goals for using social media, it also demonstrated the key hurdles relating to social media usage for business model development. These hurdles include the complexities of locating human resources talent, proving social media's potential to increase return on investment, social execution of business activities, adequate resourcing and using social media as a business function (Kenan, 2022; Sprout Social Index™, 2021). When used to support the development of a business innovation model for SMEs, social media can support the Merchant model. This can involve digital firms such as Facebook.com serving as infomediaries (information intermediaries) that either collect data about consumers or collect data about producers and their products and then sell it to firms, which can mine it for important patterns and useful information to better serve their clients (Panda et al., 2017). These clients can be SMEs that mine such data to better serve their clients. Alternatively, manufacturing SMMEs can harness the manufacturer model, where they use their digital platforms to reach out to customers directly through the Internet in ways that compress the distribution channel (Panda et al., 2017; Rappa, 2001). The subscription model would ideally allow consumers of SMMEs products and services to subscribe for a fee (monthly or daily) to social media platforms where SMMEs produce online content, networking services and Internet services providers (Rappa, 2001).

One of the most successful social media-based platforms in Zimbabwe is Muzinda Hub. Founded by Econet Wireless in 2014, Muzinda Hub is reputable for empowering young Zimbabweans, aged 18–35 years, by teaching them to code. The company provides globally competitive digital skills training that cultivates employment opportunities and allows young girls to make positive social transformation within their communities. Apart from this technology hub having enrolled over 3,500 youths onto its flagship training programme, the company has provided affordable access to digital training (Gwata, 2019). In 2019, Muzinda Hub partnered with Theirworld (Code Club initiative) to provide wider access to basic technology and coding courses to 120 young girls aged 10–20 in Harare, Zimbabwe. The project teaches girls computer literacy, basic coding, how to create applications including crucial life skills such as confidence, creativity and critical thinking. The Code Club initiative reflects the growing focus on the rise of digitalisation, automation, artificial intelligence and robotics, and the implications they will have on the workplace of the future (Gwata, 2019). Attracting some of its clients via Facebook and its website, the partnership is credited with having deepened gender balance within all cohorts of Muzinda Hub's pre-existing Digital Skills Training and Alumni Placement Programmes, by increasing exposure and recruitment of women and girls to tech-related activities.

Tockenisation and Securitisation of Assets

The process of tockenisation gives effect to the blockchain securitisation and transforms the dynamics of modern finance and lending models. In tokenisation, the issuing agent (called special purpose vehicle (SPV)) owning illiquid assets converts them into "tokens" that represent individual securities sold to investors on the blockchain. Subsequently, these tokens are distributed to each individual investor and serve as proof of ownership of each individual security issued by the SPV (Herath, 2022). Since assets are held despite the seller's bankruptcy and lack of legal interests in them (Herath, 2022), this process democratises access and use of assets the owner possesses and facilitates the sellers' engagement in business.

To the extent that tockenisation often falls outside the purview of normal financial regulation, it has been popularised as the new funding model for most startups with constrained access to loans or incapable of generating equity. Token sales on the public market coupled with bootstrapping projects founded on proceeds from token allocations have spurred the massive adoption of token-based business models (Tasca, 2018). Moreover, tockenisation and securitisation present multiple benefits to SMEs. For instance, securitisation of blockchain implies that cashflows and transactions between parties in the blockchain are recorded, allowing for faster and accurate cashflow reporting including greater transparency in executions (Herath, 2022). The elimination of the middleman that blockchain technologies afford is envisaged to increase business model sustainability through cost savings and efficiency enhancements.

The Reserve Bank of Zimbabwe (RBZ) is preparing to launch its inaugural peer-to-peer platform, which seeks to facilitate simpler financial transactions using digital gold tokens between individual users. The aim of this digital currency is to reduce Zimbabweans' reliance on the US dollar, reduce currency volatility and arrest a hyperinflationary environment in the country. The digital currency users must have gold token-based bank accounts with local commercial banks, and these accounts will allow their digital gold assets to be converted into monetary value, benchmarked in US dollars for transactions. The users can also use their debit cards or electronic wallets to access their digital tokens (Nnabuenyi, 2023).

Big Data-Driven Decision-Making

Data-driven insights have been key to supporting entrepreneurial and strategic decision making of firms. While artificial intelligence and big data analytics have been instrumental in availing data in high volume, velocity, variety and veracity (Cheah & Wang, 2017), the exploitation of such data enables data-driven strategies for business model innovation (Mostaghel et al., 2022). For instance, even though SMMEs traditionally relied on repetitive sales and customer behaviours availed through sales data to determine future customer loyalty, the exploitation of big data analytics has significantly transformed the tracking and monitoring of customer purchases and market trends to support strategic decision making. Big data analytics and IoT have availed firms with real-time, accurate data about the actual usage of products and services (Hoyer et al., 2020), transforming their relationships with customers, while changing their operational management and revenue streams (Kamble et al., 2019). The use of big data analytics also allows firms to visualise trends of products consumption across geographic, sectoral and individual levels to determine areas where process improvements are necessary including which niche markets to target.

Big data platforms are credited with improving operational efficiencies and generating greater revenue streams and enhanced growth of firms (Chaudhary et al., 2015). Moreover, big data is credited with delivering greater understanding of business value and ensuring business growth (Chaudhary et al., 2015). By using data visualisation techniques, for example, a firm may develop a holistic picture of which products and services are purchased most by customers, from which social demographic, and which locations. Therefore, data visualisation analysis techniques are posed to enhance firms' strategic, managerial and operation capabilities that need attention and those that must be sustained.

With reference to Namibia, one of the big data management-based firm is HData Systems. They use big data analytics and business intelligence services involving their collation, integration and generation of reports and data from their clients' competitors in ways that increase their clients' return on investment. By using business intelligence services and big data analytics, this firm is helping startups and large firms to achieve their business goals and to strategise based on this intelligent and trustworthy data (Top App Development Companies, 2023).

Artificial Intelligence (AI)-Informed Business Processes

Artificial intelligence employs machine learning (data mining and predictive analytics) to predict future patterns of behaviours, actions and activities (e.g., investment patterns, resourcing requirements) in business organisations. Machine learning allows automatic algorithmic performance to facilitate the recognition, acquisition, discovery of new knowledge and uncover predictions based on generalisable regularities in the data (Strohmeier, 2022). It facilitates the acquisition of systematic background information on specific management functions through the process of understanding and auditing input data (Abdallah et al., 2017). Moreover, it enhances data preparation (manipulating data into a form ready for analysis, model generation, evaluation) (Webb, 2017) and model application (i.e., applying data of one or more cases to the model to gain information on these new cases and use information in business contexts (Strohmeier, 2022).

Artificial intelligence is hailed for facilitating and predicting informed decision-making ranging from automating and evaluating the suitability of potential employees (Laumer et al., 2022), making predictions on staffing developments such as net employee requirements, reserve employee requirements and future attrition of employees (Meier & Laumer, 2022). Other benefits include the automation of processes and operations in already implemented digital applications and closing process automation gaps (Fettke & Strohmeier, 2022). In short, through machine learning, artificial intelligence facilitates a range of decision-making ranging from human resource management, investment decisions, marketing trends, customer base determination leading to the development of business process innovations that can change the sustainability trajectory of firms.

8 Proposed Conceptual Framework

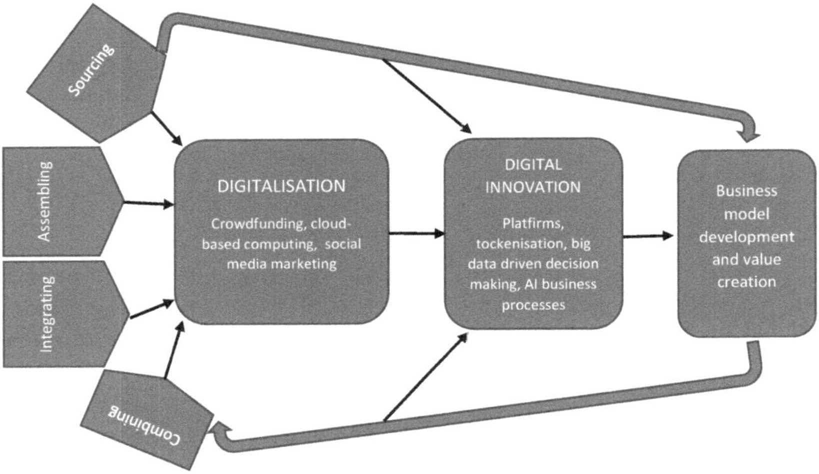

The central argument embedded in this conceptual framework is that any firm striving to develop its business model and create value for itself or customers must demonstrate a strong commitment to source (acquire), assemble, integrate and combine a diversified range of resources, capabilities and competencies from within the organisation and its outside environment. The assemblance of resources stimulates the process of digitalisation, which manifests itself in different dimensions, configurations and processes ranging from crowdfunding, cloud-based computing to social media marketing. These variations of digitalisation facilitate the firm's engagement in digital innovation processes such as platfirmisation, tokenisation, big data-driven decision-making and AI-based business processes. The fostering and stimulation of such digital innovation contribute to the development of new business models that create, deliver and capture value for SMEs. It is postulated that such processes create a new wave of sourcing, assembling, integrating and combining of new sets of heterogeneous resources, capabilities and competencies for the firms, thereby pivoting a self-perpetuating, recursive and self-regulating system.

9 Implications

Theoretical Implications

Drawing on the Theory of Disruptive Technology (Christensen, 1997), we demonstrated how small firms in developing economies navigate the introduction digital technologies to size hold of their business model innovations in ways that create, capture and deliver value for their business and customers. Consistent with previous works on digitalisation and digital innovations (Jarvenpaa et al., 2020), we demonstrated that these firms employ digitalisation by harnessing technology affordances such as ***decoupling, disintermediation*** and ***generativity*** (Autio et al., 2018; Tilson et al., 2010). Through decoupling, these small firms allow new combinations of specialised knowledge, activities, products, services and materials to happen quickly (Jarvenpaa et al., 2020). A typical example is how securitisation and tockenisation have disrupted the complexity and complexion of the venture capital market by abruptly availing tokens that allow people without immovable property to transact digital assets and eliminate their dependence on traditional banks. Disintermediation reduces small firms' dependencies and allows new and unforeseen linkages and associations to be formed to capture new niche markets (Jarvenpaa et al., 2020). There is clear and demonstrable evidence to suggest that platifirms have changed the nature, character and fluidity of firms' transactions with customers. Prominent examples include Uber, Bolt, Airbnb and Alibaba that have disrupted traditional service providers by revolutionising transportation, hospitality and commerce by eliminating intermediaries and creating new associations between customers and firms. Generativity captures the overall capacity to produce unprompted change driven by large, varied and uncoordinated audiences (Jarvenpaa et al., 2020; Zittrain, 2006). While socialites, for example, gain traction and revenue through availing content online (with likes, following, sharing, downloads), social media platforms also benefit from these personalities by marketing products and services via these socialites' accounts.

While the notion of disruptive innovations and technologies presume the presence of an efficient and effective ecosystem where new entrants benefit from efficiency in production processes, increases in product value availed at low cost and convenience (Thunderbird School of Global Management, 2022) by incumbent firms, in developing economies perfect markets rarely exist. While arguments about disruptive innovations and technologies are premised on Silicon-based notions of the existence of serial entrepreneurs in regions, research institutions and other sources of innovative knowledge, easy access to markets and customers and an entrepreneurial culture that supports risk taking and trustful institutions, these qualities rarely exist in emerging market (Jarvenpaa et al., 2020). Therefore, the development of digital capabilities and innovations in developing regions is undermined by excessive bureaucracy, turbulent environments characterised by high inflationary pressures, poor contract enforcement, lack of respect or property rights, policy inconsistencies, unwarranted political interventions and corruption. Consequently, the ability of new entrants to introduce digitalisation, disruptive innovations and technologies that transform the market and topple incumbent firms is a function of the capacity of these new firms to navigate and negotiate institutional voids ranging from contract enforcement, payment of taxes, negotiation of incentives among other considerations.

Policy Implications

As the initial low hanging fruits recede pertaining to the unfettered exploitation of user generated data as data protection laws demand compliance with responsible data generation, curation and aggregation, perturbing questions are being posed regarding how to address stunted growth of platform-based firms. As such, platifirms have concentrated on transitioning and appropriating adjacent markets in different areas with different set of rules. For instance, Amazon has moved into entertainment and groceries, Google into autonomous vehicles, Facebook into virtual reality and payments, and Apple into news and streaming music, while Tencent and Alibaba are moving into digital banking (Parker et al., 2019). With this new trend, pertinent questions are raised regarding which policy strategies can be implemented to ensure that such oligopolies do not raise barriers to entry, thereby blocking new entrants. The creation of competitive environments that increase the intensity of rivalry requires that such oligopolies do not dominate the market and policy and regulations democratise participation in adjust areas.

Research Implications

Given that one of the prime explanations for the productivity paradox is the lack of strong business model innovation subsequent to the adoption of digital technologies and ICTs by small firms (Velu, 2016), research scholarship must target comprehensive sector-specific and firm-based examination of how the domestication of emerging technologies impact specific business process (e.g., logistic value chains, production, manufacturing, sales, human resources development) in the value chain in developing economies. This is key to unlocking the business value creation and value enhancement processes as the adoption of new digital innovations often requires some reconfigurations of the entire business value chain. We must accede that technology adoption often alters the congruence between business components, which triggers reverse salience. Reverse salience is situation whereby components of the system are no longer in alignment with each other as efficiency and process improvements that technology adoption enables creates constant conflicts with adjacent processes or avails processes for redesign due to new value proposition to the customer (Velu, 2020). The need for future research on resource orchestration to address business innovation within the entire organisation regardless of its size is fundamental because managers (especially of SMEs) often adopt new technology for process improvement with little regard for possibilities of redesigning the whole organisational system—a process called piecemeal syndrome (Skinner, 1986, Velu, 2020). Therefore, future research on digital technologies and digital innovation needs to consider how the piecemeal syndrome could undermine or enhance business model innovation as well.

Practical Implications

The prevalence of blockchain technologies and platifirms among SMEs in the developing world implies that smart contracts might be the digital practices of future SMEs. Therefore, more efficient and effective methods of contract enforcement and building durable relationships may be centred on smart contracting. The increasing ubiquity of AI might also mean that AI architecture can be expanded to the entire value creation and value capture process by incorporating ethical sourcing, green production and consumption of products drawing on AI capabilities. This will require the identification and validation of focal areas and business units where efficiency improvements are key in the firm's value chains.

10 Research Limitations

While this study employed a conceptual approach to reviewing contemporary literature and documenting its findings, its emphasis on peer-reviewed literature published in English meant that other relevant literature written in other languages were excluded. The emphasis on peer-reviewed journal articles also implied that relevant and compelling materials contained in books, work in progress and non-peer-reviewed research materials were eliminated from the study. However, efforts were made to accommodate all published and peer-reviewed articles covering the concepts under investigation.

11 Conclusion

Drawing on the Theory of Disruptive Technology and institutional voids, this study presented and discussed a range of digital technologies and innovations that have potential to improve business model development and value creation. Specifically, digital platforms ("platifirms"), crowdfunding, cloud-based computing, social media marketing, tockenisation and securitisation of assets, big data-driven decision-making and artificial intelligence (AI)-informed business processes were identified as important technologies and innovations that could shape, transform and inform business model development and impact digital futures of African SMEs. The study also acknowledged the complexities and institutional hurdles on the African continent that constrain digital innovations and business model development. Therefore, rather than expecting entrepreneurial firms in developing countries to purchase or possess resources that imitate firms in developed countries, emerging economy firms must innovate and develop their own proprietary innovations (Cao, 2018; Peng et al., 2018).

References

Abdallah, Z., Du, L., & Webb, G. (2017). Data preparation. In C. Sammut & G. I. Webb (Eds.), *Encyclopedia of machine learning and data mining* (pp. 318–327). Springer.

Abuhashesh, M. Y. (2014). Integration of social media in businesses. *International Journal of Business and Social Science, 5*(8), 202–209.

Agri-Technovation Pvt Ltd. (2013). Services. https://agritechnovation.co.za/services/

Agri-Technovation Pvt Ltd. (2023a). https://agritechnovation.co.za/

Agri-Technovation Pvt Ltd. (2023b). About us. https://agritechnovation.co.za/about-us-2/

Aguera, P., Berglund, N., Chinembiri, T., Comninos, A., Gillwald, A., & Govan-Vassen, N. (2020). *Paving the way towards digitalising agriculture in South Africa*. Research ICT Africa.

Ahlstrom, D., Bruton, G. D., & Yeh, K. S. (2008). Private firms in China: Building legitimacy in an emerging economy. *Journal of World Business, 43*(4), 385–399.

Amit, R., & Zott, C. (2012). Creating value through business model innovation. *MIT Sloan Management Review, 53*, 41–49.

Antonova, A., Gourova, E., & Roumen, N. (2009). Extended architecture of knowledge management system with web 2.0 technologies. In *Paper presented at the 10th European Conference on Knowledge Management* (pp. 48–55). Kidmore End: Academic Conferences Ltd.

Augustine, S. (2022, September 23). *IaaS, FaaS, CaaS, PaaS & SaaS: What's the Difference?* https://www.bayleafdigital.com/iaas-faas-caas-paas-saas-whats-the-difference/

Autio, E., Nambisan, S., Thomas, L., & Wright, M. (2018). Digital affordances, spatial affordances, and the genesis of entrepreneurial ecosystems. *Strategic Management Journal, 12*(1), 72–95.

Baden-Fuller, C., & Haefliger, S. (2013). Business models and technological innovation. *Long Range Planning, 46*(6), 419–426.

Barlatier, P. J., & Josserand, E. (2018). Delivering open innovation promises through social media. *Journal of Business Strategy, 39*(6), 21–28.

Bashir, N., Papamichail, K. N., & Malik, K. (2017). Use of social media applications for supporting new product development processes in multinational corporations. *Technological Forecasting and Social Change, 120*, 176–183.

Bouwman, H., Nikou, S., Francisco, J., Molina-Castillo, F. J., & de Reuver, M. (2018). The impact of digitalization on business models. *Digital Policy, Regulation and Governance, 20*(2), 105–124.

Bruton, G., Khavul, S., Siegel, D., & Wright, M. (2015). New financial alternatives in seeding entrepreneurship: Microfinance, crowdfunding, and peer-to-peer innovations. *Entrepreneurship: Theory and Practice, 39*(1). https://doi.org/10.1111/etap.12143

Burström, T., Parida, V., Lahti, T., & Wincent, J. (2021). AI-enabled business-model innovation and transformation in industrial ecosystems: A framework, model and outline for further research. *Journal of Business Research, 127*, 85–95.

Cao, Z. (2018). Entrepreneurial ecosystems in emerging economies (E4s). What is similar and what is different? *Academy of Management Proceedings.*

Carillo-Hermosilla, J., Kiefer, C. P., & Del Rio, P. (2019). Taxonomy and dimensions of eco-innovation from a resource-based perspective. In F. Boons & A. McMeekin (Eds.), *Handbook of sustainable innovation* (pp. 78–100). Edward Elgar.

Chau, M., & Chen, H. (2003). Comparison of three vertical search spiders. *Computer, 36*(55), 56–62.

Chaudhary, R., Pandey, J. R., & Pandey, P. (2015). Business model innovation through big data. In *International Conference on Green Computing and Internet of Things*. IEEE.

Cheah, S., & Wang, S. (2017). Big data-driven business model innovation by traditional industries in the Chinese economy. *Journal of Chinese Economic and Foreign Trade Studies, 10*, 229–251.

Chen, T., Chuang, T.-T., & Nakatani, K. (2016). The perceived business benefit of cloud computing: An exploratory study. *Journal of International Technology and Information Management, 25*(4), Article 7. https://doi.org/10.58729/1941-6679.1297

Christensen, C. M. (1997). *The innovator's dilemma: When new technologies cause great firms to fail*. Harvard Business School Press.

Christensen, C. M., & Raynor, M. (2013). *The innovator's solution: Creating and sustaining successful growth*. Harvard Business Review Press.

Christensen, C. M., Raynor, M., & McDonald, R. (2015). What is disruptive innovation? *Harvard Business Review*. https://hbr.org/archive-toc/BR1512

de Carbon, A. (2016, August 5). Precision agriculture: Its benefits and limitations. CARRHURE Consulting. https://www.carrhure.com/precision-agriculture-benefits-limitations

Doh, J., Rodrigues, S., Saka-Helmhout, A., & Makhija, M. (2017). International business responses to institutional voids. *Journal of International Business Studies, 48*, 293–307.

Donnery, L. (2022). Cloud computing for small business: A game changer in small business, cloud, startups. Salesforce. https://www.salesforce.com/eu/blog/2022/03/cloud-computing-for-small-business.html. Posted March 2, 2022.

Endres, H., Stoiber, K., & Wenzl, N. M. (2019). Managing digital transformation through hybrid business models. *Journal of Business Strategy, 41*(6), 49–56.

Evans, D. S. (2002). *The antitrust economics of two-sided markets*. AEI-Brookings Joint Centre of Regulatory Studies, Related Publication 02-13, September 2002.

Evans, D. S. (2003). Some empirical aspects of multi-sided platform industries. *Review of Network Economics, 2*(33), 191–209.

Fettke, P., & Strohmeier, S. (2022). HR robotic process automation. In S. Strohmeier (Ed.), *Handbook of research in artificial intelligence in human resource management* (pp. 187–206). Edward Elgar.

Fink, A. (2005). *Conducting research literature reviews: From the internet to paper* (2nd ed.). Sage.

Godin, B., & Gaglio, G. (2019). How does innovation sustain 'sustainable innovation'. In F. Boons & A. McMeekin (Eds.), *Handbook of sustainable innovation* (pp. 27–37). Edward Elgar.

Guo, L., & Xu, L. (2021). The effects of digital transformation on firm performance: Evidence from China's manufacturing sector. *Sustainability, 13*(22), Article 12844.

Gupta, G., & Bose, I. (2019). Digital transformation in entrepreneurial firms through information exchange with operating environment. *Information and Management, 2019*, 103243.

Gwata, V. (2019). Muzinda Hub x Theirworld: Creating the next generation of coders and entrepreneur. *Their World*. https://theirworld.org/news/muzinda-hub-x-theirworld-creating-the-next-generation-of-coders-and-entrepreneurs/

Hamilton, F. (2021). What is a conceptual paper? Sydney, New South Wales, Australia. https://www.linkedin.com/pulse/800209-what-conceptual-paper-felix-nguyen. Accessed May 18, 2023.

Harvard Business Review. (2016). *The Platform Age*.

Herath, K. (2022). Blockchain securitization—A revolution in global structured finance. https://www.acuitykp.com/blog/blockchain-securitisation-a-revolution-in-global-structured-finance/. Posted December 7, 2022.

Hoyer, W. D., Kroschke, M., Schmitt, B., Kraume, K., & Shankar, V. (2020). Transforming the customer experience through new technologies. *Journal of Interactive Marketing, 51*, 57–71.

Hilmersson, F. P., & Hilmersson, M. (2020). Networking to accelerate the pace of SME innovations. *Journal of Innovation & Knowledge, 6*(1), 43–49.

Hwang, J., & Christensen, C. M. (2008). Disruptive innovation in health care delivery: A framework for business-model innovation. *Health Affairs, 27*(5), 1329–1335. https://doi.org/10.1377/hlthaff.27.5.1329

Jarvenpaa, S. L., Elsie L. Echeverri-Carroll, E. L., & Aura Pedraza-Avella, A. (2020). Digital innovation and entrepreneurship in and around institutional voids: The case of Fundacin Cardiovascular (FCV) in Colombia. In S. Nambisan, K. Lyytinen, & Y. Yoo (Eds.), *Handbook of digital innovation* (pp. 41–63). Edward Elgar.

Jayanti, R. K., & Raghunath, S. (2018). Institutional entrepreneur strategies in emerging economies: Creating market exclusivity for the rising affluent. *Journal of Business Research, 89*, 87–98.

Jesson, J. (2011). Doing your literature review: Traditional and systematic techniques. *Educational Research and Evaluation, 24*, 219–221.

Kamble, S. S., Gunasekaran, A., Parekh, H., & Joshi, S. (2019). Modeling the internet of things adoption barriers in food retail supply chains. *Journal of Retailing and Consumer Services, 48*, 154–168.

Kenan, J. (2022). Social media marketing: What it is and how to build your strategy. https://sproutsocial.com/insights/social-media-marketing-strategy. Posted September 22, 2022.

Khanagha, S., Taghi, M., Zadeh, R., Mihalache, O. R., & Volberda, H. W. (2018). Embracing bewilderment: Responding to technological disruption in heterogeneous market environments. *Journal of Management Information Systems, 55*(7), 1079–1121.

Klein, A., Sorensen, C., de Freitas, A. S., Pedron, C. D., & Elaluf-Calderwood, S. (2020). Understanding controversies in digital platform innovation processes: The Google Glass case. *Technological Forecasting and Social Change, 152*, Article 119883.

Kleemann, F., Voß, G. G., & Rieder, K. (2008). Un(der) paid innovators: The commercial utilization of consumer work through crowdsourcing. *Science, Technology & Innovation Studies, 4*(1), 5–26.

Klems, M. (2008). Merrill Lynch estimates cloud computing to be $ 100 billion market, cloud expo: Article. Last retrieved on November 29, 2016 from http://web2.sys-con.com/node/604936

Kudoti. (2023). https://kudoti.com/

Lafont, J., Ruiz, F., Gil-Gomez, H., & Oltra-Badenes, R. (2020). Value creation in listed companies: A bibliometric approach. *Journal of Business Research, 115*(C), 428–434.

Laumer, S., Maier, C., & Weitzel, T. (2022). HR machine learning in recruiting. In S. Strohmeier (Ed.), *Handbook of research in artificial intelligence in human resource management* (pp. 105–126). Edward Elgar.

Leeflang, P. S., Verhoef, P. C., Dahlstrom, P., & Freundt, T. (2014). Challenges and solutions for marketing in a digital era. *European Management Journal, 32*(1), 1–12.

Lorenzo-Romero, C., Cordente-Rodriguez, M., & Alarcon-del-Amo, M. D. (2019). Open collaboration as marketing transformation strategy in online markets: The case of the fashion sector. *Resources, 8*(4), 25. https://doi.org/10.3390/resources8040167

Luo, Y., & Child, J. (2020). A composition-based view of firm growth. *Management and Organisation Review, 11*(3), 379–411.

Mahdi, S., D'Este, P., & Neely, A. (2008). Citation counts: Are they good predictors of RAE scores? Advanced Institute of Management Research.

Mawson, S., & Ball, C. (2020). The use of crowdfunding by environmental entrepreneurs: Is it all about cash? In I. Fillis & N. Telford (Eds.), *Handbook on entrepreneurship and marketing* (pp. 99–111). Edward Elgar.

Mei, L., Zhang, T., & Chen, J. (2019). Exploring the effects of inter-firm linkages on SMEs' open innovation from an ecosystem perspective: An empirical study of Chinese manufacturing SMEs. *Technological Forecasting and Social Change, 144*, 118–128.

Meier, F., & Laumer, S. (2022). Machine learning in HR staffing. In S. Strohmeier (Ed.), *Handbook of research in artificial intelligence in human resource management* (pp. 127–148). Edward Elgar.

Miller, D. C., & Salkind, N. J. (2002). Elements of research design. In D. C. Miller & J. J. Salkind (Eds.), *Handbook of research design and social measurement*. Sage.

Modisane, P., & Jokonya, O. (2021). Evaluating the benefits of cloud computing in small medium and micro-sized enterprises. *Procedia Computer Science, 181*, 784–792.

Monkey Pesa. (2021). Top Fintech companies in Zimbabwe. Apophia. https://www.monkeypesa.com/post/top-fintech-companies-in-zimbabwe. Posted Aug 12, 2021.

Mostaghel, R., Oghazi, P., Parida, V., & Sohrabpour, V. (2022). Digitalization driven retail business model innovation: Evaluation of past and avenues for future research trends. *Journal of Business Research, 146*, 134–145.

Nambisan, S. (2017). Digital entrepreneurship: Toward a digital technology perspective of entrepreneurship. *Entrepreneurship Theory and Practice, 41*(6), 1029–1055.

Nambisan, S., Lyytinen, K., Majchrzak, A., & Song, M. (2017). Digital innovation management: Reinventing innovation management research in a digital world. *MIS Quarterly, 41*(1), 223–238.

Nambisan, S., Lyytinen, K., & Yoo, Y. (2020). Digital innovation: Towards a transdisciplinary perspective. In S. Nambisan, K. Lyytinen, & Y. Yoo (Eds.), *Handbook of digital innovation* (pp. 2–12). Edward Elgar.

Nel, C. (2016, March 15). Keep track of your cattle 24/7. *Farmer's Weekly* https://www.farmersweekly.co.za/agri-technology/useful-products/keep-track-of-your-cattle-24/7

Nnabuenyi, C., Jr. (2023). Reserve Bank of Zimbabwe to launch P2P digital gold token platform. https://cryptotvplus.com/2023/06/reserve-bank-of-zimbabwe-to-launch-p2p-digital-gold-token-platform/. Posted June 20, 2023.

Olago, V. (2019, August 2). AB InBev Using Blockchain to empower farmers across Africa. Ledger Africa. https://www.ledgerafrica.com/ab-inbev-using-blockchain-empower-farmers-africa

Oshri, I., Henfridsson, O., & Kotlarsky, J. (2018). Re-representation as work design in outsourcing: A semiotic view. *MIS Quarterly, 42*, 1–23.

Panda, R., Mehta, B., & Karani, A. (2017). Business models on social media. *International Journal of Marketing & Financial Management, 5*, 34–42.

Parker, G. G., Van Alstyne, M. W., & Choudary, S. P. (2016). *Platform revolution: How networked markets are transforming the economy and how to make them work for you*. W. W. Norton.

Parker, G. G., Van Alstyne, M. W., & Evans, P. (2019). The four biggest challenges digital platforms need to address: Regulation, growth, and new technologies may become roadblocks for once unstoppable firms. https://medium.com/mit-initiative-on-the-digital-economy/the-four-biggest-challenges-digital-platforms-need-to-address-a842413ee3c7. Accessed February 24, 2023.

Parida, V., Sjödin, D., & Reim, W. (2019). Reviewing literature on digitalization, business model innovation, and sustainable industry: Past achievements and future promises. *Sustainability, 11*(2), 391. https://doi.org/10.3390/su11020391

Pelizzon, L., Riedel, M., & Tasca, P. (2016). Classification of crowdfunding in the financial system. In *Banking beyond banks and money* (pp. 5–16). New Economic Windows. Springer.

Peng, M., Lebedev, S., Vlas, C., Wang, J., & Shay, J. (2018). The growth of the firm in (and out of) emerging economies. *Asian Pacific Journal of Management, 35*(4), 829–857.

Pomykalski, P. (2019). Revenue and valuation of companies with digital platform business models. *Management Sciences, 24*(1), 11–18.

Porter, M., & Heppelmann, J. E. (2014). How smart, connected products are transforming competition. *Harvard Business Review*. https://hbr.org/2014/11/how-smart-connected-products-are-transforming-competition

Pousttchi, K., & Hufenbach, Y. (2014). Engineering the value network of the customer interface and marketing in the data-rich retail environment. *International Journal of Electronic Commerce, 18*(4), 17–42.

Priyono, A., Moin, A., & Putri, V. N. (2020). Identifying digital transformation paths in the business model of SMEs during the COVID-19 pandemic. *Journal of Open Innovation: Technology, Market, and Complexity, 6*(4), 1–22.

Rajapathirana, R. J., & Hui, Y. (2018). Relationship between innovation capability, innovation type, and firm performance. *Journal of Innovation & Knowledge, 3*(1), 44–55.

Rappa, M. (2001). Business models on the web: Managing the digital enterprise. https://digitalenterprise.org/models/models.html

Reim, W., Pirjo Yli-Viitala, P., Juha Arrasvuori, J., & Parida, V. (2022). Tackling business model challenges in SME internationalization through digitalization. *Journal of Innovation & Knowledge, 7*(3), 100199. https://doi.org/10.1016/j.jik.2022.100199

Richter, A. (2020). Locked-down digital work. *International Journal of Information Management, 55*, 102157. https://doi.org/10.1016/j.ijinfomgt.2020.102157

Ruggieri, R., Savastano, M., Scalingi, A., Bala, D., & D'Ascenzo, F. (2018). The impact of digital platforms on business models: An empirical investigation on innovative start-ups. *Management & Marketing, 13*(4), 1210–1225.

Sabwa, B. A. (2013). *Cloud computing adoption by small and medium enterprises (SMEs) in Nairobi County* (Masters' dissertation). University of Nairobi.

Santos, J., Spector, B., & Van der Heyden, L. (2015). Toward a theory of business model change. Business model innovation. In N. Foss & T. Saebi (Eds.), *Business model innovation: The organizational dimension* (pp. 43–63). Oxford University Press.

Schaefer, B. (2022). What is the theory of disruptive innovation? Ccecosystems. https://ccecosystems.news/en/what-is-the-theory-of-disruptive-innovation/. Posted on August 27, 2022.

Skinner, W. (1986, July–August). The productivity paradox. *Harvard Business Review*, pp. 55–60.

Singh, S. (2021). Top 10 Agritech Startups in Africa. https://www.vcbay.news/2021/06/18/top-10-agritech-startups-in-africa/. Posted June 18, 2021.

Sprout Social Index™. (2021). New research shows social media has created a more competitive landscape for brands, but is simultaneously key for staying ahead in their industry. https://investors.sproutsocial.com/news/news-details/2021/New-research-shows-social-media-has-created-a-more-competitive-landscape-for-brands-but-is-simultaneously-key-for-staying-ahead-in-their-industry/default.aspx. Posted June 15, 2021.

Strohmeier, S. (2022). HR machine learning—An introduction. In S. Strohmeier (Ed.), *Handbook of research in artificial intelligence in human resource management* (pp. 25–45). Edward Elgar.

Tasca, P. (2018). Token based business models. In T. Lynn & J. G. Mooney (Eds.), *Disrupting finance FinTech and strategy in the 21st century* (pp. 135–146). Palgrave Studies in Digital Business and Enabling Technologies. Palgrave Macmillan.

Teece, D. J. (2010). Business models, business strategy and innovation. *Long Range Planning, 43*(2–3), 172–194.
Teng, X., Wu, Z., & Yang, F. (2022). Impact of the digital transformation of small- and medium-sized listed companies on performance: Based on a cost-benefit analysis framework. *Hindawi Journal of Mathematics, 2022*, 1–14. https://doi.org/10.1155/2022/1504499
Thunderbird School of Global Management. (2022). *Disruptive innovation and the business models that make them successful.* ASU University Technology Office Arizona State University. https://thunderbird.asu.edu/thought-leadership/insights/disruptive-innovation-and-business-models-make-them-successful. Accessed February 27, 2023.
Tilson, D., Lyytinen, K., & Sørensen, C. (2010). Digital infrastructures: The missing IS research agenda. *Information Systems Research, 21*(4), 748–759.
Top App Development Companies. (2023). Top 10+ big data analytics companies in Namibia. https://topappdevelopmentcompanies.com/na/directory/big-data-analytics/namibia. Posted September 15, 2023.
Uman, L. S. (2011). Systematic reviews and meta-analyses. *Journal of the Canadian Academy of Child and Adolescent Psychiatry, 20*, 57–59.
Van Alstyne, M. W., Parker, G. G., & Choudary, S. P. (2016). Pipelines, platforms, and the new rules of strategy. *Harvard Business Review, 94*(4), 54–62.
Van Ark, B. (2016). The productivity paradox of the new digital economy. *International Productivity Monitor, 31*, 3–18.
Velu, C. (2016). Evolutionary or revolutionary business model innovation through coopetition? The role of dominance in network markets. *Industrial Marketing Management, 53*, 124–135.
Velu, C. (2017). A systems perspective on business model evolution: The case of an agricultural information service provider in India. *Long Range Planning, 50*(5), 603–620. https://doi.org/10.1016/j.lrp.2016.10.003
Velu, C. (2020). Business model cohesiveness scorecard: Implications of digitization for business model innovation. In S. Nambisan, K. Lyytinen, & Y. Yoo (Eds.), *Handbook of digital innovation* (pp. 179–197). Edward Elgar.
Vouk, M. A. (2008). Cloud computing—Issues, research and implementations. *Journal of Computing and Information Technology, 16*(4), 235–246.
Wang, R., & Chebo, A. K. (2021, July–September). The dynamics of business model innovation for technology entrepreneurship: A systematic review and future avenue. *Sage Open, 11*(3), 1–12.
Warner, K. S., & Wäger, M. (2019). Building dynamic capabilities for digital transformation: an ongoing process of strategic renewal. *Long Range Planning, 52*(3), 326–349.
Webb, G. I. (2017). Model evaluation. In C. Sammut & G. I. Webb (Eds.), *Encyclopedia of machine learning and data mining* (pp. 844–845). Springer.

Whetten, D. (1989). What constitutes a theoretical contribution? *Academy of Management Review, 14*, 490–495.

Xie, X., Han, Y., Anderson, A., & Ribeiro-Navarrete, S. (2022). Digital platforms and SMEs' business model innovation: Exploring the mediating mechanisms of capability reconfiguration. *International Journal of Information Management, 65*, 102513. https://doi.org/10.1016/j.ijinfomgt.2022.102513

Yaseen, H., Al-Adwan, A. S., Nofal, M., Hmoud, H., & Abujassar, R. S. (2022). Factors influencing cloud computing adoption among SMEs: The Jordanian context. *Information Development, 39*(2), 317–332.

Yoo, Y. (2010). Computing in everyday life: A call for research on experiential computing. *MIS Quarterly, 34*(2), 213–231.

Yoo, Y., Henfridsson, O., & Lyytinen, K. (2010). The new organizing logic of digital innovation: An agenda for information systems research. *Information Systems Research, 21*(4), 724–735.

Zabalza, J., Rio-Belver, R., Cilleruelo, E., Garechana; G., & Gavilanes, J. (2012, July 18–20). Benefits related to cloud computing in the SMEs. In *6th International Conference on Industrial Engineering and Industrial Management*. XVI Congreso de Ingeniería de Organización. Vigo.

Zhang, F., & Zhu, L. (2021). Promoting business model innovation through social media strategic capability: A moderated mediation model. *European Management Journal, 40*, 56–66.

Zhu, F., & Furr, N. (2016). Products to platforms: Making the leap. *Harvard Business Review, 94*(4), 72–78.

Zittrain, J. (2006). The generative Internet. *Harvard Law Review, 119*(7), 1974–2040.

Managerial & Policy Perspectives

Entrepreneurship and Small and Medium-Sized Enterprises (SMEs) in Africa: Old and New Realities in the Light of COVID-19

Gwendoline Vusumuzi Nani and Samuel John Chiromo

1 Introduction

Entrepreneurship is considered to be the driving force of economic and social development in most developed and developing countries (Ajide & Soyemi, 2022). It is the process of innovation and establishing new businesses in hazardous conditions through discovering opportunities and utilisation of resources with Small and Medium Enterprises (SMEs) being the cornerstone of this development (Ajide & Soyemi, 2022; Jafarnejad et al., 2013). According to Mutula and Van Brakel (2006), SMEs are important drivers of the economy and they are the source of employment,

G. V. Nani (✉)
National University of Science and Technology (NUST), Bulawayo, Zimbabwe
e-mail: gwendoline.nani@nust.ac.zw

S. J. Chiromo
Department of Applied Management, University of South Africa (UNISA), Pretoria, South Africa
e-mail: echirosj@unisa.ac.za

P. Rambe and R. E. Hinson (eds.), *The Future of Entrepreneurship in Southern Africa*, Palgrave Studies in Technology and Innovation in Africa, https://doi.org/10.1007/978-3-031-55935-8_5

flexibility and innovation, globally. The significance of SMEs to economic growth, innovation and job formation and social cohesion are major keys for various economies in the world (Bayraktar & Algan, 2019).

The advent of the COVID-19 pandemic threw most businesses into a quagmire that they had never imagined. SMEs suffered huge setbacks such as significant reduction in employee numbers, restricted physical movements and banned face-to-face business interaction. According to Dai et al. (2020), the outbreak of the pandemic cast a heavy toll on SME operations, with eighty per cent of them temporarily closing at the time of the first wave. Setyoko and Kurniasih (2022), concur that the Coronavirus Disease (COVID-19), came as an economic and labour market shock and negatively impacted all businesses globally, especially SMEs.

Governments, throughout the world, had to take precautionary measures to curtail the spread of the pandemic. According to Meyer and Prescott (2020), the US Government instituted travel bans to many countries. State-mandated lockdowns temporarily shattered many non-essential businesses. Economic activity as measured by real Gross Domestic Product contracted at an annual rate of 5% in the 1st quarter and by an outstanding 32% in the second quarter, made the COVID-19 crisis, the swiftest and most severe economic shock the United States has ever experienced in modern times. Walter-Toews (2020) agrees that most entrepreneurs were caught by surprise, thereby exposing their lack of preparedness. Disruptions caused by the COVID-19 pandemic occurred in various sectors and at various levels causing most SMEs to succumb to its effects. Businesses suffered from supply chain disruptions, leading to loss of income, reduced demand for goods and services, loss of employment, wage cuts and weak marketing performance (Ebersberger & Kuckertz, 2021). This resulted in difficulties for SMEs to keep their businesses alive. Consumer spending fell dramatically and business investments dried up. Most SMEs in the services and retail industries which mainly depended on face-to-face interactions were hard hit as some of them had fewer resources or no insurance at all.

In Indonesia, the main sectors that suffered the COVID-19 backlash were tourism, transportation, trade and the investment sector (Mhlungu, 2021). The pandemic affected coffee shops, hotels, restaurants and travel agents due to restricted travel and banned face-to-face interaction. Sixty per cent of the customers' orders had to be refunded in full because their services could not be fulfilled. Some SMEs took loans or just closed, while others declared bankruptcy. Mhlungu (2021) further asserts that the South African economy was not spared. It suffered a double blow as it was already in recession before the outbreak, and the pandemic further deepened its economic downturn.

Many studies, by for example, Adam and Alarifi (2021) and Engidaw (2022) have focused on the challenges caused by the COVID-19 pandemic. However, statistics of people infected by the pandemic continue to decline, hence the need for a paradigm shift to focusing on the post-COVID-19 era. Mhlungu (2021) asserts that due to the devastating effect of COVID-19 on SMEs, their sustainability pandemic is yet to be fully examined. This study, therefore, seeks to address the current gap in the academic literature regarding life after COVID-19 for SMEs.

Entrepreneurs suffered huge financial setbacks but they need to be encouraged that there are still opportunities beyond the pandemic as Farouk (2020), alludes to the view, by saying that South African entrepreneurs need to remain entrepreneurial even in challenging times so that they can take full view of the opportunities that exist and are unveiled by the pandemic. This applies to all businesses that suffered the trail of destruction left by the pandemic.

The Coronavirus pandemic presented a global health and economic crisis, severely affecting societies in all aspects of life (Ozili & Arun, 2020). SMEs had never experienced a pandemic of this magnitude and they seemed to have been the most affected because unlike big businesses, they did not have financial resources to fall back on. This chapter is therefore crucial because its findings will not only assist entrepreneurs to handle similar pandemics in future but also add to the body of knowledge on how to conduct businesses in a different environment, “the new normal”. This chapter, therefore, seeks to unravel the difficulties experienced by SMEs during the COVID-19 pandemic and also delve into the creative and innovative measures that have enabled them to remain afloat to date. According to Dangol et al. (2020), SMEs were hit hard as they did not have strategies and resources to cope with crises.

2 The Schumpeter Theory in the Survival of SMEs During COVID-19 Crisis

This chapter made use of the Schumpeter theory as the basis for innovation used by SMEs as a survival strategy during the COVID-19 crisis.

Schumpeter (1934) defined innovation as the introduction of new or qualitative change in existing products, processes, markets, sources of supply of inputs and organisations. This implies that innovation encompasses a creative activity, the element of novelty, as well as the disruptive change (Assink, 2006). Schumpeter examined the importance of SMEs in the context of the innovation process in one of his pioneer works (Schumpeter Mark 1 presented in Schumpeter, 1934). He argued that SMEs are likely to be the source of most innovations, searching creatively for the new market opportunities.

Schumpeter (1934) suggested that innovation is crucial for the survival of SMEs during a crisis. The Schumpeter theory was developed based on Western ideology and the question that whether it can be applied in the African context is still a contentious issue. However, Van Beers et al. (2014) argue that the Schumpeter theory could be an analytical toolkit that can assist in understanding the phenomenon of innovations in relation to economic transformation in Africa. Hanusch and Pyka (2007) indicated that the Schumpeter theory consists of dynamic processes of innovation in their various and multifaceted forms and the related co-evolutionary processes. Therefore, it provides useful avenues to analyse innovation, hence its usefulness in dealing with economic crisis in Africa. In other words, the Schumpeter theory is more relevant to the survival of SMEs during the COVID-19 pandemic because it addresses innovation in the entrepreneurial setting.

In his seminal work, Schumpeter (1934) highlighted that innovation plays a crucial role in economic growth by allowing SME owners to seek opportunities; innovation also provides the instrument for exploiting change as an opportunity for SMEs. For SMEs to achieve commercial success, innovation is required to make the necessary infrastructure and capital for addressing market needs (Hanusch & Pyka, 2007). Potier (2015) in citation to Schumpeter (1934) argued that innovations promote increased production and investment, which create new jobs, inspire imitators and generate growth. They directly or indirectly lead to investment, which tends to increase with the emergence of new industries.

According to Ehrenberger et al. (2015), innovation is an important aspect of every SME's activity due to the fact that it creates a new space for potential specialisation and future growth. In addition, it allows pushing up the boundaries. Today's globalised and interconnected world makes innovation a necessity rather than an option for SMEs which want to survive on the market and develop further. Innovation also embodies positive benefits both for their inventor and their user. The inventor usually earns a reward in the form of money or respect. The user then gets a result with improved quality, availability, diversity or increased quantity of goods and services.

Following the Schumpeter theory, the importance of innovation for firm growth has been highlighted by many scholars (e.g. Aghion & Howitt, 1988; Carreiro & Oliveira, 2019; Colombelli et al., 2013; Mansfield, 1962; Rosenbusch et al., 2011; Santos et al., 2021; Syahadiyanti & Subriadi, 2018) since the seminal contribution of Schumpeter (1934). However, internal and external factors to the firm can affect the probability of success to transform innovation into growth, as well as the firm's incentive to innovate (Mansfield, 1962). These internal factors include the firm's size and age management capacity, workforce skills, financing capacity and ownership. In this perspective, each firm possesses a unique set of resources and capacities which have been acquired and developed over time. Their exclusive resources and capacities further determine the degree of efficiency and therefore firms' strategic decisions like whether to get involved in innovation or not. For instance, the skill with which firms acquire their technological knowledge determines their level of innovativeness. The age of a firm represents the experience and knowledge accumulated throughout its history and is related to a better management of communication and of necessary creativity to innovate, and to a more effective capacity for absorption. On the other hand, older age may also make knowledge, abilities and skills obsolete, and therefore induce organisational decay (Loderer & Waelchli, 2009). Regarding the size of the firm, Schumpeter (1942) argued that the degree of innovation is positively correlated with firm size. Generally, due to capital market imperfection, large companies have more resources to innovate and support risky activities than do SMEs.

However, external factors focus on macroeconomic conditions such as public policies, size of the market, customers, users and competition, regulation, government support, subsidies, tax system, public infrastructure, knowledge flows and networks (Santos et al., 2021). For example, the SME's jurisdictional location and its proximity to product and labour markets can influence costs and awareness of consumer demand.

According to Edquist (2005), public policies can influence business activities in direct and indirect ways. The regulatory and enforcement framework influences how SMEs can appropriate the outcomes of their innovation efforts and the multiple relationships and transactions that SMEs engage in, whereas the tax system affects the cost of business activities. Santos et al. (2021) argued that other factors such as delivery of infrastructure services and the management of macroeconomic policy can affect the ability of SMEs to launch and successfully exploit innovations. Bloch and López-Bassols (2009) are of the opinion that these various external factors exhibit a great deal of overlap and interaction with each other. For example, public policy can influence the evolution of SME's business environment through markets by regulating monopolies or by using market mechanisms to mitigate the negative environmental effects of business activities. Nonetheless, Krugman (1991) argued that markets, governmental and social institutions and norms can underpin the availability of useful knowledge that firms draw upon for innovation and shape the knowledge flows and networks.

While firms can, to a certain extent, overcome internal weaknesses, they cannot easily mitigate the negative effects of external factors, such as macroeconomic conditions. Downturns or economic crises are exogenous shocks essentially related to market contraction, unemployment, loss of confidence in investment, liquidity constraints, loss of income and uncertainty. Ebersberger and Kuckertz (2021) noted that the COVID-19 crisis seems to be different from previous crises. The origin of the COVID-19 crisis stems from a health crisis which then increased health costs and expenditures to find a treatment; and the disease control practices related to this health crisis (Ebersberger and Kuckertz (2021). Given the particular nature of this crisis, SMEs were faced with different problems that severely impacted their business activities.

Nevertheless, and despite previous crises, the COVID-19 crisis strongly stimulated research and development (R&D) and innovation in SMEs, especially in the health sector. As indicated by Ebersberger and Kuckertz (2021), facing an unprecedented situation during COVID-19, SMEs had to reinvent themselves by embracing innovation in their practices. However, a clear understanding of the changes in innovation patterns and of the role of innovation to mitigate the effects of the COVID-19 crisis are still unclear.

The patterns of innovation can be traced back to the Schumpeter theory, and there have been great technological innovations that have had a very important historical importance on industries and SMEs:

- The first Industrial Revolution (1770–1830), resulting from
- Innovations in the textile industry in England;
- The spread of the railway (1840–1890);
- Electrification, the chemical industry, the internal combustion engine (1890–1930);
- Mass production according to the methods prescribed by Fordism (1930–1980) and,
- Mass communication technologies (1980–present).

According to the Schumpeterian theory, a successful innovation can provide a competitive advantage to a firm in the market. This is supported by Backman et al. (2017) who argued that innovation has become a major tool that ensures SMEs survival through the stimulants of what Schumpeter (1934) calls the "gales of creative destruction". Fritsch (2017) defined "gales of creative destruction" as the energy used by entrepreneurs to outperform competitors in the market. SMEs are operating in an economic cycle dominated by the paradigm of communication and information, which began in the 60s with the advent of the first software and hardware tools which is the basis for the current information age (Spadoni, 2020). The Schumpeter theory of innovation fits into this period, in which innovation plays a fundamental role and opens the doors to the information society. This is consistent with the assertion made by Knorringa and Leliveld (2014) who stated that Schumpeter theory is crucial to African crisis as it provides useful instruments to critically analyse innovation in Africa.

The crucial role of innovations in times of crises has been extensively analysed against the circumstances surrounding the previous crises (Archibugi et al., 2013; Bessant et al., 2012; Chipunza, 2014; Hausman & Wesley, 2014; Spadoni, 2020). Giotopoulos et al. (2017) assert that, during crises, innovation assists businesses to effectively harness windows of opportunity to exploit unmet market needs. Weick (1993) concurs that SMEs appear to be capable of rapidly responding to crises by actively using their relational capabilities and creatively developing solutions using existing resources. In reference to the concept of crisis-driven innovations, Bessant et al. (2012) and Weyrauch and Herstatt (2017) alluded that innovations often take the form of simplified, low-cost adaptations of existing solutions characterised by creative recombination stemming from different and unrelated fields. SMEs seem to act as agents consolidating and assimilating knowledge, following a more explorative approach towards new solutions (Bessant et al., 2012). As a result, these businesses are better able to cope with crises compared to large businesses.

In the studies conducted by Rakas and Hain (2019), Fransman (2018), Phillips and Ritala (2019), it was revealed that any innovation process is a "multiplayer game" involving a complex network of multiple actors and institutions within an innovation system or innovation ecosystem. SMEs are the important actors and institutions of innovations during crisis (Chipunza, 2014). Similarly, owing to the complex dynamic nature of the COVID-19 crisis and the imposed lockdown regulations, different pronounced human needs emerged in society, leading to different domains of innovations emerging from SMEs (Dahlke et al., 2021).

The survival of SME depends on SMEs' capacity to deal with external shocks (Pfeffer & Salancik, 1978). As a result, innovation is described as a means of survival during external shocks (Pfeffer & Salancik, 1978). Innovation is the key to SMEs' survival and resilience in the face of external shocks (Hillman et al., 2009), hence its usefulness in the COVID-19 context. During COVID-19, most SMEs experienced resource constraints that accelerated their inability to survive. According to Hillman et al. (2009), existing resource constraints may be managed through product and service innovation since these increase both resilience in the face of external shocks, and also the discovery and utilisation of new resources. Therefore, SMEs with strong innovative capacities are more likely to have avoided closure during the COVID-19 pandemic.

Besides, Pfeffer and Salancik (1978), Sherer and Lee (2002) proposed a range of external and related internal measures to maximise survival chances, namely, mergers and vertical integration, joint ventures and alternative inter-organisational relationships, boards of directors, political action and executive succession. Despite these measures, Sherer and Lee (2002) noted that SMEs should follow other similar SMEs in seeking legitimacy by creating strong relationships with other SMEs. Such relationships potentially create SMEs' mutual gains rather than simply new dependencies. According to Brown et al. (2020), access to financial resources has been a major issue for SMEs during the pandemic. In creating strong links with other SMEs, their key external relationship is likely to be with state apparatuses at national, regional and local levels. However, these measures can only be embraced by innovation. For example, during COVID-19 pandemic funds were provided to SMEs to assist them to survive. Nonetheless, some SMEs did not survive despite the fund reliefs that they received due to lack of innovation in the use of the funds provided (Brown et al. 2020).

In a nutshell, the Schumpeter theory mind set played a crucial role during the COVID-19 crisis as it is the basis for innovation during any kind of economic crisis. Despite that the Schumpeter theory was developed and based on Western ideology, it plays a significant role in embracing innovation in Africa for SMEs' survival during crises such as the COVID-19 pandemic. Besides sustaining growth of the firm, innovation is the instrument for mitigating internal and external factors such as macroeconomic conditions, that negatively affect the survival of SMEs during a crisis. Innovation provides a competitive advantage to a firm in the market by effectively harnessing windows of opportunity to exploit unmet market needs. SMEs that embrace innovation appear to be capable of rapidly responding to crises by actively using their relational capabilities and creatively developing solutions using existing resources. SMEs that use innovation seem to act as agents consolidating and assimilating knowledge, following a more explorative approach towards new solutions. Owing to the complex dynamic nature of the COVID-19 crisis and the imposed lockdown regulations, different pronounced human needs emerged in society, leading to different domains of innovations emerging from SMEs. During COVID-19, most SMEs experienced resource constraints that accelerated their inability to survive. However, SMEs with strong innovative capacities were more likely to have avoided closure during the COVID-19 pandemic. Proposed measures such as mergers and vertical integration, joint ventures, alternative inter-organisational relationships and access to financial resources, could only materialise during COVID-19 if they could embrace innovation.

The Innovative Strategies that SMEs Deployed During the COVID-19 Pandemic

Although there are numerous innovative strategies that SMEs deployed during the COVID-19 pandemic, most scholars acknowledge the following innovative strategies:

- **Entrepreneurial innovation**

Entrepreneurial innovation is the ability to turn an idea into reality by finding new ways to do things and making them better, creating new products or services, improving processes or finding new markets for existing products or services (Adam & Alarifi, 2021; O'Regan & Ghobadian, 2006). Many scholars agree that entrepreneurship innovation involves the implementation of creative and risk-driven strategies, optimal deployment of available resources, building external relationship, availability of funding, building networking with both internal and external stakeholders, incorporating technology in business processes and creating mergers and vertical integration (Brem et al., 2021; Ebersberger & Kuckertz, 2021; Engidaw, 2022; Shafi et al., 2020; Valdez-Juárez et al., 2022).

The COVID-19 pandemic took control of most countries and affected the daily lives of billions of people around the world (Setyoko & Kurniasih, 2022). The pandemic has had an unprecedented impact on how people communicate, work, produce, consume and live (Ebersberger & Kuckertz, 2021). According to Ohrnberger (2022), COVID-19 caused effects on personal healthcare, social lives, employment, businesses and the overall economy, causing the disruption in the global supply chain, business continuity and growth. However, Dangol et al. (2020) noted that despite these drawbacks, there was an increase in the use of mobile technology and digitisation during COVID-19. Baskota (2020) also reported an increase in internet users by 35% over the last 4 months, during the lockdown. In support of Dangol et al. (2020), Engidaw (2022) also stated that, the emerging of the COVID-19 pandemic caused SMEs to start trading online. The internet was used for digital ordering tools, service delivery tools, digital payment tools, conducting sales online and creating new ways to connect with customers.

Klein and Todesco (2021) concur that the increase of e-commerce (electronic commerce) was a strong response from SMEs. For example, in the United States, 51% of SMEs increased online interactions with their clients; 36% of SMEs that utilised online tools conducted all their sales online; and 35% of businesses that have changed operations have expanded the use of digital payments. SMEs in Brazil used combinations of easy entrance technologies for each of their essential activities. Social networks were widely used to promote sales, and bank apps were used to collect the payment. Sales were promoted directly on social networks, for example, Instagram, Facebook and WhatsApp. Payment transactions were made through applications provided by their banks, and some SMEs paid for the first time for online advertisements. Despite these technological advancements, Adam and Alarifi (2021) argued that many SMEs lacked sustainability due to lack of innovation in their business practices.

From an SME perspective, innovation presents new products or processes that address customer needs more competitively and profitably than existing ones (O'Regan & Ghobadian, 2006). Sometimes scholars use the term "innovative practices" to refer to the effective implementation of new solutions to challenges faced by SMEs, which include, among others, effective implementation of new ideas in relation to the enterprise's products, services or processes; new marketing mechanisms; or new administrative practices and upgraded performance (Adam & Alarifi, 2021; O'Regan & Ghobadian, 2006).

- **Crisis Management**

Although the COVID-19 pandemic created uncertainty in terms of the survival of SMEs, some SMEs survived the pandemic by deploying innovative, creative and risk-driven strategies. Morrish and Jones (2020) state that during the COVID-19 pandemic, entrepreneurs initially thought of the extent of the impact considering the nature of their businesses. Business recovery was possible firstly, by identifying the physical impacts on business operations which is applicable in the short term, secondly, in a long time, by analysing the age and financial position of the business, economic sectors, direct and indirect disaster impact, and operations disruptions. Hossain et al. (2022) also stated that, during COVID-19, the formation of the crisis management team by various governments assisted the entrepreneurs to understand the crisis and be able to put in place the crisis management strategies.

According to Martinelli et al. (2018), natural disasters pose unpredictable and significant threats to the incumbency and continuity of enterprises, thus directly affecting their ability to offer products and services to customers. Hence, entrepreneurs should embrace different roles to initiate change and create opportunities by deploying available resources. To craft the opportunities with current resources during COVID-19 crisis moment, SME owners focused on different issues like relying on relational capabilities, building financial capacity, assistance recipients' mismatch, collaborating with other stakeholders like an employee, suppliers, distributors, competitiveness of product-service solutions, reorganisation of the workplace and logistics pipeline. Besides, Brem et al. (2021) noticed that to some extent, a crisis can promote the development of new opportunities and stimulate the identification of the latest opportunities. Kuckertz et al. (2020) concur that during the COVID-19 crisis, entrepreneurs had opportunities to learn new things like the digitalisation of business. There were also opportunities arising from the crisis itself such as developing hygiene or digital work solutions. This clearly demonstrates that the ability of the SMEs is one of the instruments to help continue the business sustainably even in a crisis time like a COVID-19 pandemic.

- **Resilience Strategy**

Martinelli et al. (2018) suggested that resilience capabilities and plans are crucial in times when SMEs are in crisis, thus to maintain continuity, future success and sustainability of SMEs in times of crisis. SMEs must have capabilities and plans. During the COVID-19 crisis, some SMEs embraced the "organisation resilience view" which means SMEs should have the ability to absorb effectively, provide a unique response to the impact and engage in transformative strategies to capitalise on the impact of the crisis that potentially threatened the survival of SMEs. Resilience means both adaptive capacity and the ability to respond to a new environment to combat the disruption and it is a key instrument which individuals, systems and organisations should use to combat unexpected crisis.

Shafi et al. (2020), Rapaccini et al. (2020), are of the opinion that SMEs can adopt different types of resilience strategies to manage the

COVID-19 crisis. Some of these strategies include the reconfiguration, leveraging, sensing and interpreting, learning and knowledge integration, social capital, digitalisation and digital servitisation. SMEs should also encourage positive employee relationships to enhance resilience during a crisis. All these strategies can only be possible if there is entrepreneurial innovation, hence, the entrepreneurs' innovative and adaptive capacity can help SMEs to manage the situation smoothly. Valdez-Juárez et al. (2022) note that the scarcity of financial resources and other inputs triggered by the COVID-19 pandemic pushed SMEs to be more resilient and encourage innovation to fight competitively. Some SMEs were able to develop marketing strategies and innovative actions during the crisis.

Methods of Research Used in the Study

The study was non-empirical and insights were drawn from available literature in the area of entrepreneurship, entrepreneurs and SMEs in the face of the COVID-19 pandemic. The aim of using this literature review approach was to produce a thorough analysis, and subsequent conceptual framework development, that will be tested in future research endeavours. Refereed journal articles and books constituted the sources of information. The fact that the COVID-19 pandemic caused inexplicable damage to businesses, the lessons derived from its effects, aroused interest for the focus of discussion in this chapter. This study is one of the very few studies that explicitly explored what the entrepreneurs never knew they were capable of, that they could survive in business through embracing technology, until the COVID-19 pandemic hit them.

The Preferred Reporting Items for Systematic Reviews and Meta-Analysis (PRISMA) was used since the current study involves a review of prior research on the phenomenon in question. PRISMA is a fundamental collection of evidence-based components for systematic review reports, and it helps systematic reviewers to properly articulate the review's purpose and the authors' objectives (Liberati et al., 2009). It is endorsed as a best practice in the most prestigious publications (Nguyen, & Nguyen, 2022).

In order to meet the requirements of PRISMA the following processes were conducted during systematic literature review:

- **Source selection**: Relevant sources were searched from various databases by using titles, abstracts and keywords on entrepreneurship, innovation and COVID-19. In addition, the snowball approach was applied to assess prospective articles that may have been overlooked throughout the search effort. In this regard, each research paper was exhaustively analysed by examining each reference. This research analyses the publication's title, abstract, objectives, methodology, findings and conclusions to determine its relevance to the current study. Initially, researchers reviewed any literature on pandemics and the impact caused by these pandemics to businesses. The search identified theoretical and empirical studies on pandemics such as cholera, Spanish Flu, Severe Acute Respiratory Syndrome (SARS) and COVID-19. The first search produced one hundred and fifty articles.
- **Search criteria**: To include articles in the corpus, the following prerequisites must be met: (1) entrepreneurship search phrase: at least one entrepreneurship term must occur in an article's title, abstract or author keywords. (2) COVID-19 search phrase: at least one COVID-19 term must occur in an article's title, abstract or author keywords. (3) factors search term: at least one factor term must appear in an article's title, abstract or author keywords. To focus on the factor analysis, the article's title, abstract and keywords must contain at least one of the following terms: entrepreneurship, innovation, pandemic, COVID-19, survival strategies, innovation, entrepreneurial resilience and sustainability adaptive behaviour.
- **Eligibility evaluation**: The first researcher personally assessed the entry criteria specified by evaluating the titles and abstracts of the acquired publications to decide whether or not the obtained articles were acceptable for inclusion in the study. When it was determined that a definitive verdict could not be reached, the second researcher was consulted to discuss the publication's other facets, notably the methodology and the factor analysis. Only articles that can fulfil the following requirements are kept in the corpus: (1) The article was peer-reviewed for inclusion in the databases. Due to the credibility of peer-reviewed journals and the rigorous peer-review processes, only publications from relevant databases were included in this study. (2) The

topic of an article was relevant to factor analysis in entrepreneurship and COVID-19. (3) The article was written in English, and (4) only journal articles were evaluated.

- **Processing and data extraction**: In order to carry out the analysis, the current study extracted relevant factors, theoretical frameworks, hypotheses that were supported, and hypotheses that were rejected. After the data were obtained, they were cleaned by either being changed to include synonym names or by having their abbreviations converted to their full names. The studies on the COVID-19 pandemic that had initially been identified were narrowed down to studies that focused on challenges and strategies employed by SMEs specifically in handling their businesses during the COVID-19 pandemic. This was the screening exercise, where only studies relating to the COVID-19 pandemic were isolated and grouped (Table 1).

Findings of the Study

SMEs are acknowledged by scholars as having created value to the economy despite challenges they met (Jafarnejad et al., 2013; Mutula & Van Brakel, 2006). This is evidenced during the COVID-19 pandemic whereby, despite suffering setbacks, SMEs were acknowledged as the driving forces for economic and social development in not only African countries, but also globally (Ajide & Soyemi, 2022; Dai et al., 2020).

Innovation was acknowledged as having played an integral part in any setbacks of SMEs (Hillman et al., 2009; Pfeffer & Salancik, 1978). This was apparent during COVID-19. Those SMEs that intensively integrated innovation into their processes survived the pandemic by mitigating internal and external factors (Dahlke et al., 2021). Internal factors included, firm's size and age management capacity, workforce skills, financing capacity and ownership, whereas external factors included macroeconomic conditions, size of the market, customers, users and competition, regulation, government support, subsidies, tax system, public infrastructure, knowledge flows and networks (Hillman et al., 2009).

By having SMEs survive means that entrepreneurs outperform their competitors in the market. This is only possible if innovation is a major tool that ensures SMEs' survival. During the COVID-19 pandemic, those

Table 1 Challenges faced by SMMEs during the COVID-19 pandemic

Source & date	*Study focus- challenges*	*Key highlights & insights*	*SMEs responses*	*Recommendations*
Dai et al. (2020) Setyoko and Kurniasih (2022) Ebersberger and Kuckertz (2021)	Financial	The majority of SMEs suffered huge financial setbacks Businesses suffered from supply chain disruptions Business investments dried up Reduced demand for goods and services Loss of income	Most SMEs closed down Some customers' orders had to be refunded Some applied for bank loans Others declared bankruptcy	Selling online Scale down operations and focus only on essential services
Setyoko and Kurniasih (2022)	Human Resources	Significant reduction in employees COVID-19 came as a labour shock		
Meyer and Prescott (2020)	Policy and legislative challenges	Travel bans State-mandated lockdowns	Selling online	Need to embrace technology

Source & date	*Study focus- challenges*	*Key highlights & insights*	*SMEs responses*	*Recommendations*
Fubah and Moos (2022)	Loss of Customers and Clients	Loss of customers as a result of COVID-19, implies that SMEs had little or no business	Some SMEs had to constantly advertise their services to stay in business. They also had to contact and update their clients via email about whether or not they were open for business	Intensive advertisement
Fubah and Moos (2022)	Lack of Government Support	Lack of government support was a major challenge faced by the majority of the SMEs	Finding alternative funding approach such as loans	Alternative funding approach
Fubah and Moos (2022)	Unable to pay rent and employees	Some businesses that were run in the rented premises were unable to pay rent. Some businesses were also unable to pay employees	Searching for funding such as loans and applying for COVID-19 relief programme	Search for alternative funding options

SMEs with no innovation seemed to have been outperformed because of lack of innovation in their processes. For example, digital innovation plays a fundamental role and opens the doors to the information society, which allows digital communication between SMEs and stakeholders during the COVID-19 pandemic. Innovation has to be diffused to accelerate its function in surviving SMEs. This is evident during the COVID-19 pandemic whereby the diffusion of innovation, which is the process that analyses and evaluates the way in which new services, ideas and products are adopted, was found to be crucial. The diffusion of innovation process allowed SMEs to move from the pre-adoption stage to the adoption and post-adoption stages of innovative ideas during the pandemic.

Therefore, SMEs' survival depends on SMEs' capacity to deal with external shocks and innovation as a means of survival during external shocks such as the COVID-19 pandemic, hence, its usefulness in the COVID-19 context. The existing resource constraints may be managed through product and service innovation since these increase both resilience in the face of external shocks, and also the discovery and utilisation of new resources. It is proposed that there should be external and related internal measures to maximise survival chances of SMEs during pandemic such as COVID-19. These measures include mergers and vertical integration, joint ventures and alternative inter-organisational relationships, boards of directors, political action and executive succession. In addition, SMEs must create strong links with other SMEs. Such links potentially create SMEs' mutual gains rather than simply new dependencies. In creating strong links with other SMEs, their key external relationships must be with state apparatuses at national, regional and local levels. The literature also indicates that access to financial resources has been a major issue for SMEs during the pandemic. Therefore, the governments and other funding institutions must continue to fund SMEs during pandemics to assist them to survive.

Based on the findings of this study, it is recommended that policy intervention and industrial actions that promote virtual connection and innovative e-commerce for SMEs operations have to be implemented. The findings imply that policy interventions need to be sensitive and tailored to the different types of SMEs in terms of industry, sector, market type and size rather than adopting a one-size-fits-all approach and should not only focus on SMEs' survival in the short term but building resilience for long-term operation through innovation. It is also recommended that financial bailout and/or Internet infrastructure and support for SMEs could also make them more resilient to the adverse impact of the COVID-19 pandemic.

Contribution of the Study to Theory and Practice

Framework for Survival Strategies of SMEs During COVID-19

This study resulted in the development of a framework meant to assist businesses weather the storm in case of future pandemics. The study contributes to existing literature in times of pandemics and identifies survival and sustainability strategies during a long-lasting crisis (Fig. 1).

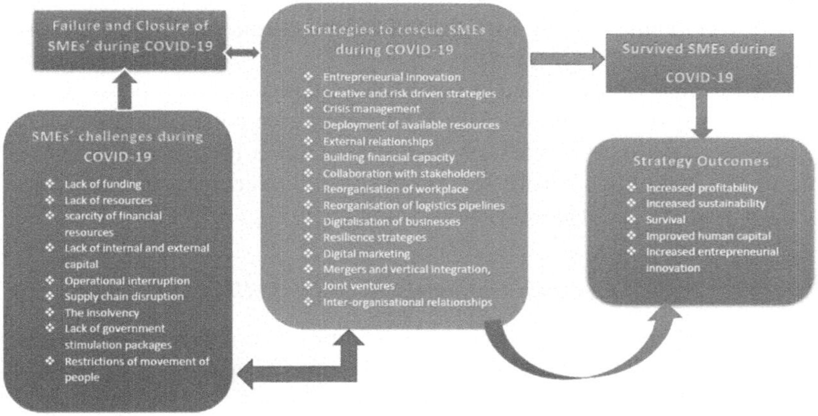

Fig. 1 Framework for survival strategies of SMEs during COVID-19

Contribution of the Study to Practice

The contribution that this chapter made is that the COVID-19 pandemic exposed the digital divide between small and big businesses, as before the pandemic, most businesses were not worried about ownership of technological gadgets. In light of the effects of the pandemic, SMEs needed to align themselves with the digital wave and transform the way they do business as alluded to by Dangol et al. (2020) who noted that, there was an increase in the use of mobile technology and digitisation during COVID-19. Ebersberger and Kuckertz (2021) and Kuckertz et al. (2020) concur that facing an unprecedented situation during COVID-19, SMEs had to reinvent themselves by embracing innovation in their practices.

The COVID-19 pandemic gave rise to the creation of different creative and innovative strategies that SMEs used to ensure that their only means of survival remained operational. The pandemic taught SMEs that the brick-and-mortar model would not always work. There was a need for them to be creative and innovative. For example, to address the logistical challenges some SMEs embraced technology and operated their businesses online. Instead of watching helplessly like entrepreneurs of the past would do, entrepreneurs of today came up with strategies of reorganising work structures and worked remotely from home. The implications may neither be conclusive nor prescriptive since the virus is still with us but will offer guidelines to entrepreneurs on how to conduct their businesses in the event of future pandemics.

Innovation was acknowledged as having played an integral part in any setbacks of SMEs (Hillman et al., 2009; Pfeffer & Salancik, 1978). This was apparent during COVID-19. Those SMEs that intensively integrated innovation into their processes survived the pandemic by mitigating internal and external factors (Dahlke et al., 2021).

Contribution of the Study to Policy

Most researchers, through their studies, aim at equipping policymakers with new knowledge on amending and coming up with new policies which will govern the way businesses are conducted.

Edquist (2005) asserts that public policies can influence business activities in direct and indirect ways. The regulatory and enforcement framework influences how SMEs can appropriate the outcomes of their innovation efforts and the multiple relationships and transactions that SMEs engage in.

The lessons learnt from this pandemic could influence all aspects of business and policymakers for years to come. The lessons derived are not only for the benefit of SMEs but policymakers too. One of the lessons that policymakers are likely to derive from this chapter is the need to put in place infrastructure that will entice SMEs to use technology and also offer training on the necessary digital and technological skills to enhance their entrepreneurial capabilities. The study impresses upon governments to make risk analysis and to accelerate development of e-commerce, e-marketing, banking, digital payment mechanisms, e-financial services, robust digital communication systems within government and other office activities, globally.

Implications for Future Research

This chapter focused on challenges experienced by SMEs during the COVID-19 pandemic and the survival and resilience strategies that they crafted. Further studies could be conducted on the effectiveness and the sustainability of the survival and coping strategies post-COVID-19 pandemic.

3 Conclusion

While the COVID-19 pandemic provided catastrophic challenges for businesses generally, and SMEs specifically, the study unravelled opportunities that entrepreneurs never dreamt of. SMEs came up with survival and resilience strategies such as adopting digital technologies, doing business online, partnering up and co-existing with big companies and diversification, among others. SMEs, no matter how small, have to realise that transacting digitally is no longer an option. They should strategise on how to transact and do business in the new normal. SMEs will have to take risk management lessons and better still, the government should put in place training on risk management, business continuity management, emergency management, crisis management and supply chain security. These strategies will help nascent and practising entrepreneurs to come up with ways of strengthening their businesses in times of environmental uncertainties. These findings will also benefit researchers who want to conduct future empirical studies on pandemics that may occur. Governments also stand to benefit from the study in that the findings will help policymakers in crafting, training and funding programmes and policies and global cooperation to rebuild international order.

References

Adam, N. A., & Alarifi, G. (2021). Innovation practices for survival of small and medium enterprises (SMEs) in the COVID-19 times: The role of external support. *Journal of Innovation and Entrepreneurship, 10*(1), 1–22. https://doi.org/10.1186/s13731-021-00156-6

Aghion, P., & Howitt, P. (1988). *Growth and cycles through creative destruction* (Unpublished). University of Western Ontario.

Ajide, F., & Soyemi, K. (2022). Oil rent, entrepreneurial start-ups, and institutional quality: Insights from African oil- rich countries. *Entrepreneurial Business and Economics Review, 10*(1), 35–49.

Archibugi, D., Filippetti, A., & Frenz, M. (2013). The impact of the economic crisis on innovation: *Evidence from Europe, Technological Forecasting & Social Change, 80*(7), 1247–1260. https://doi.org/10.1016/j.techfore.2013.05.005

Assink, M. (2006). Inhibitors of disruptive innovation capability: A conceptual model. *European Journal of Innovation Management, 9*, 215–233.

Backman, M., Klaesson, J., & Öner, Ö. (2017). Innovation in the hospitality industry: Firm or location? *Tourism Economics, 23*(8), 1591–1614.

Baskota, R. (2020, July 15). *Nepal hydroelectricity sector gets COVID-19 shock.* https://www.nepalitimes.com/latest/nepal-hydroelectricity-sector-gets-covid-19-shock/

Bayraktar, M., & Algan, N. (2019). The importance of SMEs on world economies. *International Conference on Eurasian Economies.* https://doi.org/10.36880/c11.02265

Bessant, J., Rush, H., & Trifilova, A. (2012). Jumping the tracks: Crisis-driven social innovation and the development of novel trajectories. *Die Unternehmung, 66*(3), 221–242. https://doi.org/10.5771/0042-059x-2012-3-221

Bloch, C., & López-Bassols, V. (2009). Innovation indicators. *Innovation in Firms: A microeconomic perspective.* OECD Publishing. https://doi.org/10.1787/9789264056213-en

Brem, A., Viardot, E., & Nylund, P. A. (2021). Implications of the coronavirus (COVID-19) outbreak for innovation: Which technologies will improve our lives? *Technology Forecasting and Social Change, 163*, 120451.

Brown, R., Liˇnares-Zigarra, J. M., & Wilson, J. O. S. (2020). *Innovation and borrower discouragement in SMEs* (CBRF Working paper 20–2014). University of St Andrews.

Carreiro, H., & Oliveira, T. (2019). Impact of transformational leadership on the diffusion of innovation in firms: Application to mobile cloud computing. *Computers in Industry, 107*, 104–113.

Chipunza, L. T. (2014). *Driving innovation in small accommodation businesses: A comparative study of Zimbabwe and South Africa* (Doctoral dissertation, Bloemfontein: Central University of Technology, Free State).

Colombelli, A., Haned, N., & Le Bas, C. (2013). On firm growth and innovation: Some new empirical perspectives using French CIS (1992–2004). *Structural Change and Economic Dynamics, 26*, 14–26. https://doi.org/10.1016/j.strueco.2013.03.002

Dahlke, J., Bogner, K., Becker, M., Schlaile, M. P., Pyka, A., & Ebersberger, B. (2021). Crisis-driven innovation and fundamental human needs: A typological framework of rapid-response COVID-19 innovations. *Technological Forecasting and Social Change, 169*, 1–29.

Dai, R., Feng, H., Hu, J., Ji, Q., Li, H., Wang, R., Wang, R., Xu, L., & Zhang, X. (2020). *The impact of COVID-19 on small to medium enterprises: Evidence from two-wave phone surveys in China* (Working Paper 549). Centre for Global Development www.cgdev.org.

Dangol, J., Chitrakar, S., & Yoo, K. S. (2020). Impact of COVID-19 on Nepalese small and medium enterprises. *Journal of Business and Social Sciences Research, 5*(2), 1–14.

Ebersberger, B., & Kuckertz, A. (2021). Hop to it! The impact of organization type on innovation response time to the COVID-19 crisis. *Journal of Business Research, 124*, 126–135.

Edquist, C. (2005). Systems of innovation: Perspectives and challenges. In *The Oxford handbook of innovation* (pp. 181–208). Oxford University Press.

Ehrenberger, M., Koudelková, P., & Strielkowski, W. (2015). Factors influencing innovation in small and medium enterprises in the Czech Republic. *Periodica Polytechnica Social and Management Sciences, 23*(2), 73–83. https://doi.org/10.3311/PPso.7737

Engidaw, A. E. (2022). Small businesses and their challenges during COVID-19 pandemic in developing countries: In the case of Ethiopia. *Journal of Innovation and Entrepreneurship, 11*(1), 1–14.

Farouk, L. (2020). *The way forward: How startups and SMEs can navigate the COVID-19 crisis: Entrepreneur*. https://www.google.com/amp/s/www.entrepreneur.com/amphtml/349225

Fransman, M. (2018). *Innovation ecosystems: Increasing competitiveness*. Cambridge University Press. https://doi.org/10.1017/9781108646789

Fritsch, M. (2017). The theory of economic development–An inquiry into profits, capital, credit, interest, and the business cycle. *Regional Studies, 51*(4), 654–655.

Fubah, C. N., & Moos, M. (2022). Exploring COVID-19 challenges and coping mechanisms for SMEs in the South African entrepreneurial ecosystem. *Sustainability, 14*, 1944. https://doi.org/10.3390/su14041944

Giotopoulos, I., Kontolaimou, A., Korra, E., & Tsakanikas, A. (2017). What drives ICT adoption by SMEs? Evidence from a large-scale survey in Greece. *Journal of Business Research, 81*, 60–69.

Hanusch, H., & Pyka, A. (2007). Principles of Neo-Schumpeterian economics. *Cambridge Journal of Economics, 31*, 275–289.

Hausman, A., & Wesley, J. J. (2014). The role of innovation in driving the economy: Lessons from the global financial crisis. *Journal of Business Research, 67*, 2720–2726.

Hillman, A. J., Withers, M. C., & Collins, B. J. (2009). Resource dependence theory: A review. *Journal of Management, 35*(6), 1404–1427. https://doi.org/10.1177/0149206309343469

Hossain, M. R., Akhter, F., & Sultana, M. (2022). SMEs in covid-19 crisis and combating strategies: A systematic literature review (SLR) and a case from emerging economy. *Operations Research Perspectives, 9*, 100–222.

Jafarnejad, A., Abbaszadeh, M. A., Ebrahimi, M., & Abtahi, S. M. (2013). Analysis of barriers to entrepreneurship in small and medium-sized enterprises (SMEs). *International Journal of Academic Research in Economics and Management Sciences, 2*(4), 207.

Klein, V. B., & Todesco, J. L. (2021). COVID-19 crisis and SMEs responses: The role of digital transformation. *Knowledge and Process Management, 28*, 117–133. https://doi.org/10.1002/kpm.1660

Knorringa, P., & Leliveld, A. (2014, April 9–10). *Understanding frugal innovation in Africa: Schumpeter revisited—Discussion Paper for REPOA's 19th Annual Research Workshop 'Transformation, job creation and poverty eradication'*. Dar es Salaam, Tanzania. https://courses.edx.org/c4x/DelftX/RI101x/asset/Understanding_Frugal_Innovation_in__Africa.pdf

Kuckertz, A., Brändle, L., Gaudig, A., Hinderer, S., Morales Reyes, C. A., Prochotta, A., … Berger, E. (2020). Startups in times of crisis—A rapid response to the COVID-19 pandemic. *Journal of Business Venturing Insights, 13*, e00169. https://doi.org/10.1016/j.jbvi.2020.e00169

Loderer, C., & Waelchli, U. (2009). *Firm age and performance* (Working Paper). University of Bern, Bern.

Mansfield, E. (1962). Entry, Gibrat's law, innovation and the growth of firms. *American Economic Review, 52*, 1023–1051.

Martinelli, E., Tagliazucchi, G., & Marchi, G. (2018). The resilient retail entrepreneur: Dynamic capabilities for facing natural disasters. *International Journal of Entrepreneurial Behavior & Research, 24*(7), 1222–1243.

Meyer, B. H., Prescott, B., & Sheng, X. S. (2022). The impact of the COVID 19 pandemic on business expectations. *International Journal of Forecasting, 38*(2), 529–544.

Mhlungu, M. B. (2021). *Key success factors for developing and managing small and medium-sized enterprises post covid-19 pandemic*. Dissertation, Master of Commerce. University of Kwazulu-Natal (pp. 1–316).

Moher, D., Liberati, A., Tetzlaff, J., Altman, D. G., The PRISMA Group. (2009). Preferred reporting items for systematic reviews and meta-analyses: The PRISMA statement. *PLoS Medicine, 6*(7). https://doi.org/10.1371/journal.pmed.1000097

Mutula, S. M., & Van Brakel, P. (2006). E-readiness of SMEs in the ICT sector in Botswana with respect to information access. *The Electronic Library, 24*(3), 402–417. https://doi.org/10.1108/02640470610671240

Nguyen, V. T., & Nguyen, C. T. H. (2022). A systematic review of structural equation modeling in augmented reality applications. *Indonesian Journal of Electrical Engineering and Computer Science, 28*(1), 328–338. https://doi.org/10.11591/ijeecs.v28.i1

O'Regan, N., & Ghobadian, A. (2006). Perceptions of generic strategies of small and medium sized engineering and electronics manufacturers in the UK. *Journal of Manufacturing Technology Management, 17*(5), 603–620. https://doi.org/10.1108/17410380610668540

Pfeffer, J., & Salancik, G. (1978). *The external control of organizations: A resource dependence perspective*. Harper & Row.

Phillips, M. A., & Ritala, P. (2019). A complex adaptive systems agenda for ecosystem research methodology. *Technological Forecasting and Social Change, 148*, 119739. https://doi.org/10.1016/j.techfore.2019.119739

Potier, J. (2015). Joseph A. Schumpeter and the economic climate of the 1930s–1940s: Depression, stagnation or harbingers of the decline of capitalism? *Economic Review, 66*, 993–1019.

Ohrnberger, J. (2022). Economic shocks, health, and social protection: The effect of COVID-19 income shocks on health and mitigation through cash transfers in South Africa. *Health Economics, 31*(11), 2481–2498. https://doi.org/10.1002/hec.4592OHRNBERGER2498

Ozili, P. K., & Arun, T. (2020). Spillover of COVID-19: Impact on the global economy. *Electronic Journal*. https://doi.org/10.2139/ssrn.3562570

Rakas, M., & Hain, D. S. (2019). The state of innovation system research: What happens beneath the surface? *Research Policy, 48*(9), 103787. https://doi.org/10.1016/j.respol.2019.04.011

Rapaccini, M., Saccani, N., Kowalkowski, C., Paiola, M., & Adrodegari, F. (2020). Navigating disruptive crises through service-led growth: The impact of COVID-19 on Italian manufacturing firms. *Industrial Marketing Management, 88*, 225–237.

Rosenbusch, N., Brinckmann, J., & Bausch, A. (2011). Is innovation always beneficial? A meta-analysis of the relationship between innovation and performance in SMEs. *Journal of Business Venturing, 26*(4), 441–457. https://doi.org/10.1016/j.jbusvent.2009.12.002

Santos, M., Haegeman, K., & Moncada-Paternò-Castello, P. (2021). *The impact of Covid-19 and of the earlier crisis on firms' innovation and growth: A comparative analysis*. European Commission, JRC, unit B7, Seville, Spain. jrc125490.pdf.europa.eu

Schumpeter, J. A. (1934). *The theory of economic development—An inquiry into profits, capital, credit, interest, and the business cycle*. Harvard Economic Studies 46, Translated by Redvers Opie (p. 255).

Schumpeter, J. A. (1942). *Socialism, capitalism and democracy*. Harper & Brothers.

Setyoko, P. I., & Kurniasih, D. (2022). Impact of the Covid 19 pandemic on small and medium enterprises (SMEs) performance: A qualitative study in Indonesia. *Journal of Industrial Engineering & Management Research, 3*(3), 315–324. https://doi.org/10.7777/jiemar.v3i3.406

Shafi, M., Liu, J., & Ren, W. (2020). Impact of COVID-19 pandemic on micro, small, and medium-sized Enterprises operating in Pakistan. *Research in Globalization, 2*, 100018. https://doi.org/10.1016/j.resglo.2020.100018

Sherer, P., & Lee, K. (2002). Institutional change in large law firms: A resource dependency and institutional perspective. *Academy of Management Journal, 45*, 102–119.

Spadoni, M. E. (2020). *Schumpeter's theory of innovation during the Coronavirus Pandemic: New opportunities and future challenges for the sharing economy*. Master in International cooperation, finance and development- Università telematica. https://www.academia.edu/50295708/Schumpeter_s_theory_of_innovation_during_the_Coronavirus_Pandemic_new_opportunities_and_future_challenges_for_the_sharing_economy

Syahadiyanti, L., & Subriadi, A. P. (2018). Diffusion of innovation theory utilization online financial transaction: Literature review. *International Journal of Economics and Financial Issues, 8*(3), 219.

Valdez-Juárez, L. E., Castillo-Vergara, M., & Ramos-Escobar, E. A. (2022). Innovative business strategies in the face of COVID-19: An approach to open innovation of SMEs in the Sonora region of Mexico. *Journal of Open Innovation: Technology, Market, and Complexity, 8*(1), 47.

Walter-Toews, D. (2020). *On pandemics: Deadly diseases from bubonic plague to Coronavirus*. Greystone Books.

Weick, K. E. (1993). The collapse of sensemaking in organizations: The Man Gulch disaster. *Administrative Science Quarterly, 38*(4), 628–652.

Weyrauch, T., & Herstatt, C. (2017). What is frugal innovation? Three defining criteria. *Journal of Frugal Innovation, 2*(1), 1–17. https://doi.org/10.1186/s40669-016-0005-y

Yaya, S., Otu, A., & Labonté, R. (2020). Globalisation in the time of COVID-19: Repositioning Africa to meet the immediate and remote challenges. *Globalization and Health, 16*(1), 1–7.

Ethical Dilemmas Faced by Human Resource Management Practitioners in African Small Micro and Medium Enterprises

Mildred Mahapa and Lekhooa Matela

1 Introduction

In any society, the issue of what is wrong and what is right always takes precedence. A workplace is no exception as employees interact on a daily basis. Employees are regarded as the most important resources available to an entrepreneur in the creation, development and sustenance of thriving Small, Medium and Micro Enterprises (SMMEs). The ever-changing employee expectations and competitions have made the human resource function very critical in business competitiveness because people are the sources of business competitive advantage (Ekuma & Akobo, 2015). Human resource (HR) practitioners ensure that competent candidates are selected and placed in an organisation. The proper selection and placement of candidates into an organisation result in having the relevant

M. Mahapa (✉) · L. Matela
Department of Business Administration, National University of Lesotho, Roma, Lesotho
e-mail: m.mahapa@nul.ls

L. Matela
e-mail: l.matela@nul.ls

P. Rambe and R. E. Hinson (eds.), *The Future of Entrepreneurship in Southern Africa*, Palgrave Studies in Technology and Innovation in Africa, https://doi.org/10.1007/978-3-031-55935-8_6

people doing the right job, which eventually enhances the future performance of a thriving business. It is also the role of the HR practitioners to ensure strict adherence to ethics and ethical behaviours in organisations (Israel & Kazungu, 2019). Therefore, the SMMEs are seized with the need to act ethically as they deal with employees.

It is important to note that standards, values, morals and ethics have become increasingly complex in a postmodern society, and as such, the function of the HR has been experiencing remarkable growth and rapid professionalisation in the last decades. Despite the remarkable developments in Human Resource Management (HRM), one part of the people's management that has not been examined properly from a scholarly perspective is ethical dilemmas mostly in the SMMEs. This is a complex and yet interesting subject that needs to be interrogated through research. The core ethical challenge for the HR managers, according to Armstrong (2010), lies in the differences in the interests of employers and employees and the complexity of their competing interests.

The ethical dilemmas occur in uncertain situations, which bring about conflicting interests, values and beliefs relating to multiple stakeholders. Renwick (2003) argues that even though the main function of the HR department is to protect the employees' well-being, it is ironic that the same department has been critiqued for tampering with the employees' well-being. In other words, while the HR practitioners are often charged with the responsibility to deal with ethical issues, they are paradoxically responsible for the generation of ethical dilemmas. Conflict of interest often leads to ethical dilemmas, which often involve prioritising and choosing from competing values. Armstrong (2010) states that resolving conflict requires all the parties to recognise that the HR practitioners can both represent the needs of employee and implement management agendas. They can also be the voice of both the employees and management, and they also act as a partner to both employees and managers. This makes their role to be complicated, and therefore, can be another source of ethical dilemmas. Due to the size of the SMMEs, the duties of the HR are mostly done by the owner of the business or other general administrators who in most cases do not possess an HR qualification. In that scenario trying to act ethically then becomes a challenge, which results in the ethical dilemmas.

Because of the aforementioned conflicts, companies that challenge unethical behaviour still rely more and more on the HR department for best performance, and thus, this department gets increased responsibility.

Daniel (2011) opines that the ethical values in an organisational setting are accentuated and reinforced mainly through value-based leadership. This denotes the relationship between the leaders and co-workers based on the shared and internalised values, which are acted upon by the leaders. In short, the HR function is to seek to implement ethical practices, which aim at imparting an ethical culture. Therefore, this research seeks to explore the ethical dilemmas faced by the HRM practitioners in the SMMEs in Lesotho, and the factors that influence ethical decision-making process.

There is empirical evidence which suggests that adopting the HRM practices in SMMEs has several benefits, such as reducing staff turnover and the development of human and entrepreneurial capital. Not only are the benefits limited to the organisation, but the economy also enjoys the benefits. SMMEs with good HRM practices foster economic development in developed and developing countries by driving creativity and innovation, and making a significant contribution to countries' Gross Domestic Product (GDP). The organisations that focus on improving the HRM practices are better performers as the people are the backbone of any organisation (Nzonzo & Matashu, 2014).

Despite the SMMEs' remarkable and indisputable contribution to the Lesotho's aggregate economic performance, specifically in terms of employment generation, business creation and development, they are still the victims of ethical dilemmas when managing their activities. The purpose of this research is to identify the types of ethical dilemmas, which can arise in the practice of the HR management in the SMMEs and understand what influences the ethical decision-making process. The following main research questions have formulated: What types of ethical dilemmas do human resources management officials in Lesotho face, and what influences the decision-making process?

This paper begins by looking at the theoretical development focusing on what previous studies say about ethical dilemmas and the importance of this research as it fills the research gaps on ethical dilemmas in the SMMEs. It further looks at the methodology that was adopted to carry out the study. The findings and discussions follow thereafter.

2 Theoretical Development

Ethical considerations are part of the organisational strategy for the decision making on responsibility. Both internal and external stakeholders enjoy immense benefits when the organisations encourage good ethical behaviour. This fact is also critical for a small business that wants to grow and enjoy competitive advantage. Ethics is the standard of behaviours in an organisation, and it includes the set of values, which usually complies with social norms and contributes to the existence of community (Amadasu, 2020). Ethics is defined by Turyakira (2018) as a system of moral principles, a sense of right and wrong, goodness and badness of actions and the motives and consequences of these actions.

From the business perspective, Ahmed (2019) asserts that ethical and unethical behaviours are behaviours exhibited by the employees in the workplace as they perform their daily tasks (Rice & Perry, 2013). Amadasu (2020) defines business ethics as right or wrong conduct exhibited by a leader or workers. It is worth noting that ethics are based on both individual beliefs and social concepts; they vary from person to person, from situation to situation and from culture to culture. Ekuma and Akobo (2015) have categorised ethics in 3 ways, namely, descriptive ethics (what people think is right), meta-ethics (what 'right' means) and normative ethics (how people should act).

Having unpacked ethics, it becomes prudent to understand the meaning of ethical dilemmas. An ethical dilemma is characterised as a moral situation where any decision, which is made, is equally undesirable (Fernando, 2009). Treviño and Nelson (2010) define an ethical dilemma as a situation where two or more important values, rights and/or responsibilities are in conflict, and a choice has to be made between equally unpleasant alternatives. It should be noted that the ethical dilemmas emanate from moral problems. A moral problem has been defined by Turyakira (2018) as a situation in which a problem or dilemma is experienced between one's own values and norms and those of other people. This implies that it is a situation, which by one's own account, is not correct or should not occur. In the Human Resource Management, the ethical dilemmas involve personal, professional and organisational considerations (Corbin & Strauss, 2015). It is, therefore, of paramount importance to study these dilemmas in the SMMEs as the HR practitioners play the key role in developing and creating the policies and programmes for the organisations. The policies and programmes that exhibit the ethical climate or culture developed and maintained in their organisations have become an important responsibility for the HR department in all organisations globally (Daniel, 2011). Treviño and Nelson (2010) outlined common ethical dilemmas related to business.

a. *People Issues*

People issues ethical dilemmas might occur when people work together. They include privacy, discrimination, sexual and other types of harassment, or how people get along. An important word when the people issue is being considered is fairness.

b. *Conflicts of Interest*

The conflict of interest ethical dilemma might occur when the judgement or objectivity is compromised. This ethical dilemma could also be an incompatible relationship with someone. Therefore, the ethical dilemma may occur if a decision has to be made upon someone whom a decision maker has a personal relationship with. If the conflict of interest occurs, it is recommended to include other colleagues in the decision-making process.

c. *Use of Corporate Resources*

The use of corporate resources ethical dilemma may occur when the employees have access to corporate resources, including their finances and reputation. The HR practitioners, therefore, have to be cautious because they speak on behalf of the company.

d. *Managing the Diverse Workplace*

Managers might get into the diverse workplace ethical dilemma when dealing with the individuals of both sexes and the people of different ages, races, religions, ethnic groups or sexual orientation.

Ethical dilemmas are very rampant and sometimes difficult to overcome. This is because there are environmental factors that bring about the ethical dilemmas, especially to the HR function. These environmental factors include demographic trends, legislative or regulatory climate, economic climate and social trends. An example of how the economic factors can contribute to the ethical dilemma might be when an economy is facing recession, and the rooms in a five-star hotel are half-empty, so there might be no need to keep each member of staff. Who should the HR managers dismiss first and why? This is a typical dilemma for a big hotel. If such big organisations are faced with such huge dilemmas, it becomes apparent that the small firms also face dilemmas. This, therefore, creates the need to investigate how the SMMEs are seized with ethical dilemmas.

In addition, the HR managers may wish to behave according to a certain ethical standard as prescribed by their professional body and may endeavour to do so on a day-to-day basis. Unfortunately, their power is often limited and lack wider support, so they may not be able to endeavour in ethical means and ethical goals (Ahmed, 2019). Rice and Perry (2013) have pointed out that some of the common obstacles in ethical decision in the HR include failure to recognise that ethics and management decisions are interrelated, failure to integrate ethics into the way of doing business, a belief that an individual is above the rules and laws of ordinary men, a rush into judgement, poor moral awareness and lack of ability to resolve ethical conflicts. Ethical awareness is the ability to see the ethical dimensions in a situation or in a certain decision and can be developed within the firm and its employees. If the employees are aware of the company's values, then it is easier for them to recognise an ethical aspect in the situation.

There is a growing need to pay attention to the ethical business practices because they form an important code of conduct, which directs all the human behaviour (Jili et al., 2017). Despite the fact that the ethical dilemmas are rampant in any organisational setting, they have to be effectively managed as they can negatively affect businesses. People need to be morally sensitive and aware of these dilemmas, and then work towards minimising them, especially in the SMMEs firms. However, people have a different level of sensitivity in terms of perceiving ethical issues, which is caused by dissimilar personal, situational and cultural factors. Daniel (2011) supports the fact that individuals need to recognise the moral issues first. The recognition of moral issues consists of two aspects, which include a person recognising that their decision and action will affect others (decision and actions have consequences for human beings), and that some choice must be involved (a person has volition). Everyone in the organisation should also be aware of how their behaviour impacts others, and that consequences of each chosen strategy may follow. Therefore, moral sensitivity becomes a pivotal component on how to deal with the ethical dilemmas because without that, moral agent would not even notice that one is present. Thus, the research focused on the ethical dilemmas faced by the HR practitioners in the SMMEs in Lesotho.

It is also imperative to understand the ethical decision making as this is the other objective of the paper. According to Ekuma and Akobo (2015), ethical decision is a decision, which is legal and morally acceptable to the larger community. In contrast, unethical decision is an illegally or morally unacceptable decision. In business, ethics involves the basic categories, concepts, language of ethics, rights and responsibilities, goodness, fairness, justice, virtue, kindness, loyalty, trustworthiness and honesty (Corbin & Strauss, 2015). The first step in the ethical decision-making process in business is to recognise the presence of ethical issue.

It is important to note that the problem in management across the nations of Africa is that human rights or universal rights are subject to different interpretations. What is valued as right in a country may not be so in another. Thus, few laws apply on an international scale to provide substantial guidelines for corporate conduct. In the international management, there has also been the concern with ethical relationships with the people who are directly affected by the decisions of foreign companies. Nonetheless, the researchers noted that the most prevalent unethical behaviour in business is corruption and bribery. Corruption and bribery are prevalent in the most African countries. It is the practice of paying money or providing benefits to someone in business or government to obtain an inappropriate market, workplace or economic advantage. This behaviour (corruption and bribery) is widely condemned as an unethical practice. In too many cases, bribery in the African nations transcends the level of being referred to as unethical to being a common practice.

This research has been guided by the Utilitarianism Ethical Theory, which propounds that ethics depends on one's capacity to envisage the imports of activity and the decision that yields the best value for most people (Chonko, 2012). The theory is based on two assumptions, namely, act utilitarianism and rule utilitarianism. On the one hand, act utilitarianism focuses on the person's ability to accomplish the task that is beneficial to most of the people irrespective of personal feelings or the societal limitations, such as laws. On the other hand, Chonko notes that rule utilitarianism takes the law into account and is concerned with fairness. Utilitarianism Ethical Theory values justice and aligns with the principle of beneficence (Chonko, 2012).

Utilitarianism is a form of consequentialism. For consequentialism, the moral rightness or wrongness of an act depends on the consequences that it produces. On consequentialist grounds, actions and inactions whose negative consequences outweigh the positive consequences will be deemed morally wrong while actions and inactions whose positive consequences outweigh the negative consequences will be deemed morally right. On the utilitarian grounds, actions and inactions, which benefit few people and harm more people, will be deemed morally wrong while actions and inactions, which harm fewer people and benefit more people, will be deemed morally right. The utilitarian's concern is how to increase net utility. Vance and Trani (2008) posit that utilitarianism philosophy ought to be adjudicated regarding the measure of bliss or despondency that they bring while stressing that nobody's joy is considered more significant than anybody else's. The essential import of this theory is to give the utmost best to the majority while the ethical estimation of action is exclusively dictated by its commitment to the overall usefulness.

3 Methodology

There have been a number of researches on entrepreneurship in Lesotho (Amadasum, 2020; Amadasum & Mutezo 2022; Makheta & Sebolelo 2015; Nketekete & Motebang, 2006). However, the issue of the HR ethical dilemmas is contested, which necessitated the researchers to undertake the study. This is a critical topic that will assist in formalising the HR functions in SMMEs since most people are venturing into this space. It also assists in ensuring that proper systems are put in place for competitiveness and growth. The purpose of this research is to develop understanding of ethical dilemmas faced by the HR managers in the Lesotho SMMEs and the factors that influence the dilemmas. Understanding these dilemmas brings about moral sensitivity, which is key in transforming today's SMMEs. The researchers therefore, adopted qualitative research as a research strategy. Corbin and Strauss (2015) describes qualitative research as a technique that emphasises words rather than quantification in the collection of data and focuses on how the people interpret their social word. The human element plays the main role in the qualitative research in both collecting and analysing data.

Lesotho is divided into 10 administrative districts, each district with its own town. The research was done in 3 major districts in Lesotho, namely, Leribe, Butha-Buthe and Maseru. These were purposively selected as they represent the bigger districts in terms of population in Lesotho, where there are some SMME activities. For qualitative research, it is generally more favourable to choose non-probability sampling because researchers intend to collect rich information that enhances understanding of the problem under the study (Daniel, 2011). As a result, purposive sampling was used to select the participants, where the researchers identified the individuals who are already in the SMMEs.

The interest of this paper is to get understanding about the ethical dilemmas faced by the Human Resource Management officials in the Lesotho's SMMEs and what influences the ethical decision-making process. In the case of this study, the people involved in the research were the HR personnel with at least one year of work experience in this job role. The reason for such a decision was that at least a person with a year's experience or above would understand the HR issues better. To ensure validity of findings, the researcher also chose the HR personnel in the SMMEs aged between 25 and 50 years. For this paper, the combination of purposive sampling and snowball sampling in selecting the participants were used. First, snowballing was used to get in contact with other three participants who were involved in the HR management, and the researchers were not aware of. Snowballing was done in Leribe as the researchers were not really knowledgeable on the HR issues. This allowed them to get more insights and views on the HR dilemmas. Snowball sampling is another type of non-probability sampling, which is handy, especially if it is not easy to locate people who are suitable for the interview. Corroborating these sampling techniques helped the researcher to find the people who had experience and were knowledgeable in the area understudy.

Data were collected using interviews. The main goal was to identify common themes in the interviews carried out with the HR officials in the SMMEs. These interviews focused on the ethical dilemmas that the HR officials experience, and what influences their ethical decision-making process. The researcher used semi-structured interviews as a data collection method. Data collected through the interviews and the spoken words were recorded, and then transcribed. The participants had a leeway on how to reply and the researchers could add new questions as they arose following the response of interviewee. All the interviews lasted from minimum of 30 minutes to maximum of 50 minutes.

Overall, 15 semi-structured interviews were conducted with the HR officials working in Maseru, Leribe and Butha-Buthe. Therefore, five interviews were conducted in each district. Due to the nature of the topic, the actual research was very sensitive. The HR officials who took part in the research ensured that their real names were not mentioned in the research. However, they intentionally changed only the size of the company and its orientation, but the name of the company was not mentioned in the research. Only the people with at least one year of work experience in the HR role were invited for the interview, and those who had working experience in the HR field from Lesotho. The researchers also reviewed the job tasks of all the HR officials involved in the research as a part of the triangulation of data. Due to the nature of the HR activities, their daily-based job tasks were pretty much very similar. All of them were involved in the recruitment, HR planning and dealing with employees' relations, such as the conflicts or misconduct of behaviour. As a technique for data analysis, the researchers chose a combination of open and axial coding for the purpose of this paper. As Corbin and Strauss (2015) have outlined that the process of interpretation begins with open coding, where the researcher breaks down and fractures the data, and then examines, compares, conceptualises and categorises.

Lesotho is a small country located in Southern Africa and landlocked by the Republic of South Africa. It is a small, mountainous country that covers an area of 30,355 square kilometres (Zijlma 2017). Lesotho is divided into ten administrative districts and has a population of approximately two million, and most of the people live in rural areas (World Population Prospects, 2017). Sesotho and English are the official languages even though there are also Xhosa, Zulu (Zijlma 2017) and Phuthi speakers.

The Ministry of Trade and Industry, Co-operatives and Marketing refers small, medium enterprises (SMEs) as micro, small, medium enterprises (MSMEs) in Lesotho. However, for the purpose of this study, the researchers adopted the SMME terminology, not the MSMEs. The SMMEs are usually defined by the adjectives indicating the size of organisation, hence the economists' division of the SMMEs into classes based on some quantitative measurable indicators. According to Nansadiqa et al. (2019), the most common criteria to distinguish between large and small businesses are the number of employees and the amount of annual turnover. Martin-Oriega and Methven (2017) also propound that in the developing countries, the SMMEs are mostly characterised as one-person businesses in which the working staff can be family members who are often unpaid, but are active in the enterprise. Jili et al. (2017) also define small to medium enterprises as the businesses that employ 150 people or fewer and are not a subsidiary of a public limited company. The working definition in this research is according to the MSMEs policy of Lesotho, which is based on the number of employees.

According to the policy, a micro business employs 1 to 5 employees, including the business owner. A small business employs 6 to 20 people, and medium-size businesses has 21 to 50 employees. According to Makheta and Sebolelo (2015), the SMMEs are the backbone of nearly all the economies throughout the world because of their importance in job generation and personalised service offering. They have a significant impact on the sustainable development process of both the developed and developing countries because they promote economic growth and alleviate poverty. According to Berry et al. (2002), the increasing predominance of flexibility in the SMMEs and specialisation have influenced many business analysts to believe in the crucial role that the SMMEs play in the industrial structure of any developing country. In Lesotho, despite the average of 4.83% economic growth, unemployment remains high, and poverty is widespread (FinScope MSME Survey Lesotho, 2015).

In terms of employment, the government of Lesotho, the mining sector and the textile industry are the major employers (FinScope MSME Survey Lesotho, 2015). FinScope MSME Survey Lesotho states that to reduce the dependence of the economy on the public sector, the government aims to encourage rapid and sustained private sector development. It is widely recognised that the SMMEs are a significant contributor to job creation, development and economic growth. According to Turyakira (2018), the SMMEs in Africa are mostly affected by the ethical dilemmas since they lack the funds, strategic information and relevant alliances to implement ethical practices. This, however, is not receiving the attention necessary because the SMMEs in Africa are prioritising the matters that affect them like access to finance, business management skills and competition (Nzonzo & Matashu 2014). Lesotho is no different; most of the discussions on the SMMEs in Lesotho have addressed the issues on the lack of access to finance and the development of human capital. The government has put some funds aside to ease access to finance to increase the number of the SMMEs and address the issue of unemployment.

4 Findings and Discussion

This section deals with the presentation and analyses of the data collected throughout the research process. The researcher presented data collected from the interviews in the selected 3 districts in Lesotho from HR officials. Data presentation was done employing thematic analysis since research study was qualitative in nature.

Reward System

Since the same questions were asked in all the districts, the data were collectively presented as the answers were more or less similar. The ethical dilemma faced at work is related to the allocation of bonuses, which are not always based just on measurable reasons. One of the HR officers highlighted that the biggest ethical dilemma was the issue of awarding employees' bonus based on merit. They felt that the most merit increases were not always based on performance. They indicated that,

(1) *You would say that a person is getting merit increase and others don't, yet the performance would be similar*

Recruitment and Selection

Recruitment was also pointed out as an HR activity, which often leads to an ethical dilemma because of possible discrimination issue. One participant highlighted that,

(2) *Recruitment, especially if you are stuck with the new employee whom you think might be right for the job, but you have somebody else coming to you who might be even better, but you are not able to hire them due to some qualification or some legal requirements to do with foreign employees.*

The informants went further to highlight that recruitment is full of ethical dilemmas. Since an interview is a lot about appearance, sex, nationality and culture, the HR officer thinks that the person is likely to fit in business culture. One officer clearly pointed out that,

(3) *For me, it is also an ethical dilemma when I already know that I won't hire someone, but you can't tell it to him because it is ethically wrong*

In explaining a current dilemma, one participant said.

(4) *We had some interviews, and in those interviews, we had friends who were put forwards from colleagues. That gave a lot of ethical dilemmas. One of the candidates who was forwarded by a colleague has a good CV but failed the interview, which is very important. Unfortunately, we had to disappoint her that she was not good enough for the job; however, the colleague who put her forward tried to convince us otherwise, and that was a dilemma.*

For all the HR officials involved in the research, recruitment is part of their duty. However, all of them acknowledged that recruitment is a source of ethical issues, which often leads into ethical dilemmas. According to the HR officials, recruitment brings two types of ethical dilemmas for the HR managers. The first one is the conflict of interest, which occurs when decision about 'to hire or not to hire' must be made upon someone whom they have a personal relationship with. The second type of ethical dilemma arises when the HR managers face possible discrimination because of race, religion, national origin, sex, disability or age while recruiting.

Conflict Management

Another type of ethical dilemma arises when the HR officials managing conflicts with an employee or between employees should act fairly, but they admitted that it is difficult to be completely impartial because of favouritism. One of the managers said,

(5) *It is very easy for you to go harder on an employee who does not perform well and soft on those who do their jobs better*

One HR officer also said that when one manager favours certain team members or even guests (if working in the hotel) over another gets her into ethical dilemma.

The findings in this study coheres with the conclusions made by Onomogbo (2016) that the common unethical practices in businesses include padding expense accounts, seeking reimbursement for questionable or non-existent business expenses, taking business property or materials for personal use, soliciting or offering kickbacks and price fixing. Botha (2012) also states that the most common ethical concerns about misconduct in the business environment include bribery, coercion or bullying, theft, discrimination, fraud, harassment, dishonesty, cover-ups and pornography.

From the findings, it can be noted that the Utilitarianism Theory influences how the people react to certain issues. The theory highlights that the rightness or wrongness of actions is determined by their tendency to produce good or bad consequences or outcomes. Utilitarianism says that the right action in any situation is the one that will produce the best outcomes as measured by the impact on everyone involved. In the case of the SMMEs, the HR officials are employees, and some are the owners of the organisations, and they encounter ethical dilemmas as depicted from the findings. However, the decisions that are good for the company must be upheld to ensure that the organisations succeed. Chonko (2012) highlights that utilitarianism focuses on the person's ability to accomplish a task that is beneficial to most people irrespective of their personal feelings or the societal limitations, such as laws. Rule utilitarianism takes the law into account and is concerned with fairness. It is important to note that moral awareness is the backbone of an individual's' sense of moral behaviour and ethical decision making.

Factors that Influence Ethical Decision-Making Process

Time and Information

Lack of time and of information in the SMMEs were stated by all the participants as factors that influence ethical decision making. Failure to gather the relevant facts and rushing to judgement were described as an obstacle in making good ethical decisions. One officer indicated that they felt that in certain situations, they need to take a bit more time to explore the dilemma properly, read conversation between the people who are involved and explore possibilities to be able to decide instead of blaming someone. Tarus and Nganga (2013) also affirm that lack of information, credit, scale economies, quality and reputation make most SMEs very uncompetitive. They also highlight that the SMMEs are aware of the large scale of unethical practices taking place in large companies and government departments, which they see as standard or acceptable practice. Therefore, this may influence their behaviour and perceptions and even make them more open to dishonest behaviour. In some instances, the SMEs see these unethical actions as necessary for survival.

Training

Fourteen out of fifteen interviewees agreed that they had not experienced or attended any ethical training in their companies. These indicated that they lacked knowledge on the general practice of ethics in business. Their business lacked general knowledge of good governance, which is why they were faced with many ethical dilemmas.

The evidence also revealed that thirteen HR officials did not undertake any ethical training at work, which Hamric et al. (2014) identified as a potential internal obstacle to the application of the ethical decision-making competency. The HR officials had a view that sometimes lack of some facts about actual ethical dilemma affect the making of good ethical decisions. Rice and Perry (2013) summarised the obstacles in ethical decision making. These include failure to recognise that ethics and management decisions are interrelated, and failure to integrate ethics into the way of doing business. This finding from the research is also in line with the narrative of Turyakira (2018) who highlights that the SMMEs in the developing countries lack awareness and understanding of the importance of business ethics and its advantages. The SMMs lack long-term vision and focus more on the survival in the short term.

Training is necessary to get everyone on a common understanding of ethics (Putnam 2016), and it should focus on business ethics, and how the SMMEs can introduce the concept in their structure. The SMME's owners and their employees need to become more educated and more aware of the need for the ethics in business. They need to understand what ethics means, and how to apply the stakeholders' model of including everyone in making ethical decisions (Donovan 2013).

Finance

The data from thirteen HR officials indicated that their managers often consider just financial part of business, which is one of the biggest obstacles in good ethical decision making. One manger indicated that,

(6) *They care about business. They are interested in a person who is willing to stay overtime, and who is flexible and hardworking; so, sometimes decisions are made to better complete your task at work than, for example, to help people. Therefore, they often decide in the interest of your organisation than in the interest of people. You want to complete your job task correctly, and not to lose job.*

The above findings are attributed to the fact that the SMMEs need to survive, and as they tend to be small, they experience more difficulties. The SMMEs are vulnerable to the practice and consequences of unethical business behaviour (Medlin & Green, 2014) due to their size, limited finances and funding sources, their dependence on word-of-mouth strategies to market products, dependence on sometimes overpowering customers, difficulty in building a reputation and their tendency to take shortcuts when doing business. Turyakira (2018) emphasises that due to lack of financial resources to build a formal ethical culture, the SMMEs in some countries, like Pakistan, embrace unethical practices to remain afloat.

Individual Attributes

Ferrell et al. (2012) mentioned that ethical decision making in a business is influenced by individual factors (person having values and principles) and organisational factors. These authors also assert that an organisation's values often play a bigger role in the decision-making process than a person's own values. This is also in support of the Utilitarian Ethical Theory that the decisions are influenced by many factors and in most cases people. The organisational influence, as a source of ethical challenges, also puts the HR officials into ethical dilemmas when their personal values compete with the organisational main objective, which is placed around revenue and business. Their person values include giving a chance to everyone regardless of where they come from, being caring, helpful and fair with people, respecting people and teamwork. This was admitted by all the HR managers who mentioned that they feel pressure when making ethical decision. Turyakira (2018) also affirms that the SMMEs are primarily driven by the personal beliefs and values of their owners and also face significant resource pressure.

Also, two HR officials confirmed their 'failure to integrate ethics into the way of doing business'. This has also been identified by Rice and Perry (2013) as the obstacles in the ethical decision making when the managers consider only the financial side of business. Hamric et al. (2014) further highlights that, ethical policies present in the companies inform the employees that the organisation is particular about ethical standard. Ethical culture also has an important role in passing codes, guidance and norms onto employees. It does not have to be necessarily taken as a failing to integrate ethics, but it has to be taken in consideration.

Implications for Theory, Policy and Practice

The study may lead to practical and effective application of human resource functions, which will help in the proper management of the human capital in the SMEs. It will also assist in having fair and transparent HRM policies that enhance effective employment relations. The research will also help filling the literature gap that currently exists on the HR ethical dilemmas in the SMEs in Africa.

5 Conclusion

The main objective of the research was to identify the ethical dilemmas and from the research, the human resources officials identified three main sources of the ethical issues, which often lead into ethical dilemmas which are recruitment, employee relations and organisational influence. To be more specific, most HR managers acknowledged recruitments as a source of ethical issues. Recruitment brings two types of ethical dilemmas: the conflicts of interest and dilemmas arising due to possible discrimination. Again, in this study, it is concluded that employee relations bring three types of ethical dilemmas, which are, the conflicts of interest when a decision is made upon an employee whom they have a personal relationship with, favouritism when managing conflict between the employees, as well as balancing possible competing stakeholders' interest in relation with wages and bonuses.

References

Ahmed, K. M. (2019). The role of small and medium-sized enterprises (SMEs) participation in public procurement implementation: A case of Banadir region. *EPRA International Journal of Research and Development (IJRD), 21*(2), 123–133.

Amadasu, D. O. E. (2020). *The influence of market driven strategies and access to finance on competitive growth of small and medium–sized enterprises in selected districts of Lesotho*. PhD thesis. University of South Africa, Pretoria.

Amadasum, D. O. E., & Mutezo, A. T. (2022). Effects of market driven strategies on competitive growth of SME's in Lesotho. *Journal of Innovation andEntrepreneurship, 11*(13), 117–129.

Armstrong, M. (2010). *Armstrong's essential human resource management practice: A guide to people management*. London: Kogan Page Publishers.

Berry, L. L, Seiders, K., & Crewal, D. (2002). Understanding Service Convenience. *Journal of Marketing, 66*, 1–7. https://doi.org/10.1509/jnkg.66.3.18505. Accessed 8 July 2023

Botha, H. J. (2012). *Investigating the ethical considerations faced by small business entrepreneurs in the informal sector: Zandspruit township, Johannesburg.* http://www.uj.ac.za/EN/Faculties/management/departments. Accessed 11 July 2023.

Chonko, L. (2012). *Ethical theories*. http://www.dsef.or/wp-content/uploads/2012/07/Ethical/theories.pdf. Accessed 31 August 2023.

Corbin, J. & Strauss, A. (2015). *Basics of qualitative research: Techniques and procedures for developing grounded theory*. New York: Sage.

Daniel, J. (2011). *Sampling essentials: Practical guidelines for making sampling choices*. New York: Sage.

Donovan, A. M. (2013). The importance of business ethics to small ventures. *Entrepreneurship and Innovation Management Journal, 1*(1), 50–59.

Ekuma, K. J., & Akobo, L. (2015). Human resource management ethics and professionals' dilemmas: A review and research agenda. *Human Resource Management Research, 5*(3), 47–57.

Fernando, A.C. (2009).*Business Ethics: An Indian Perspective*. New Delhi: Pearson Education.

Ferrell, O. C., Fraedrich, J., & Ferrel, L. (2012). *Business ethics and ethical decision making and cases (9th Ed)*. Accessed May 2023 from http://book.google.co.in/

FinScope MSME Survey Lesotho. (2015). The government of Lesotho (GoL). FinScope Maseru.

Hamric, A. B., Hanson, C. H. M., Tracy, M. F., & O´grady, E. T. (2014). *Advanced practicenursing: An integrative approach*. Saunders Elsevier.

Israel, B., & Kazungu, I. (2019). The role of public procurement in enhancing growth of small and medium sized-enterprises: Experience from Mbeya Tanzania. *International Journal of Social Sciences, 12*(5), 34–43.

Jili, N. N., Masuku, M. M., & Selepe, B. M. (2017). SMMEs promoting local economic development (LED) in UMlazi Local Municipality, KwaZulu-Natal. *African Journal of Hospitality, Tourism and Leisure, 6*(1), 1–10.

Makheta, L., & Sebolelo, P. (2015). Problems and prospects of SME's loan management: Case of Lesotho. *International Journal of Recent Research Interdisciplinary Science (IJRRIS), 2*(1), 24–31.

Martin-Oritega, O., & Methven O'Brien, C. (2017). Advancing respect for labour rights globally through public procurement. *Politics and Governance, 5*(4), 69–79.

Medlin, B., & Green, K. W. (2014). Impact of management business on employee engagement. *Academy of Strategy Management Journal, 13*(2), 21–36.

Nansadiqa, L., Masbar, R., & Majid, M. S. A. (2019). Does economic growth matter for poverty reduction in Indonesia? *East African Scholars Journal of Economics, Business and Management, 2*(2), 46–52.

Nketekete, M. E., & Motebang, M. L. (2006). Entrepreneurship education in Lesotho secondary schools: Pedagogy challenges. *Education Knowledge and Economy. 2*(2), 121–135

Nzonzo, J. C., & Matashu, M. (2014). An insight into the human resource management practices adopted by entrepreneurs in South Africa. *Journal of Small Business and Entrepreneurship Development, 2*(3), 73–87.

Putnam, M. S. (2016). *Ethical values for business success*. Bothel, WA.

Rice, J. & Perry, F. (2013). *Healthcare leadership excellence: Creating a career of impact*. Chicago: Health Administration Press.

Tarus, D. K., & Nganga, S. I. (2013). Small and medium size manufacturing enterprises growth and work ethics in Kenya. *Developing Country Studies, 3*(2), 51–59.

Turyakira, P. K. (2018). Ethical practices of small and medium-sized enterprises in developing countries: Literature analysis. *South African Journal of Economic and Management Sciences, 21*(1), 1–7.

Vance, N. R., & Trani, B. V. (2008). The ethical grounding to 21st century public leadership. *International Journal of Organisation Theory and Behaviour, 11*(3), 373–381.

Zijlma, A. (2017). *Lesotho facts and information*. http://goafrica.about.com/od/. Accessed 12 September 2023.

Reflections on Enabling Legislative Regimes for African Women-Owned Businesses: A Post-COVID-19 Perspective

Emem O. Anwana

1 Introduction

African women entrepreneurs have been acknowledged as contributing significantly to innovation, job and wealth creation, poverty reduction, and household welfare (Anwana & Aroba, 2022; Ojong et al., 2021; Rashid & Ratten, 2020; SADC, 2022; UN Women & the ILO, 2021). According to AFAWA (Affirmative Finance Action for Women in Africa), an African female entrepreneur will typically reinvest up to 90% of her income in the education, health, and nutrition of her family and community, compared to up to 40% for men (AfDB AFAWA, 2023). Ojong et al. (2021) contend that, if taken more seriously, women entrepreneurs on the continent 'can add millions' to their economies. According to the (UNDP, 2020) report, African women account for 74% of informal sector workers, with the majority of African women-owned businesses being

E. O. Anwana (✉)
Faculty of Management Sciences,
Durban University of Technology, Durban, South Africa
e-mail: emema@dut.ac.za

P. Rambe and R. E. Hinson (eds.), *The Future of Entrepreneurship in Southern Africa*, Palgrave Studies in Technology and Innovation in Africa, https://doi.org/10.1007/978-3-031-55935-8_7

classified as small and micro enterprises (SMEs). The African Development Bank (AfDB) in establishing AFAWA (Affirmative Finance Action for Women in Africa) recognised that women constitute the driving force behind the African economy, with the continent boasting the highest proportion of women entrepreneurs globally. Additionally, they observed that African women entrepreneurs often reinvest a substantial portion, as high as 90%, of their earnings into areas such as education, healthcare, and nutrition for their families, a figure that surpasses the reinvestment rate of up to 40% seen amongst men. This according to the AfDB underscores the transformative potential of investing in women entrepreneurs (AfDB AFAWA, 2023). However as noted by the UNDP (2023), although many governments have sustained efforts to promote gender equality through legal frameworks, employment promotion, innovation, and workplace improvements, women entrepreneurs on the African continent continue to face obstacles and challenges. According to the report, achieving gender equality in entrepreneurship requires sustained commitment and multifaceted initiatives, some of which are discussed in this chapter.

Africa requires urgent intervention if it is to attain the United Nations (UN) Sustainable Development Goals (SDGs), particularly SDG 1(no poverty), SDG 5 (gender equality), SDG 8 (decent work and economic growth), and SDG 10 (reduced inequality). To attain economic development and improve the socio-economic conditions of Africans, the continent will need to create enabling environments for entrepreneurial expansion and economic development. Women must not be left out of the economic development plans if the SDGs are to be achieved (African Development Bank (AfDB) Group, 2023). Within the SADC region, women comprise over 50% of the population and eligible voters in their member states. However, they still face significant under-representation in political and public decision-making roles across most countries in the region (SADC & SARDC, 2022).

SADC recognises that the economic empowerment of women and inclusion of women in economic development plans not only positively impacts their own life situations, but is also central to mobilising their potential for sustainable development and poverty alleviation (SADC & SARDC, 2022). According to SADC (2022), women's economic independence is essential because it fights against exploitation, the feminisation of poverty, and discrimination. SADC maintains that gender equality at the economic level contributes directly to poverty reduction and overall development, noting that women in the SADC constitute more than

50% of the impoverished population in the region. Additionally, SADC recognises that to effectively combat poverty, specific initiatives targeting substantial groups amongst the impoverished are essential.

As the world continues to grapple with the aftermath and effects of the COVID-19 pandemic on small and medium enterprises (SMEs), it has become increasingly imperative for women-owned businesses, particularly those in Africa and the SADC that were disproportionately affected by the pandemic, to be supported through gender-sensitive instruments from government to at least return to the pre-pandemic era.

This chapter examines how gender-sensitive perspectives can bring about transformative strategies that support gender equality and empower women entrepreneurs. The chapter is underpinned by the Feminist and Capability theories as they relate to female entrepreneurship. The chapter also explores the intersection of women's entrepreneurship and policy, focusing on the existing legal framework for women-owned businesses in the SADC region. It intends to identify shortcomings and deficiencies in current regulations while proposing key elements of effective legislation that can foster women's entrepreneurship in the post-COVID-19 era.

2 Theoretical Development

The Feminist and Capability theories underpin this study. The chapter adopts the feminist perspective based on the established principles that women-owned businesses have grown in importance globally, as well as in Africa. Women entrepreneurs represent a practical demonstration of women's empowerment and economic independence. According to the Feminist theorist, women entrepreneurs differentiate themselves from their male counterparts in terms of their values and experiences in managing and growing their business enterprises and, as a result, they make a unique and positive contribution to entrepreneurship (Foss et al., 2019). Feminist theorists view feminism from two distinct perspectives, namely those that focus on the individual woman and the importance of adapting to her needs and desires, referred to as Social Feminism, and those that recognise patriarchal oppression and advocate a complete overhaul of the social system, referred to as Radical Feminism. In relation to women entrepreneurs, these two variants of the Feminist theory focus on issues such as growth, training, networking, finance, traditional and cultural practices, feminine ways, and values. According to Pruchniewska (2018), doing business is synonymous with feminism because it entails taking control of one's economic destiny and empowering other women to do the same. This viewpoint emphasises entrepreneurship's transformative potential in confronting patriarchal systems and creating spaces for feminist values to be practised and promoted. Feminist theory promotes diversity, inclusivity, and equality by questioning traditional gender norms and biases. It encourages collaborative decision-making, empowers women, and supports women-owned enterprises. Feminist ideals enhance organisational performance and the societal well-being of women while addressing the systemic hurdles faced by women in their entrepreneurial endeavours.

The study also adopts the Capability theory in recognition that women entrepreneurs, although making a unique and positive contribution to entrepreneurship, will have to adopt certain strategic capabilities that are essential for the sustainability of their businesses in order to become successful and sustainable (Teece, 2019). According to Teece (2019), the Capability theory deals with the ability of how a firm or business can leverage its competitive advantage. Teece (2019) states further that the pursuit and maintenance of competitive advantage, to the extent that it is derived from innovation rather than some type of market constraint, are arguably more seminal than an investigation into (static) efficiency because it focuses on how firms develop, learn and, in some cases, become 'great' and benefit their stakeholders. Hence, women-owned businesses will have to adopt certain strategic capabilities in order to become sustainable in a post-COVID-19 era. The next section of the chapter delves into the impact of COVID-19 on SMEs owned by women in the SADC region. Following that, the chapter explores the strategic capabilities essential for the sustainability of all businesses, including those owned by women.

3 Effect of COVID-19 on Women-Owned SMEs in the SADC Region

The impact of the COVID-19 pandemic on entrepreneurship, as highlighted by GEM (2023), had a disproportionate effect on women entrepreneurs compared to their male counterparts. This imbalance can primarily be attributed to the increased burden placed on women, who had to shoulder a larger share of responsibilities related to remote and domestic work. Additionally, women entrepreneurs are more prevalent in customer-oriented service sectors, rendering their businesses particularly vulnerable to the challenges posed by the lockdown measures. The financial strain caused by business closures, which were a direct result of the lockdown regulations imposed at the peak of the pandemic regrettably pushed a significant number of female entrepreneurs and their employees back into the unemployment statistics of their respective countries (Khwela-Mdluli & Beharry-Ramraj, 2020; Panda, 2022; United Nations, 2020).

The pandemic also disrupted essential services, making it harder for women to access help, especially for those in dangerous domestic situations. Lockdown regulations, primarily aimed at preventing the spread of the virus, did not adequately address the safety of women in their homes or the protection of their livelihoods. Women often found themselves confined with their abusers and unable to access help due to the closure of centres that provided such services (United Nations, 2020). While some countries offered COVID-19 relief to their citizens, these government efforts and credit facilities were often insufficient to revive women's informal businesses (Anene, 2021). Furthermore, the stringent eligibility requirements further limited women's access to available credit facilities (Anwana & Aroba, 2022).

Stephan (2023) emphasises that COVID-19 has had a profound negative impact on women in all aspects of life—social, domestic, political, and economic. The author opines that solutions should adopt a gender-focused perspective, with policies formulated and implemented to address the specific challenges faced by women. In Africa, although gender equality has been widely discussed through structures like the African Union (AU) and regional organisations such as the Economic Community of Central African States (ECCAS), Economic Community of West African States (ECOWAS), East African Community (EAC) and SADC, limited progress has been made in implementing existing policies or developing gender-specific legislation. The chapter delves into the shortcomings of the current legislative framework within the SADC. However, it also recognises that legislation, on its own, is insufficient to ensure the long-term viability of women-owned businesses. To secure growth and sustainability, women business owners must embrace specific strategic competencies. The subsequent section of the chapter delves into the significance of women business owners adopting these essential capabilities for the enduring success of their enterprises.

4 Strategic Capabilities of Women-Owned Businesses in a Post-COVID-19 Era

Many studies on entrepreneurship have shown that strategic capabilities are crucial for business success, particularly in the 'gig economy', a phenomenon which has grown tremendously in the last decade and which refers to labour markets that are short-term, on-demand, irregular, and task-based (Montgomery & Baglioni, 2021). Over the years, the gig economy has expanded to encompass work in a much broader range of industries, including food and beverages, transportation and education, amongst others (Tan et al., 2021). The gig economy presents numerous opportunities for female-owned SMEs in the SADC region post-COVID-19. It allows female entrepreneurs to tap into a larger customer base and expand their networks beyond geographical boundaries. Additionally, participating in the gig economy can provide women entrepreneurs with valuable experience in managing remote teams and utilising digital platforms for their business operations.

Post-COVID-19, the gig economy has become even more crucial for female-owned SMEs as many female entrepreneurs have embraced the gig economy as a means of expanding their businesses and reaching new markets, even as they seek flexibility in their working arrangements. However, for female-owned SMEs operating in the 'gig economy' to be sustainable, they will need to adopt certain strategic capabilities such as managerial skills, technological proficiency, and adaptability to changing market dynamics. According to Pandey (2021), although women have dominated the gig workforce in areas such as caregiving and housekeeping, few women have ventured into the delivery and transportation sector of the gig market. Although the number of women in the transportation sector of the gig economy is increasing in the West, the same cannot be said of African women entrepreneurs. Therefore, if female entrepreneurs are to participate in the gig economy post-COVID-19, there is need for the development of an enabling legislative regime, as well as training and exposure in strategic capabilities for female-owned businesses in the post-COVID-19 era. The next section discusses four strategic capabilities that female-owned business within the SADC must adopt to be sustainable post-COVID-19.

I. **Managerial and Leadership Capability**

Managerial and leadership capability plays a crucial role in the success of SMEs, and female-owned SMEs cannot be an exception. As stated above, although women entrepreneurs face unique challenges, the ability to effectively manage their businesses is essential for growth and sustainability. One aspect of managerial strategic capability is leadership. According to Atiku and Randa (2021), the type of leadership required for business sustainability post-COVID-19 is that of an ambidextrous leader, which according to Martínez-Climent et al. (2019) is a leader that can explore future business opportunities while utilising the current opportunities, and having the ability to switch in-between. Atiku and Randa (2021) state that this type of leadership is one that has the flexibility to transition between different situations, and is essential for encouraging innovation, continuous business process improvement and resource efficiency. Through gender-focused policies and regulations, SADC governments can set up training programmes aimed at equipping women entrepreneurs with these skills.

II. **Financial Management Capability**

Another important aspect of strategic capability is financial management capability. As earlier stated, although female-owned SMEs contribute positively to economic growth, they often struggle to secure financing (Anwana & Aroba, 2022). Where they can secure financing, they often lack the necessary financial management skills, leading to losing business capital and eventually business closures. The SADC DRFC (2023), in outlining the challenges faced by SMEs in the region, noted that financial-related challenges constituted major constraints to SME survival. The DRFC noted the following as hindering factors for SMEs within SADC:

- A lack of medium-to-long-term finance for start-ups and expansions;
- Inappropriate terms and conditions for short-term credit or trade finance;
- Insufficient financing and other instruments to support the SME sector; and
- Low capitalisation and a lack of collateral for SMEs to access finance from financial institutions.

According to Anwana (2024), many of these challenges could be alleviated through gender-sensitive policies and regulations. The United Nations (UN) also advises governments to promote a gendered approach in recovery efforts from the pandemic. Development partners, such as development finance institutions (DFIs) and multilateral development banks (MDBs), are called upon to increase their gender-smart financing programmes to aid in the recovery of women entrepreneurs from the devastations of the pandemic on their businesses (UN Women, 2022). African governments are urged to provide enabling legislative environments to support these donor initiatives. According to the UN, achieving gender equality and empowering women and girls globally requires stronger legislation, policies, and institutions (UN Women, 2022).

III. **Technological Strategic Capability**

Technological proficiency is a critical requirement for SME sustainability. The COVID-19 pandemic compelled many businesses to adopt and embrace digital platforms for their operations. Embracing technology not only enhances operational efficiency, but also creates opportunities for expanding markets and acquiring new skills (Atiku & Abatan, 2021). By adopting digital tools and platforms, African women entrepreneurs can establish a competitive presence in the evolving business landscape and contribute to the broader industrialisation goals of the SADC region, as outlined in the SADC Industrialisation agenda (SADC DRFC, 2023). Proficiency in technology empowers female-owned SMEs to optimise operations, improve efficiency, and reach a wider customer base. By adopting digital tools and platforms, women-owned businesses can enhance marketing strategies, effectively manage inventory, automate tasks, and deliver seamless customer experiences.

Most of the technologies embraced by African women entrepreneurs in the SADC region have been in the areas of electronic payment methods; utilising social media for advertising their goods and services; and employing digitisation and digital technologies for product and service delivery to their customers. The SADC Regional Indicative Strategic Development Plan (RISDP) 2020–2030, in its ten-year strategic plan, outlined the enhancement of regional technological capability and capacity through science, technology, and innovation as a key intervention to drive economic development within SADC (SADC RISDP, 2020).

The RISDP key intervention strategies include:

i. Capacitating SMEs to participate in industrialisation and regional value-chains;
ii. Establishing a SADC Women in Science, Engineering, and Technology Organisation; and
iii. Developing and implementing a Regional Strategy on the Fourth Industrial Revolution.

By embracing digital tools and platforms, women-owned businesses can enhance their marketing strategies, effectively manage inventory, automate processes, and provide seamless customer experiences. SADC has called upon governments and non-profit organisations (NPOs) to develop policies and legislation that support women through training programmes to acquire technological skills to enhance their entrepreneurial endeavours.

IV. **Business Adaptability to Changing Market Dynamics**

Business adaptability to a changing market dynamic is a vital strategic capability for female-owned SMEs operating in the gig economy, especially in the post-COVID-19 era. The pandemic has accelerated digital transformation and highlighted the importance of remote work and online services. Female entrepreneurs who can quickly adapt to these changes and pivot their business models accordingly are more likely to thrive in this evolving landscape. However, adaptability in the context of women entrepreneurs comes with its unique challenges. Participation in the gig economy involves technological skills and access to resources such as the internet, smart devices, and access to finance. Hence, for women-owned businesses to fully harness the potential of the gig economy post-COVID-19, it is essential for policy-makers and stakeholders to address the various challenges that female-owned SMEs encounter. The next section of the chapter discusses gender and entrepreneurship within the SADC region (Atiku & Abatan, 2021; Mathibe & Croucamp, 2019).

5 Gender and Entrepreneurship in SADC

Rationalising gender in the context of entrepreneurial sustainability in the SADC region is both contentious and a policy dilemma in a bloc where most of the people live in poverty, with unemployment and worsening socio-economic developmental challenges. The Southern African Development Community (SADC) was founded in 1980 under the name Southern African Development Coordination Conference (SADCC). It adopted its current name in 1992 during a summit meeting held in Windhoek, Namibia. Prior to 1992, SADCC's focus was to establish strong economic co-operation amongst Southern African countries, excluding South Africa. The goal was to enhance the economies of South Africa's neighbouring nations by reducing their reliance on the apartheid South African economy. SADCC concentrated on the development of critical sectors such as transportation, communication, energy, mining, and industrial production. From 1992, when the organisation became SADC, its objectives expanded to include the establishment of an open economy built on principles of equality, mutual benefit, and balanced development. This included efforts to dismantle tariff barriers; promote trade and mutual investments; facilitate the free movement of goods, personnel and labour services; work towards unified tariffs and currencies gradually within the Community; and create a free trade zone by the year 2000 (SAHO, 2019).

The economic bloc consists of 15 member states, with a combined GDP (US$) of 737,392 and per capita of 3,152. The population of SADC is approximately 394,845,175 with a land area of 9,882,959. In August 2008, the SADC Free Trade Area (FTA) was established. Botswana, Lesotho, Madagascar, Mauritius, Mozambique, Namibia, South Africa, Eswatini, Tanzania, Zambia and Zimbabwe were the original members. Although Angola and the Democratic Republic of the Congo are not yet members, Angola as of 2019 was working through its trade ministry to create conditions for Angola's accession to the SADC Free Trade Area. On 22 October 2008, SADC, the Common Market for Eastern and Southern Africa, and the East African Community formed the African Free Trade Zone, which included 26 countries with a combined GDP of $624 billion (£382.9 billion). The agreement aims to ease access to markets and end problems caused by member countries' membership in multiple groups (SADC, 2022).

SADC has 27 legally binding protocols covering topics such as defence, development, illicit drug trade, free trade, and people movement. Before the COVID-19 pandemic, the region had made strides in the empowerment of women. Through the SADC Protocol on Gender and Development, a policy document developed in 2008 by the SADC Secretariat and the SADC Gender Protocol Alliance, consisting of 15 country networks of women regional feminists (Butale, 2023). The protocol appealed to member states to accelerate implementation efforts to achieve concrete and transformative changes in the lives of women and girls throughout the region. Article 17 of the protocol enjoined member states to undertake legislative reforms to give men and women equal rights and opportunities to economic resources; review their national trade and entrepreneurship policies to make them gender responsive; and develop strategies to ensure that women benefit equally from economic opportunities, including those created through public procurement processes (SADC, 2008).

According to SADC (2022), women have huge potential to function as a significant resource for development in the SADC area. As part of its efforts to create and implement a regional programme for women's economic empowerment, a regional framework for women's economic empowerment that is consistent with the SADC Gender Programme was created, known as the Regional Multi-Dimensional Women's Economic Empowerment Programme 2020–2030 (RMDWEEP) in 2019. The goal of RMDWEEP was to advance women's economic empowerment and gender-responsive development to advance social inclusion and justice in the region. The RMDWEEP seeks to coordinate, support, monitor, and assess regional commitments made by SADC member states towards women's economic empowerment.

6 Gender-Sensitive Legislation and Women Empowerment

Legislation can have a significant impact on women empowerment. In any country, laws and regulations can either facilitate or hinder women's ability to start and grow businesses. Legislative and regulatory frameworks encourage fair and equal treatment of businesses, particularly those competing for government contracts. Importantly, these frameworks should include special provisions for women that promote gender equality not only in public procurement processes, but also in other areas such as access to finance, skills acquisition, and property rights (Bomani & Derera, 2020).

In many SADC countries, women often face legal and regulatory barriers that limit their access to finance, property rights, and markets. For example, in some countries, women are prohibited from owning property or inheriting family land. This makes it difficult for women entrepreneurs to access credit or collateral (Simba et al., 2022). Gender-sensitive legislation is critical for promoting women's economic empowerment and achieving the SDGs as well as the AU Agenda 2063, which the SADC countries have signed up to. Legislation with gender-sensitive elements enables the recognition of the unique challenges that women face in starting and growing businesses and creates room to address these challenges through regulations. Gender-sensitive legislation also enables the promotion of equal opportunities for women and men in all spheres of life. It can help to reduce gender-based discrimination and promote gender equality. The SADC Protocol on Gender and Development describes 'gender sensitivity' to mean acknowledging and taking into account both men's and women's specific gender needs at all levels of planning, implementation, monitoring, and evaluation (AFDB, 2022).

The role of legislation in empowering women in all spheres of live has been a growing topic of interest in Africa. Several studies have been conducted to examine the impact of enabling legislation on women entrepreneurs and their businesses. These studies have highlighted the importance of legal frameworks that support women's economic empowerment and that provide them with equal opportunities to access resources and markets. A study conducted by the International Labour Organization (ILO) found that countries with supportive legal frameworks for women entrepreneurs tend to have higher rates of female entrepreneurship. The study also highlighted the need for legislation that addresses the specific challenges faced by women entrepreneurs, such as access to finance, property rights, and discriminatory practices. Another study by the United Nations Development Programme (UNDP) found that while some countries had made progress in promoting gender equality through legislative reforms, there were still significant gaps in implementation and enforcement (ILO, 2023; UNDP, 2020).

Overall, these studies suggest that enabling legislation is critical for promoting women-owned businesses. However, it is not enough to simply pass laws and develop policies, as there must be a concerted effort to ensure that these laws and policies are effectively implemented and enforceable. According to Maeresera and Runganga (2020), the persistent issues that threaten to reverse gains in gender equality and women's empowerment are, amongst other things, gender-insensitive electoral policies; a lack of resources; and prevalent gender stereotypes based on customs and traditions. The next segment of the chapter explores the legislative inadequacies and gaps that prevent women entrepreneurs in the SADC region from reaching their full entrepreneurial capability.

7 Legislative Inadequacies and Gaps in Promoting Women-Owned Business in SADC

In Africa generally, and in SADC, it has been documented that even where policies that support women's entrepreneurship exist, they are rarely put into practice and implemented. There is also a general lack of clear policies and regulations that support women-owned businesses. This has resulted in limited access to government contracts and procurement opportunities, which are crucial for business growth (Ojong et al., 2021). Ogundana et al. (2021) contend that in as much as there have been efforts to promote women-owned businesses in the SADC region, there are still legislative inadequacies and gaps that hinder their growth. One of the major challenges identified by the authors is the lack of access to finance. According to them, the ability to access finance is a critical factor for business success, but women entrepreneurs often face difficulties in accessing credit due to discriminatory lending practices, lack of collateral, and limited financial literacy. Other factors include:

I. *Restrictions to ownership of property rights*: In some SADC countries, laws restricting married women from acquiring rights to land, immovable property, and other types of property still exist.

II. *Taxation:* Informal businesses are made to pay multiple levies and taxes to different municipal operators or risk getting their goods confiscated and destroyed.

III. *Bureaucratic business registration:* In some SADC countries, the process of starting and registering a business is complicated, expensive, and time-consuming. Hence many women-owned businesses are unregistered and operating only in the informal sector.

IV. *Poor service delivery:* Poor public services such as water, electric power, sanitation, transportation, etc. negatively impact women entrepreneurs, thus making access to markets expensive and often unsafe.
V. *Energy:* Insufficient and inadequate energy supplies negatively impact women entrepreneurs who operate mostly in the service sector. Alternative energy is often expensive and out of reach for most female entrepreneurs.
VI. *Corruption:* Pervasive corruption continues to be a hindering factor for women entrepreneurs. Police, municipal operators, and public procurement implementers extort, harass, and prevent women from participation.
VII. *Sexual harassment and gender-based violence (GBV):* Women face sexual harassment in almost all aspects of their lives, thereby preventing them from participating in many sectors of the economy that are dominated by men (Ojong et al., 2021).
VIII. *Harmful cultural and traditional beliefs and practices:* Such as child/early marriages, school dropout, and prevention from acquiring education and skills, as well as the burden of caring for children, elderly, and sick relatives are all hindering factor to a sustainable business environment for women.

Overall, addressing legislative inadequacies and gaps will require concerted efforts from policy-makers, civil society organisations, and other stakeholders. It is only through collaborative action that an enabling environment can be created for women-owned businesses to thrive in the SADC region in the post-COVID-19 era. Table 1 depicts the efforts as well as the legislative gaps by SADC member states in developing and implementing gender-sensitive legislative measures for women empowerment and entrepreneurship in the region.

The above table illustrates the endeavours made by SADC nations to embrace gender-focused policies and legislation aimed at empowering women. Nevertheless, the shortcomings and insufficiencies in these initiatives primarily manifest in their execution and implementation. Corruption, deficiencies in managerial and technical skills, bureaucratic hurdles, limited access to information, patriarchal systems, gender-based violence, and various other challenges hinder women from fully benefiting from these measures. The next section of the chapters makes recommendations on possible ways forward.

Table 1 Gender-sensitive legislative measures adopted by SADC member states and noticeable gaps

No	*SADC country*	*Existing gender-sensitive legislative initiatives and institutions*	*Gaps and obstacles*
1	Angola	• Article 18 of the 1992 Angolan Constitution guarantees equal rights for all its citizens • Poverty Reduction Strategy Plan (PRSP) 2003–2005 • Post-conflict Rehabilitation and Reconstruction Programme (PRRP) 2003–2005 • Convention on the Elimination of all Forms of Discrimination Against Women (CEDAW) ratified in 1984 • Convention on the Rights of the Child (CRC) ratified in 1989 • The National Labour Code provides for equal rights in the workplace for men and women	• Very low representation of women in the established political institutions • Access to resources such as productive land, cash, and credit • Access to tools and agricultural inputs like seeds, fertiliser, and pesticides • Access to skills and technological knowledge • Access to market institutions • Involvement in income-generating projects
2	Botswana	• Companies Act (2018): The Act allows provides equal opportunities for women to own and manage businesses • Industrial Property Act (2010): This legislation protects intellectual property rights, ensuring that women entrepreneurs have legal safeguards for their innovations and creations • Trade and Consumer Protection Act (2009): This law ensures fair competition in the market and protects consumers. It also offers women entrepreneurs the opportunity to participate in the marketplace on equal footing • The Women's Economic Empowerment Policy (2004): This policy framework promotes women's economic inclusion and empowerment. It provides support for training, access to credit, and capacity-building programmes for women entrepreneurs • The National Gender Policy (2003): This policy promotes gender equality and women's participation in all sectors of society, including entrepreneurship. It aims to reduce gender disparities in economic opportunities	• Most women-owned business are unregistered and operating in the informal sectors • Inadequate representation of women at decision-making levels • Inadequate access to resources including land and credit

(continued)

Table 1 (continued)

No	*SADC country*	*Existing gender-sensitive legislative initiatives and institutions*	*Gaps and obstacles*
3	Comoros	• Constitution of the Union of the Comoros guarantees equal rights and opportunities for all citizens, regardless of gender • Labour Code: The Labor Code of Comoros includes provisions that prohibit discrimination in employment • Public procurement legislation encourages women's participation in public procurement • The Growth and Poverty Reduction Strategy Paper (PRGSP) • General Commission for Solidarity and Gender Promotion (CGG) housed in the Ministry of Health, • Department of Female Entrepreneurship • Establishment of Gender Focal Points (GFP) in each Ministry • National Gender Equity and Equality Policy (PNEEG)	• Absence of updated gender-disaggregated data. • Bureaucracy and political interference and interest in public procurement • CGG lacks qualified and sufficient staff to perform the duties assigned to it • GFPs are not set up at an appropriate decision-making level and with adequate resources
4	Democratic Republic of Congo	• The Constitution of the Democratic Republic of Congo 2006 prohibits discrimination based on gender • In 2015 the government passed legislation requiring at least 10% of women to be employed by businesses with more than 50 employees • DRC established national funds for women's entrepreneurs to provide funding and training to female business owners • The Gender and Family Code • The National Gender Policy	• Insecurity caused by conflicts, • Lack of infrastructure • Access to finance and resources

No	*SADC country*	*Existing gender-sensitive legislative initiatives and institutions*	*Gaps and obstacles*
5	Eswatini	• The Constitution of Eswatini recognises the principles of gender equality and non-discrimination • The Public Procurement Act of Eswatini includes provisions that give preference to women-owned businesses in public procurement processes • The Companies Act of Eswatini provides a legal framework for business registration and operation • The Ministry of Commerce, Industry, and Trade established a Women in Business Desk to provide assistance and resources to female entrepreneurs	• Education and Skills Gaps • Access to Technology • Gender Bias and Stereotypes • Limited access to Finance
6	Lesotho	• Formation of the Women's Bureau in 1973 • Ministry of Gender, Youth Sports and Recreation in 2000 (MGYSR) • Lesotho National Development Corporation (LNDC) has implemented a preferential procurement policy that gives preference to women-owned businesses in public procurement processes • Married Persons Equality Bill • National Plan of Action on Women and Girls and HIV/AIDS	• Women's limited access to and control over resources, • Heavy workload leading to time constraints, • Cultural norms, attitudes, and practices that regard women as perpetual dependents, • Institutional barriers related to gender integration • Exclusion from making household decisions • Lack of economic, social, and political control
7	Madagascar	• National Strategy for Gender Equality and Equity (2018–2022) that aims to promote women's economic empowerment by providing credit, training, and technical assistance • The government created a Women's Entrepreneurship Fund to provide financial assistance to women-owned businesses	• Some of the barriers to women-owned SME growth include limited access to finance, a lack of business skills and networks, as well as cultural differences

(continued)

Table 1 (continued)

No	*SADC country*	*Existing gender-sensitive legislative initiatives and institutions*	*Gaps and obstacles*
8	Malawi	• National Gender Policy and the Malawi Growth and Development Strategy (MGDS), five-year (2017–2022) development aspirations recognises gender equality • Public Procurement Act includes affirmative action provisions in favour of women-owned businesses in public procurement processes • Ministry of Gender, Child Development and Community Development developed the National Gender Policy (NGP) • National Plan of Action to Combat Gender-Based Violence in Malawi (2016–2021) • National Action Plan for Women Economic Empowerment (2016–2021) • National Strategy on Ending Child Marriages (2018–2023) • The National Agricultural Policy (NAP)	• Limited business networks • Limited access to finance, financial institutions have stringent requirements, and women may lack collateral or credit history
9	Mauritius	• National Women Entrepreneur Council (NWEC) to support and guide female entrepreneurs. The NWEC provides training programmes, mentorship opportunities, and financial assistance to women who want to start or grow a business	• Lack of access to resources, market opportunities, and networking • Training and skills gap exist in areas of managerial, technological, and financial
10	Mozambique	• Constitution of the Republic of Mozambique recognises gender equality and prohibits discrimination based on gender • The National Gender Policy • National Strategy for Women's Economic Empowerment	• Lack of access to resources, market opportunities, and infrastructure

No	*SADC country*	*Existing gender-sensitive legislative initiatives and institutions*	*Gaps and obstacles*
11	Namibia	• The Namibian Constitution 1990 provides for equal rights for women in marriage, during marriage and in divorce • ratification of the Convention on the Elimination of All forms of Discrimination Against Women(CEDAW) (1992), • ratification of the CEDAW Optional Protocol (2000), • ratification of the SADC Declaration on Gender and Development, • ratification of the Beijing Platform for Action, • ratification of the African Regional Platform for Action (1997) • ratification of the African Charter on Women's Rights (2004) • National Gender Policy (NGP), • the National Gender Plan of Action (NGPA) • The Namibia Vision 2030 • Ministry of Gender Equality and Child Welfare (MGECW) establish the Gender Focal Points (GFPs)	• Problems, of implementation and monitoring of these acts still exist • Not all ministries have Gender Focal Points (GFPs), either due to a shortage of personnel or resistance to gender-related matters by some ministry staff
12	Seychelles	• Constitution of the Republic of Seychelles (Tenth Amendment) Act, 2022, guarantee equal rights to all citizens • The Women and Gender Equity (WGE) 2018 established to ensure that laws and policies are more gender sensitive • Seychelles Business Registration Act: ensures that women have the equal opportunities to establish and manage businesses	• Despite legal protections, some women entrepreneurs still encounter gender-related barriers in business registration, property ownership, and contract enforcement

(continued)

Table 1 (continued)

No	*SADC country*	*Existing gender-sensitive legislative initiatives and institutions*	*Gaps and obstacles*
13	South Africa	• The Broad-Based Black Economic Empowerment Act, for instance, has affirmative procurement provisions that apply to women-owned enterprises. This policy ensures that women-owned businesses have equal opportunities to participate in public procurement processes and access government contracts • The Employment Equity Act 55 of 1998, as amended, recognises gender equality, and aims to create a level playing field for all genders in the workplace by ensuring that everyone has equal opportunities for employment, training, and advancement • Constitution of South Africa provides an enabling framework that has guided the introduction of policies and laws to enforce transformation, non-discrimination, non-sexism, and equality for women in the country • The Small Business Development Act (1996) helped to create an enabling environment for small businesses to thrive and become sustainable • Small Enterprise Development Agency (SEDA), • Seda Technology Programme (STP), • Small Enterprise Finance Agency (SEFA), • Technology Innovation Agency, • National Empowerment Fund (NEF), and • Incubation Support Programme (ISP) are some of the institutions and agencies established by the South African government to assist SMEs (Mathibe & Croucamp, 2019)	• Women entrepreneurs still find it difficult to operate in male-dominated sectors such as construction, mining. transportation • GBV and femicide continue to dominate headlines • women still find themselves operating predominantly in the informal sector

No	*SADC country*	*Existing gender-sensitive legislative initiatives and institutions*	*Gaps and obstacles*
14	Tanzania	• The Ministry of Community Development, Gender, and Children (MCDGC) is the National Machinery with overall responsibility for women's and gender development • National Women and Gender Policy (2000) • Women and Gender Development Policy(WGDP, 2000) • National Strategy for Gender and Development (NSGD, 2002) • Women and Gender Policy for 2003 • All sectoral ministries have designated gender focal points (GFP) to facilitate the integration of gender perspectives, ensure gender mainstreaming, equality, and justice within their institutions and the various programmes they undertake	• Need for more comprehensive legislation that specifically targets women-owned businesses • The gender focal points (GFPs) face constraints as they are burdened with multiple responsibilities, including gender and HIV/AIDS mainstreaming, in addition to their regular professional duties within their respective departments

(continued)

Table 1 (continued)

No	*SADC country*	*Existing gender-sensitive legislative initiatives and institutions*	*Gaps and obstacles*
15	Zambia	• The National Gender Policy (NGP) • Strategic Plan for the Advancement of Women (SPAW) • Strategic Plan of Action for the National Gender Policy (SPANGP) (2003–2007) • The Gender In Development Division (GIDD) • Citizens Economic Empowerment Commission (CEEC), which provides financial and technical assistance to women and other marginalised groups who own small and medium-sized enterprises (SMEs) • Zambia's Ministry of Commerce, Trade, and Industry also launched several programmes aimed at improving the competitiveness of women-owned SMEs through training, mentorship, and networking opportunities • Programme for the Advancement of Girls Education (PAGE)	• Female entrepreneurs are constrained by lack of business and technical skills and knowledge • Bureaucratic business registration processes, • Lack of market opportunities • Insufficient access to export markets • No access to credit • Inadequate funding for gender programmes
16	Zimbabwe	• The Zimbabwe Indigenisation and Economic Empowerment Act, Chapter 14, Sect. 33 of 2007, provides opportunities for local entrepreneurs, regardless of gender, to bid for government supply contracts (Bomani & Derera, 2020) • Zimbabwe's Constitution (2013), through an expanded Bill of Rights, provides constitutional guarantees for gender equality and affirmative action • The National Gender Policy Implementation Strategy and Action Plan (2017) • The National Gender Policy Implementation Strategy and Action Plan (2019) • The Ministry of Women Affairs, Community, Small and Medium Enterprise Development responsible for coordinating gender mainstreaming • Gender-Responsive Budgeting (GRB) • Signed and ratified Convention on the Elimination of all forms of Discrimination Against Women (CEDAW) • Energy for Black Women programme. Over R885 million was invested in more than 100 service stations across the country, with black women entrepreneurs owning and managing 44% of the service stations	• Tender corruption challenges when it comes to bidding for and obtaining government contracts • Lack of managerial and technical skills required to compete for government contracts • Limited access to information about government bids and tender procedures (Basheka, 2018, Bomani & Derera, 2020) • High inflation • Policies generally lacking clear and measurable targets and indicators that monitor progress

(Authors own compilation, AFDB [2022])

8 Recommendations and Way Forward

The recommendations are categorised into two main sections. The initial set of recommendations concerns the strategic skills and abilities that female entrepreneurs should adopt to ensure their resilience in a post-COVID-19 period. The second set of recommendations centres on how policies and legislation can fortify and promote the advancement of women entrepreneurs in the SADC region.

9 Recommendations on Strategic Capabilities for Female Entrepreneurs

Ambidextrous Leadership: According to Martínez-Climent et al. (2019), ambidextrous leadership is leadership that can explore future business opportunities while utilising the current opportunities, and having the ability to switch in-between. Atiku and Randa (2021) posit that this type of leadership has the flexibility to transition between different situations and is essential for encouraging employee innovation, continuous business process improvement, and resource efficiency. With the coronavirus pandemic exacerbating the difficulties faced by small and medium-sized organisations (SMEs), ambidextrous leadership is required for businesses to survive in the post-pandemic dispensation.

Innovation: Research has proven that businesses that are receptive to innovation and willing to adapt innovation into their organisational strategy become more sustainable. Women-owned businesses need to become aware of changes in their customers' demand, become creative, ecologically friendly, and innovative. As noted by Atiku and Abatan (2021), businesses with a creative capability will outperform their competition and ensure the business's long-term viability.

Digitisation: The natural world in which people live, socialise, and work is changing as a result of digital disruption. Organisations must develop an industry-specific, long-term digital transformation strategy that begins from the outside in, with a clear operationalisation strategy that connects the front, middle, and back offices. Businesses require a unified corporate vision and an embedded change culture. This can help the sustainable digital transformation process by reducing friction and increasing connectivity, agility, and transparency, which can result in a seamless digital business model (Nyagadza, 2022). Women-owned businesses will need to embrace and adopt digital transformation strategies into their business operations if they are to become sustainable.

Financial inclusivity: COVID-19 and the ensuing lockdown procedures had a disastrous effect on small businesses, particularly those owned by women. The pandemic created significant liquidity problems. Consumers simultaneously experienced income losses, which resulted in less spending and consumption. This led to women-owned businesses losing their business capital and finding themselves in a position where they could not restart their business after the pandemic. According to available entrepreneurship literature, the most significant barriers to starting and growing a businesses is the lack of access to finance (Atiku & Randa, 2021; Moscalu et al., 2020).

Taxes: Many countries within the SADC regions impose heavy taxes on SMEs, which in turn hurts the growth and sustainability of these SMEs. Many female-owned SMEs do not understand tax implications and sometimes fall prey to multiple municipal taxes, corruption, and fraud from municipal agents. To ameliorate these challenges, SADC governments will need to develop clear policies on SME taxes. Multiple and unscrupulous tax demands need to be avoided and delinquent government officials need to be prosecuted. Furthermore, government agencies, non-profit organisations, and other women's support groups and associations need to work together to provide training for women entrepreneurs on acquiring as well as upskilling their financial management skills to understand tax implications as well as support their business growth and sustainability (Atiku & Randa, 2021; Sony & Naik, 2020).

10 Recommendations on Enabling Regulatory and Legislative Regimes for Women-Owned Businesses

i. **Access to Finance and Credit Facilities**

Access to financing and credit options should be made available with consideration for women-owned businesses. This is due to studies demonstrating that compared to their male counterparts, female entrepreneurs face greater obstacles when trying to access financing. A training and capacity-building component should be included in the legislation to help women entrepreneurs develop their skills.

ii. **The Need for Women's Inclusion in Decision-Making Processes**

Women constitute more than half of the population and electorate in SADC member states. However, they remain significantly under-represented in political and public decision-making in most of the region's countries. The pandemic has highlighted the need for women to be included in decision-making processes. Women's voices need to be heard, especially in matters that affect them directly. Women have unique perspectives and experiences that need to be considered when making decisions. If the existing gender inequalities are to be addressed, women need to be included in all levels of decision-making, from local to national levels.

iii. **The Importance of Collaboration**

Collaboration is key when it comes to addressing gender inequalities. Women's groups need to work together and collaborate with policy-makers and other stakeholders. By working together, a more inclusive and equitable society can be created.

iv. **The Role of Civil Society Organisations**

Civil society organisations play a crucial role in advocating for women's rights and promoting gender equality. These organisations work at the grassroots level and can provide valuable insights into the challenges faced by women. The pandemic put a strain on civil society organisations. Many had to adapt their operations to comply with lockdowns and movement restrictions. However, they played a crucial role in providing support to those affected by the pandemic.

v. **The Importance of Data**

Data is crucial when it comes to addressing gender inequalities. Data is needed to understand the extent of the problem and to develop effective solutions. However, data on gender inequalities is often lacking. Data on how the pandemic affected women differently from men can be used to develop targeted legislative and policy interventions.

vi. **Elimination of Gender-Based Violence (GBV) in SADC**

GBV is a pervasive problem in the SADC region. According to the United Nations Development Programme (UNDP), one in three women in SADC has experienced physical or sexual violence in their life-time. To address this issue, SADC developed a comprehensive legal and policy framework on GBV. The SADC Protocol on Gender and Development includes provisions on preventing and addressing GBV, including the development of national action plans, the establishment of specialised services for survivors, and the prosecution of perpetrators (UNDP, 2020). These policies must be implemented and made effective in order to stop GBV in all its forms.

vii. **Private Sector Engagement**

Private sector engagement is critical for promoting gender-sensitive legislation and supporting women entrepreneurs. Private sector actors can play a key role in advocating for policy reforms that promote gender equality and support women-led businesses. They can also provide financial and technical support to women entrepreneurs, such as access to credit, training, and mentorship.

viii. **Regional Co-operation**

Promoting gender-responsive legislation and assisting female entrepreneurs in the SADC region depend heavily on regional co-operation. To advance initiatives that support gender equality and women's economic empowerment, member states can share experiences and best practices amongst themselves.

ix. **Clear Definition of What Constitutes a Women-Owned Business**

For legislation to effectively promote women-owned businesses in the SADC region, it must contain certain constitutive components. There needs to be a clear definition of what constitutes a women-owned business. This will ensure that the legislation is targeting the right group of people and giving them the necessary legislative backing and support.

x. **Elimination of Gender-Based Discrimination in Procurement Processes**

Measures should be put in place to address gender-based discrimination in business practices, such as procurement processes and access to markets. This will ensure that women-owned businesses are not unfairly disadvantaged.

xi. **Gender Mainstreaming**

There is a need for SADC member states to develop and implement a gender-sensitive and supportive legal framework that fosters the growth of women-owned businesses in the region. Gender mainstreaming is seen as a means to achieve this, gender mainstreaming involves identifying gender gaps and integrating the concerns and experiences of women, men, girls, and boys into the design, implementation, monitoring, and evaluation of policies and programmes to ensure equitable benefits for all. Through gender mainstreaming SADC can develop and enforce policies promoting gender equality, combating discrimination, and inclusion of women in policy formulation to ensure their active participation in regional economic development, peace, and security measures.

xii. **Investment in the Informal Economy**

According to Burki (2020), the informal sector accounts for more than two-thirds of female employment in Africa, with most of them working or operating businesses in the service and agricultural sector, which unfortunately were the worst hit sectors during the COVID-19 pandemic due to the lockdown measures imposed by African governments to contain the spread of the virus. Hence, investment in the informal economy is crucial if gender equality and poverty elimination are to be achieved.

xiii. **Monitoring and Evaluation**

There should be monitoring and evaluation mechanisms put in place to assess the effectiveness of the legislation in promoting women entrepreneurship. This will enable policy-makers to make necessary adjustments and improvements based on feedback from stakeholders.

11 Conclusion

The COVID-19 pandemic brought about profound changes to the business landscape, with a notable expansion of the gig economy and an increased reliance on digital technology for service delivery. Women-owned SMEs have embraced this evolving economy, appreciating its flexibility, which allows for the simultaneous balancing of childcare and family responsibilities. However, to ensure the sustainability of women-owned businesses in the gig economy post-pandemic, specific strategic capabilities are essential. The chapter delved into the strategic capabilities required by women-owned SMEs in the SADC region for sustainability in the post-COVID-19 era, drawing from the framework of the Feminist and Capability theories. It underscored the critical role of legislation in addressing gender inequalities and promoting women's empowerment. By presenting the gendered legal framework profiles of SADC member states, the chapter emphasised how laws can serve as protective measures for women's rights and act as catalysts for gender equality and women's empowerment when properly resourced and implemented with a gender-sensitive approach.

The chapter concluded by emphasising that gender-sensitive legislation can serve as a powerful tool for empowering and advancing women-owned businesses. It called for the enactment of laws and the formulation of policies targeting crucial components like access to finance, education, training, mentorship, and networking opportunities for women entrepreneurs in the SADC region. However, it also highlighted that legislation alone is insufficient. Hence, concerted efforts are required for effective implementation and enforcement. While recognising some progress in the SADC region, the chapter identified significant gaps and deficiencies in existing legislation. To bridge these gaps, policy-makers were urged to prioritise the creation of an enabling environment for women-owned businesses to thrive in the post-COVID-19 era. This entails gender-sensitive policy direction, including the active involvement of women in the planning and implementation stages of policies and regulations.

References

AfDB. (2022). *Country gender profiles*. https://www.afdb.org/en/documents/category/country-gender-profiles. Accessed June 10, 2023.

AfDB AFAWA. (2023). *Why AFAWA?* https://www.afdb.org/en/topics-and-sectors/initiatives-partnerships/afawa-affirmative-finance-action-women-africa. Accessed May 20, 2023.

African Development Bank (AfDB) Group. (2023). *African women in business initiative*. https://www.afdb.org/en/topics-and-sectors/initiatives-partnerships/african-women-in-business-initiative. Accessed May 20, 2023.

Anene, C. P. (2021). The impact of COVID-19 on women contributions to Nigerian economy via the informal sector. *International Journal of Comparative Studies in International Relations and Development, 7*(1), 58.

Anwana, E. (2024). African women-owned SMEs post-COVID-19: Toward a gender-sensitive policy development strategy *SMEs and economic development in Africa* (pp. 33–46). Routledge.

Anwana, E. O., & Aroba, O. J. (2022). African women entrepreneurs and COVID-19: Towards achieving the African Union agenda 2063. *HTS Teologiese Studies/Theological Studies, 78*(2). https://doi.org/10.4102/hts.v78i2.7987

Atiku, S. O., & Abatan, A. A. (2021). Strategic capabilities for the sustainability of small, medium, and micro enterprises. In *Reshaping entrepreneurship education with strategy and innovation* (pp. 17–44). IGI Global.

Atiku, S. O., & Randa, I. O. (2021). Ambidextrous leadership for SMEs in the COVID-19 era. In *Handbook of research on sustaining SMEs and entrepreneurial innovation in the post-COVID-19 era* (pp. 19–39). IGI Global.

Bomani, M., & Derera, E. (2020). Women entrepreneurs and government tenders in Harare, Zimbabwe: Challenges and strategies for survival. *Journal of Contemporary Management, 17*(2), 126–143.

Burki, T. (2020). The indirect impact of COVID-19 on women. *The Lancet Infectious Diseases, 20*(8), 904–905.

Butale, C. T. (2023). The ambiguous conceptualisation of gender mainstreaming in the Southern African development community. *Development Southern Africa, 40*(3), 713–727.

Foss, L., Henry, C., Ahl, H., & Mikalsen, G. H. (2019). Women's entrepreneurship policy research: A 30-year review of the evidence. *Small Business Economics, 53*, 409–429.

GEM. (2023). *Global entrepreneurship monitor 2022/2023 Global report-adapting to a 'new normal'*. GEM.

ILO. (2023). *ILO vision of equality between women and men*. https://www.ilo.org/gender/Aboutus/ILOandGenderEquality/lang--en/index.htm. Accessed May 21, 2023.

Khwela-Mdluli, N., & Beharry-Ramraj, A. (2020). The effect of Covid-19 on working women in South Africa. *Gender & Behaviour, 18*(4), 16501–16512.

Maeresera, S., & Runganga, B. (2020). Gender rationalisation in the SADC standby force: Challenges and prospects. *Gender & Behaviour, 18*(4), 16581–16592.

Martínez-Climent, C., Rodríguez-García, M., & Zeng, J. (2019). Ambidextrous leadership, social entrepreneurial orientation, and operational performance. *Sustainability, 11*(3), 890.

Mathibe, D., & Croucamp, P. (2019). Policy and strategy framework for black, women-owned small and medium businesses, with reference to the Johannesburg and Tshwane metropoles. *Journal of Public Administration, 54*(4–1), 714–727.

Montgomery, T., & Baglioni, S. (2021). Defining the gig economy: Platform capitalism and the reinvention of precarious work. *International Journal of Sociology and Social Policy, 41*(9/10), 1012–1025.

Moscalu, M., Girardone, C., & Calabrese, R. (2020). SMEs' growth under financing constraints and banking markets integration in the euro area. *Journal of Small Business Management, 58*(4), 707–746.

Nyagadza, B. (2022). Sustainable digital transformation for ambidextrous digital firms: Systematic literature review, meta-analysis and agenda for future research directions. *Sustainable Technology and Entrepreneurship, 1*(3), 100020.

Ogundana, O. M., Simba, A., Dana, L. P., & Liguori, E. (2021). Women entrepreneurship in developing economies: A gender-based growth model. *Journal of Small Business Management, 59*(sup1), S42–S72.

Ojong, N., Simba, A., & Dana, L. P. (2021). Female entrepreneurship in Africa: A review, trends, and future research directions. *Journal of Business Research, 132*, 233–248.

Panda, P. (2022). COVID-19, trade disruptions, and gender: A survey of the potential interactions and consequences for economic development in Sub-Saharan Africa. *Journal of African Development, 23*(2), 347–374.

Pandey, E. (2021). *The rise of women in the gig economy.* https://www.axios.com/2021/08/26/women-gig-economy-doordash-uber-delivery-driver. Accessed August 2023.

Pruchniewska, U. M. (2018). Branding the self as an "authentic feminist": Negotiating feminist values in post-feminist digital cultural production. *Feminist Media Studies, 18*(5), 810–824.

Randa, I. O., & Atiku, S. O. (2021). SME financial inclusivity for sustainable entrepreneurship in Namibia during COVID-19. In *Handbook of research on sustaining SMEs and entrepreneurial innovation in the post-COVID-19 era* (pp. 373–396). IGI Global.

Rashid, S., & Ratten, V. (2020). A systematic literature review on women entrepreneurship in emerging economies while reflecting specifically on SAARC countries. In V. Ratten (Ed.), *Entrepreneurship and organizational change: Managing innovation and creative capabilities* (pp. 37–88). Springer International Publishing. https://doi.org/10.1007/978-3-030-35415-2_4

SADC. (2008). *SADC protocol on gender and development.* https://extranet.sadc.int/files/2112/9794/9109/SADC_PROTOCOL_ON_GENDER_AND_DEVELOPMENT.pdf. Accessed May 28, 2023.

SADC. (2022). *Women economic empowerment programme.* https://www.sadc.int/pillars/women-economic-empowerment-programme. Accessed April 28, 2023.

SADC and SARDC. (2022). *SADc gender and development monitor 2022.* SADC. https://www.sadc.int/sites/default/files/2022-08/Gender_Monitor_2022_English_final.pdf. Accessed May 29, 2023.

SADC DRFC. (2023). *Support for SMMEs.* https://www.sadc-dfrc.org/support-smmes. Accessed August 2023.

SADC RISDP. (2020). *SADC Regional Indicative Strategic Development Plan (RISDP) 2020–2030*. https://www.sadc.int/sites/default/files/2021-08/RISDP_2020-2030.pdf. Accessed August 2023.

SAHO. (2019). *Southern African Development Community (SADC)*. https://www.sahistory.org.za/. Accessed September.

Simba, A., Kalu, E., Onodugo, V., Okoyeuzu, C., & Ogundana, O. (2022). Women entrepreneurs in Nigeria. In *Women entrepreneurs in Sub-Saharan Africa: Historical framework, ecosystem, and future perspectives for the region*. Springer.

Sony, M., & Naik, S. (2020). Critical factors for the successful implementation of Industry 4.0: A review and future research direction. *Production Planning & Control, 31*(10), 799–815.

Stephan, R. (2023). Introduction why is COVID female? In *COVID and gender in the Middle East* (pp. xxi–xxx). University of Texas Press.

Tan, Z. M., Aggarwal, N., Cowls, J., Morley, J., Taddeo, M., & Floridi, L. (2021). The ethical debate about the gig economy: A review and critical analysis. *Technology in Society, 65*, 101594.

Teece, D. J. (2019). A capability theory of the firm: An economics and (strategic) management perspective. *New Zealand Economic Papers, 53*(1), 1–43.

UN Women. (2022). *Moving forward*. https://www.unwomen.org/en/annual-report/2022. Accessed January 2023.

UN Women and the ILO. (2021). *Rethinking gender responsive procurement: Enabling an ecosystem for women's economic empowerment*. https://www.unwomen.org/sites/default/files/Headquarters/Attachments/Sections/Library/Publications/2021/Rethinking-gender-responsive-procurement-en.pdf. Accessed May 20, 2023.

UNDP. (2020). *Futures report: Making the AfCFTA work for women and youth*. 10017. https://au.int/sites/default/files/documents/39689-doc-ss_afcftafuturereport.pdf. Accessed July 15, 2022.

UNDP. (2023). *Unrealized potential: Female entrepreneurship and the digital gender gap in Sub-Saharan Africa*. https://www.undp.org/publications/dfs-unrealized-potential-female-entrepreneurship-and-digital-gender-gap-sub-saharan-africa

United Nations. (2020). *The impact of COVID-19 on women, policy brief*. https://www.unwomen.org/media/headquarters/attachments/sections/library/publications/2020/policy-brief-the-impact-of-covid-19-on-women-en.pdf?la=en&vs=1406. Accessed June 10, 2023.

Conclusions and Reflections on Theory, Policy and Managerial Practice

The Future of Innovation and Entrepreneurship as Drivers of Livelihoods in Southern Africa: A Synthesis

Patient Rambe and Robert Ebo Hinson

1 Introduction

Small and medium-sized enterprises (SMEs) make a significant contribution to the world economy by increasing gross domestic product (GDP) and creating job opportunities (Hamad et al., 2018). In Southern Africa, SME's constitute 90% of the private businesses that largely contribute to GDP (40% annually) and employment (80% of the labour force) (Abisuga-Oyekunle et al., 2020; Ussif & Salifu, 2020). Thus, entrepreneurship has been recognised as a veritable tool for fuelling economic development, stimulating innovation and its significance has

P. Rambe (✉)
Central University of Technology, Free State, Bloemfontein, South Africa
e-mail: prambe@cut.ac.za

R. E. Hinson
Ghana Communication Technology University, Accra, Ghana
e-mail: rehinson@gctu.edu.gh

P. Rambe and R. E. Hinson (eds.), *The Future of Entrepreneurship in Southern Africa*, Palgrave Studies in Technology and Innovation in Africa, https://doi.org/10.1007/978-3-031-55935-8_8

been accentuated by the disruptions caused by the volatile, uncertain, complex, ambiguous (VUCA) context of the recent COVID-19 pandemic.

Entrepreneurship is deemed the driving force of economic and social development in most developed and developing countries (Ajide & Soyemi, 2022; Naidoo, 2021). It is the process of innovating and establishing new businesses in perilous conditions through the discovery of opportunities and the utilisation of resources for their (i.e. Small and Medium Enterprises (SMEs)) development (Ajide & Soyemi, 2022; Jafarnejad et al., 2013). According to Mutula and Van Brakel (2006), SMEs are important drivers of the economy, and they are the source of employment, flexibility and innovation, globally. The significance of SMEs to economic growth, innovation and job formation and social cohesion are major keys for various economies in the world (Ussif & Salifu, 2020).

Despite the power of innovation and entrepreneurship in driving economic growth and societal progress (Chomunorwa et al., 2023), research that recognises the intersection of innovation and technology in the materialisation of entrepreneurship education especially through the formation of value creating and value enhancing ventures in emerging markets is yet to take root. Yet, technological advances such as artificial intelligence, big data analysis, deep learning, clean technology and sensor technology are disrupting existing industries and creating new ones (Naidoo, 2021; Ussif & Salifu, 2020). Reflecting on the innovative technology platform, SweepSouth.co.za, Toefy and Scheepers (2019) highlight the significance of this website in transforming the supply and demand of domestic workers in South Africa, leading to better welfare for these marginalised groups by spotlighting the value of human dignity and the respect for largely female and unemployed labour force. Therefore, technological innovations have the potential to bring about transformative change, disrupt industries, and provide individuals with the opportunity to shape their own futures. As our world becomes increasingly interconnected and rapidly evolving, the importance of innovation and entrepreneurship only grows in its significance.

Even though innovation, fuelled by human innovations and technological advancements, is at the core of progress (Block et al., 2023; Chomunorwa et al., 2023), hard documented evidence is yet to emerge on the fusion of technology, innovation and entrepreneurship education in the materialisation of high growth oriented and sustainable firms, especially at the bottom of the pyramid of emerging economies. Therefore, while thinking outside the box, identifying unmet needs, and creating new solutions are critical for driving economic prosperity and addressing pressing global issues, a deeper grasp of how the institutional voids of emerging economies are implicated in facilitating and constraining entrepreneurship development is necessary. When combined with technology, innovation becomes a catalyst for creating sustainable livelihoods and turning ideas into successful ventures, especially where contextual dimensions of entrepreneurship are foregrounded. For instance, disruptive technological innovations which bridge infrastructure gaps and policy fragilities of the unbanked or underbanked population in Africa (World Bank, 2017) such as M-Pesa's pay-as-you-go models are breaching financial exclusion through collaborations between financial incumbents and financial technology businesses (Swartz et al., 2023) while reinforcing financial literacy by providing low-cost mechanisms for accessing crucial financial resources. Yet the realisation of technology and innovation leapfrogging necessitates innovations in education, functional institutions, regulations and investments in research and development (Swartz et al., 2023). Essentially, a theoretical, analytical and empirical matrix that fuses concepts and integrates them with contextual understanding is ideally suited for generating germane entrepreneurial processes, behaviours and outcomes.

While contextual sensitivity is critical, even more paramount is paying special attention to how the manifold technological advancements are transforming the way new businesses are being created, how knowledge is constructed, and how new forms of behaviours in different sectors and industries are metamorphosing. For instance, breakthroughs in artificial intelligence, robotics, biotechnology, and renewable energy are transforming existing industries while opening new avenues for entrepreneurial exploration (Shajek & Hartmann, 2023). These developments offer unprecedented opportunities for individuals to pursue their passions, chart their own course, and build successful careers, paving way for the emergence of the gig economy that is revolutionising the nature of work. The gig economy is a labour market characterised by the prevalence of short-term or freelance work arrangements, where individuals work on a project or task basis rather than holding traditional long-term employment contracts. The flexibility and autonomy the gig economy provides enables individuals to leverage their skills and talents to establish their own businesses and earn income on their own terms. However, given the need for sensitivity to contextual and spatial differences in emerging economies (Scott et al., 2020), the teaching of entrepreneurship needs to accommodate contextual technology and innovation to address the cognitive, behavioural, social and emotional needs of students in pursuit of entrepreneurship. Given the individual, regional, and country level differences in context-sensitive research (Chlosta, 2016), a more contextualised approach is needed to account for cognitive, regulative and normative processes when investigating micro and meso processes of entrepreneurial pursuits.

In African contexts where income-generating opportunities flourish (albeit in flux) but are juxtaposed with institutional blockages (e.g. unsophisticated banking systems, restrictive regulatory and institutional frameworks, poor enforcement of contracts, policy uncertainties) that continue to frustrate entrepreneurial pursuits, a fine balance between entrepreneurs' search for economic opportunities and resolving these societal and environmental challenges become peremptory. While the advent of new technologies is availing inherent opportunities for dynamising the future of innovation, the nature, shape, and complexion of nascent entrepreneurship, for example, are also transforming to accommodate the rise of social entrepreneurship. Social entrepreneurs combine business acumen with a societal mission to create positive change, leveraging innovation to tackle crucial issues such as poverty, education, healthcare, and environmental sustainability (Shajek & Hartmann, 2023). Through their efforts, they are transforming their own livelihoods, empowering communities, and contributing to a more equitable and sustainable world.

Despite these pockets of commendable strides, we are acutely aware that much of the literature on technology and innovation-driven entrepreneurship in emerging economies is informed by US studies even though the American models ignore "indigenous lenses" resulting in a general lack of proper contextualisation of studies (Bruton et al., 2018), especially those reporting on African entrepreneurship. The lack of contextualised and context-specific conceptualisations (Roper, 2013) means that entrepreneurship studies in emerging economies are poorly executed, misconceived or draw erroneous conclusions (Sinha et al., 2020). The African context is unique in the sense that it is a potpourri of both great economic promise and outrightly disappointing institutional, legal and policy affordances and hurdles. For instance, while Leke and Yeboah-Amankwah (2018) project rapid technology adoption as making the African continent geared for innovation-driven entrepreneurship, other studies (Blimpo et al., 2017; Ogundana et al., 2021) paint a more complex picture of institutional gaps, policy inconsistencies and infrastructural blockages that continue to hamper technology-driven innovations and progress on the continent. Therefore, context-sensitive and context-informed research that takes stock of the holy grail of combinational resources, combinatorial capabilities while accommodating the institutional subtleties and policy complexities will provide a more grounded yet holistic record of the African narrative on entrepreneurship.

Additionally, an account of the future landscape of African innovation and entrepreneurship is incomplete without referring to the increasing networks of collaboration and interconnectedness on the content. African entrepreneurs are now part of vibrant ecosystems that foster collaboration, knowledge sharing, and resource pooling instead of working in silos. Incubators, innovation hubs, and accelerators offer a nurturing environment where entrepreneurs can tap into mentorship, networks, and funding. This supportive ecosystem paves the way for entrepreneurial success, empowering livelihoods, and propelling innovation forward (Shajek & Hartmann, 2023). Despite this rosy picture of African entrepreneurship being portrayed, what remains unclear are the boundary conditions under which such collaboration in entrepreneurial ecosystems can be created and tapped into including how stakeholders of such ecosystems especially nascent entrepreneurs (e.g. students) can directly benefit from such ecosystems. This is particularly key given that, the combination of benefits that accrue to small venture firms are not cast in stone, and what is particularly specific to a particular context as is the case with university-based start-up ecosystems could vary radically from what constitutes generic ecosystems. Moreso, seeing beyond specificities to embrace generalities is essential to building start-up ecosystems (Novotny et al., 2020), especially in emerging economies where generalisability is plausible given the comparability of the nature and configuration of such economies notwithstanding some nuances and peculiarities.

The rest of the chapter is structured as follows: First, we provide a theoretical discussion of contextual embeddedness to demonstrate that the adoption of technology and innovation to support the materialisation of entrepreneurship education is highly context-bound and context-specific. Second, we contend that technology embeddedness provides a conceptual and analytical heuristic for developing deeper insights into not only the context-specific and situated nature of innovation materialisation and technology diffusion but also the conjoined nature of the relationship between human agency (the realisation of the outcomes of teaching of entrepreneurship education) and the embedded structure in which such agency is exercised. Third, we provide some related studies connecting technology, innovation and the manifestation of the outcomes of teaching of entrepreneurship education especially in emerging contexts. Last, we build on practical exemplars of the appropriation of technology and innovation to bridge health, education and employment hurdles.

2 Theoretical Development

Contextual Embeddedness

The interplay of innovation, technology and the material manifestation of the consequences of teaching of entrepreneurship cannot be discussed devoid of context. As such, contextual embeddedness describes how human economic actions (e.g. venture founding and entrepreneuring availed through teaching entrepreneurship education) are enabled as well as constrained by social structures (Polanyi, 1944; Uzzi, 1996). For instance, literature argues that social structures (especially regulative, policy and financial developments, power and influence) have the power to facilitate and constrain economic activities (Granovetter, 1985). The argument is that since cognitive embeddedness (i.e. the ways in which structured regularities of mental processes limit the exercise of economic reasoning) is dependent on the nature and configuration of social structures, environmental factors are posed to have a bearing on cognitive processing (Novotny et al., 2020). Therefore, the use of innovation and technology in shaping the teaching of students including the outcomes of such human development initiatives is a function of how educators interpret the interplay between their human action (i.e. teaching as a form of productive economic activity) and social structures brought to bear on such economic activity. Embeddedness, therefore, presents a veritable heuristic and analytical construct for unpacking the situated contexts and boundary conditions under which entrepreneurship education can be delivered as well as how consequences of such activities are generated.

Embeddedness is hailed as a multi-faceted concept that considers multiple layers of institutions and examines the cultural, political, structural, and cognitive embeddedness that need to be coordinated for them to thrive (Beckert, 2015). Across the different contexts where embeddedness has been applied spanning technology entrepreneurship, social entrepreneurship and rural entrepreneurship (Harima, 2022), literature suggests that this concept enables entrepreneurs to negotiate access to resources available within particular social ties and networks (Jack & Anderson, 2002; Wigren-Kristofersen et al., 2019). For instance, embeddedness in ethnic communities has been reported to facilitate shared values, trust, reciprocity, and solidarity, making localised resources available to migrant entrepreneurs (Aldrich & Waldinger, 1990; Harima, 2022; Portes & Sensenbrenner, 1993).

Technology and Innovation Embeddedness

To the extent that entrepreneurial education demands educators to account for cognitive, behavioural, affective (e.g. entrepreneurial passion), relational, and cultural aspects of the educated especially students, one needs to accommodate different properties of the embedded and situated nature of this process. Since technology and innovation can constitute social structure upon which human action such as direct instruction, supervision, and coaching as forms of knowledge development can be honed, Novotny et al. (2020) argue that different properties of embeddedness spanning cognitive structure within a social sector (i.e. cognitive embeddedness), a cultural structure in society (i.e. cultural embeddedness), relational structures among social actors (i.e. social embeddedness), and a power structure within a social boundary (i.e. political embeddedness) must be considered. Therefore, understanding technology embeddedness as a way of explaining entrepreneurial education and its associated outcomes (especially opportunity exploitation, new venture creation, entrepreneurship) requires one to consider how people enact structures which shape their technology including how such technology is developed through political processes which result in structures being embedded in the technology (Novotny et al., 2020; Orlikowski, 1990). As such, as educators harness technology and innovations as part of delivering entrepreneurship education and realising its material outcomes (e.g. wealth creation, venture development, venture financing), they are emboldened to use the social structures enabled by technology to facilitate the building of sustainable nascent businesses.

Rather than conceive innovative teaching of entrepreneurship as a "one man/woman enterprise", we embrace a collegial view of entrepreneurship education where educators together with stakeholders (e.g. venture capitalists, angel investors, incubators, accelerators, innovation platform leaders and innovators), in contexts they are situated, provide opportunities for students to co-create as well as individually construct entrepreneurial knowledge. Following Callon's (1992) view on technology innovation, we advance the notion that entrepreneurship education and its associated outcomes are embedded, enabled, nurtured and disrupted by contexts fuelled by techno-economic networks. Techno-economic networks are a coordinated set of heterogeneous actors (public laboratories, technical research centres, industrial firms, financial organisations, users and public authorities), which collectively develop and diffuse innovations (Callon, et al., 1992; Kim & Lee, 2019) making entrepreneurial pursuits possible.

Education and Entrepreneurship: Navigating Troubled Contexts

In today's rapidly changing and unpredictable world, education is essential for equipping students with the tools they need to thrive. Entrepreneurship education offers a relevant curriculum and valuable competencies that can help young people develop resilience, independence, innovation, and the ability to identify opportunities for success in a post-COVID-19 environment (Hardie et al., 2020). Since entrepreneurial initiatives leads to the creation of enterprises that create jobs, reduce poverty and significantly improve economic development, the future and quality of entrepreneurial ventures depend on the quality of today's entrepreneurial education. Block et al. (2023), for instance, assert that how we will live and quality of our lives in the future largely depend on education of future entrepreneurs.

We argue that while entrepreneurship education and training are of uttermost importance for preparing students to succeed in their uncertain entrepreneurship futures, the career path to becoming an entrepreneur is not linear but complex. For instance, the structure created by complex legislation, policy inconsistencies, and highly regulated educational regimes continually collide with the agentive forces created by collaborative networking, open innovation and amalgamation of combinational resources in emerging contexts. Therefore, entrepreneurship educators are continually confronted with a huge task of adequately motivating and preparing students or future entrepreneurs, while simultaneously being called to respond to an ever-evolving turbulent environment fuelled by disruptive technologies, changing legislation and dwindling public funding. As such, while entrepreneurship education is under pressure to deliver the mandate of a relevant, impactful, and context-informed curriculum and equipping students with skills, abilities and aptitudes for building resilience, independence, innovation, and the capacity to identify opportunities, received research is questioning whether the skills availed through entrepreneurship education are germane to leading productive and fulfilling lives, especially in the new post-COVID-19 environment (Block et al., 2023; Shajek & Hartmann, 2023).

In a digital era where adoption of digital technologies to meaningfully foster value creation and facilitate digital entrepreneurial ecosystems (Audretsch et al., 2023) are critical in fostering digitally advanced entrepreneurship, critical questions are being raised regarding the traditional approach to entrepreneurship education delivery. For instance, given arguments about the capacity of the adoption of digital technologies and an embeddedness approach within digital entrepreneurial ecosystems to foster firms' abilities and regions' capacity to be resilient, enabling business transformations and radical change (Khurana et al., 2022), it is prudent to establish if the traditional approach foregrounding business plan development and teaching "about" entrepreneurship is still relevant in the contemporary era. The irony of adopting the traditional approach is that students who are supposed to be future business developers are made to learn various aspects of running a business such as marketing, accounting, management and spend much time and energy on developing the business plan itself with little attention, time and focus on the pre-idea stage and actual problem-solving activity (Linton & Klinton, 2019).

Research has shown that the traditional approach to teaching entrepreneurship has a negative impact on students' willingness to embark on entrepreneurial ventures (Adeyemo, 2023; Hardie et al., 2020). Since entrepreneurship and entrepreneurship education are context-specific, teaching entrepreneurship with a focus on contextual innovation as well as technological innovation will better prepare future entrepreneurs to take up the challenge of creating meaningful ventures. This position is consistent with the effectuation logic which suggests that entrepreneurs need to rely on resources that are readily available at hand and co-create opportunities rather than predefining goals in highly uncertain environments (Block et al., 2023; Chomunorwa et al., 2023).

In a context where start-up entrepreneurs depend highly on the availability of knowledge and a wide range of digital technologies to manage their entrepreneurial knowledge (Audretsch et al., 2021), sectorial digital capabilities and complementarities (Bruno et al., 2024), one questions whether the simple logic of traditional teaching is compelling enough to impact aptitudes, skills and abilities of twenty-first-century students. In line with this thinking, Linton and Klinton (2019) argue that since entrepreneurship is a complex process that lacks linearity, entrepreneurship education and learning should emphasise the process that entrepreneurs go through to create successful ventures, which follows the effectuation logic rather than teaching "about" the various aspect of the business. Thus, utilising design thinking and a methodical approach, which is about learning "through" approach that focuses on the entrepreneurial process, highlighting the role of skills and mindsets will enable entrepreneurship educators to be student-centred and produce entrepreneurs that are prepared for the future rather than merely educating students "about" entrepreneurship (Killingberg et al., 2021; Linton & Klinton, 2019).

However, entrepreneurship education in most institutions still follows the causation logic, which mainly focuses on planning, control, and rational analysis to get to a predefined outcome (Adeyemo, 2023; Block et al., 2023). This is notwithstanding the survey findings of Daniel (2016) from 31 countries which concluded that following the planning and prediction approach (causation logic) discourages most students from starting a business venture. In contrast, the finding of Nabi et al. (2017) indicates that students are more likely to form an intention to start a business venture when entrepreneurship education focuses on skills and competence development. This effectual logic approach deviates from the formal education and business training in South Africa, which is deemed to have little or no impact on future entrepreneurs' employment and earning potential (Throsby, 2007). For instance, entrepreneurs in creative and cultural industries do not, for example, pursue these authentic ways of learning (Banks et al., 2000; Ebewo et al., 2023). Based on the above discussion, we conclude this section by affirming that entrepreneurial education systems that align with the effectuation logic are more likely to be effective in producing the desired entrepreneurs than those designed based on the causation logic.

Education and Innovation

Research studies have shown that education and innovation are interconnected with education serving as a foundation for innovation and innovation also serving as a driving force behind the advancements in the field of education (Chomunorwa et al., 2023; Nabi et al., 2017). Education plays a critical role in developing and nurturing creativity, critical thinking, problem-solving skills, and instilling entrepreneurial mindset in students. For instance, practically oriented entrepreneurial education such as case studies, simulations, design thinking, concept idea pitching and entrepreneurship competitions are authentic and context-bound delivery methods that have the potential to build nascent and sustainable student ventures through facilitating and foregrounding entrepreneurial processes such as business concept development, market research, market gap analysis, value proposition and unique selling points (Rambe, 2023). On the one hand, entrepreneurial education is an important component for driving innovation that equips students/learners with the ability to adapt to change, embrace new ideas and contribute to the development of innovative solutions to societal challenges (Hardie et al., 2020; Killingberg et al., 2021). On the other hand, when novel works contribute to the implementation of original and novel ideas in terms of new technologies, processes and techniques, and products (Zhou & George, 2001), which are deemed by experts to be of scientific, aesthetic, social and technological value (Shalley & Breidenthal, 2021; Vernon, 1989), they can also invariably transform the way entrepreneurial education is conceived, conceptualised and delivered. A case in point is how manifold innovations in the Silicon Valley such venture capital development, technology development and industrial cluster formation have influenced how teaching is delivered at prestigious universities in the United States.

Technological advancement has revolutionised the education landscape, offering new possibilities for teaching and learning. The recent disruptions in the educational sector caused by COVID-19 which led to mandatory closures of educational facilities have further accelerated the adoption of these technological innovations such as technology-supported remote teaching and learning, virtual and technology-enhanced collaborations and meetings, online knowledge repositories, digital databases, and AI-based learning. Such developments have served as catalysts for digital innovation and transformation across educational sectors globally as schools have shifted to remote and hybrid learning models, particularly in emerging markets like Southern Africa (Killingberg et al., 2021; Linton & Klinton, 2019). Thus, considering the ongoing digital advancement and transformation across various sectors mainly accelerated by the COVID-19 disruptions, digital transformation and innovation by educational institutions are inevitable to ensure uninterrupted academic activities and for education to remain relevant and competitive. The digital transformation of education entails moving away from traditional teaching methods towards a more learner-centric approach, driven by technology, and offering improved teaching and learning experiences (Osmundsen et al., 2018; Shajek & Hartmann, 2023; Stamatović & Zlatić, 2021). For example, technological advancements have led to the development of online teaching and learning platforms such as learning management systems and video conferencing tools, which have facilitated remote teaching and learning.

In the South Africa, a context ironically rich in the provision of entrepreneurial education yet riddled with high levels of unemployment, Shivdasani and Anwarsha developed a job-hunting application, Giraffe, to address joblessness in the nation's small yet most congested province, Gauteng, home of the country's largest city, Johannesburg. A year later, with 100,000 jobseekers signed up, they brought Giraffe to the greater metro areas of Cape Town and Durban. With over 1 million people using the platform, thousands of businesses were able to be matched to job seekers. Given that any user having a cell phone with an internet browser can use the platform, this bottom of the pyramid innovation has been able to lift many South Africans out of poverty by linking them to available job opportunities. Using any device of their choice, Giraffe website users can complete their details within minutes, which allows companies to create CVs for them, which are subsequently uploaded to their database. Therefore, if entrepreneurship education creates affordances for action-oriented teaching style that encourages experiential learning, problem-solving, project-based learning, such initiatives that are supportive of risk taking, creativity, and innovation (Schachtebeck & Tselepis, 2023) will not be out of reach.

Entrepreneurial Education and Informal Sector Innovation

A study conducted by United Nations Development Programme (UNDP, 2023) in partnership with Utrecht University (the Netherlands), the University of Johannesburg (South Africa), and MIT Sloan School of Management (USA) highlights the dynamic landscape of innovation and entrepreneurship within South Africa, which stands as a shining example of the resilience and creativity that flourishes within the country. This study demonstrates the prevalence and significance of innovation practices in the informal sector of South Africa as well as how informal innovation and entrepreneurship have the potential to reshape the country's socio-economic fabric. This collaboration serves as a critical exemplar of how universities through their entrepreneurship education programmes can serve as conduits of informal innovation, namely the creative and adaptive processes through which individuals, often within grassroots or community settings, develop novel solutions, products, services, or practices in response to local challenges or unmet needs. For instance, a local innovator in South Africa, Siphiwe Zuma, created a retractable umbrella backpack for people with disabilities (Hansen, 2023). Similarly, another innovator, Netshidzati Lucky Mashudu, created a smart glove which translates sign language into speech to communicate with his deaf parents (Wafula & Irungu, 2023). These innovations must be conceived as promising innovations coming from local innovators, some of whom are alumni of local universities operating in an emerging economy context of South Africa, plagued by multiple hurdles spanning limited access to the Internet, electricity and public transportation (Kanyane, 2023).

These exemplars highlight the importance of entrepreneurial education to bring out the best from the vast innovation and entrepreneurial landscape, skills and potentials, particularly from the youth within the sub-region. This will not only include identifying and understanding who the innovators are, but understanding the challenges and obstacles they face in their local context and how to surmount these challenges. Identifying, nurturing, supporting, and making these entrepreneurial and innovation potentials visible is the right first step towards fostering a vibrant innovation ecosystem at all levels of society to bring about the desired change of reducing unemployment, poverty and inequality. By embracing and amplifying the potentials of entrepreneurs in both formal and informal sectors, data-driven insights can be used to build capacity, provide support, and guide policy decisions that can further harness hidden potentials for positive change in the sub-region.

Health and Entrepreneurship

In the last decades, healthcare landscapes around the world have changed dramatically due to demographic and epidemiological shifts, technological innovations and rising consumer expectations. The emergence of increasingly complex health conditions has also necessitated access to specialists and treatments beyond standard practices of care. Some complex conditions include the ageing populations globally leading to an increased demand in healthcare, the rise in non-communicable disease (NCD) rates and the lack of access to quality healthcare, particularly in low- and middle-income countries (LMICs), which contribute to a high burden on national public health systems that must be overcome. The most recent

COVID-19 pandemic has accelerated these struggles due to even higher demand for primary healthcare and hospital services, strengthening the call for a major rethink and overhaul of the healthcare sector, particularly using digital solutions in the practice and delivery of care in the existing health ecosystem. These shifts are likely to persist, underlining the need to foster innovation as the key to ensuring growth in a post-crisis recovery. Access to the private health is funded mainly through private medical insurance schemes, whose membership extends to only 18% of the total African population. Indeed, many countries implement a public–private partnership model in which the public and the private sector provide healthcare infrastructures as well as delivery of healthcare services to patients. While the private sector can entail many different sectors of the economy, this paper focuses on university agencies, SMEs and start-ups in health innovation, including digital innovation, which are considered to be among most important, upcoming sectors of any developed/developing economy (Purbasari et al., 2021). When building resilient and equitable health systems, it is therefore crucial to consider the private sector as a partner which complements the activities of the public sector (Kanneganti, 2021).

For instance, the case study about Quali Health South Africa presented by Saville et al. (2020) provides a perfect example to demonstrate why there is the need to develop and nurture health entrepreneurs with an eye for technological innovations in the health sector. According to the Quali Health story, though South Africa spends 4.2% of her GDP on health making her the 75th ranked in the world in terms of public health spending as a percentage of GDP, the country is poorly ranked in the Global Competitive Report. For instance, of the 144 countries surveyed in the report, South Africa ranked in position 143 for cases of tuberculosis per 100,000 people. HIV prevalence, which stood at 17.9% of the adult population, translated into a ranking of 140 out of 144, and in measuring infant deaths per 1,000 live births, the country ranked 105 out of 144. In turn, the country's dismal state of health translated into poor socio-economic outcomes. South Africa's life expectancy stood at just 56.1 years. In actuarial terms this meant that, on average, South Africans died before they reached retirement age. By contrast, the country's high spending on health does not resonate with the quality of health provided to her citizens. If one added in private spending on healthcare (4.1% of GDP), foreign aid and the non-governmental organisation sector (0.2% of GDP), the country's total spending on healthcare makes up a total of 8.4% of the economy. By contrast, the World Health Organization (WHO) recommends that countries spend just 5% of GDP on health, and average expenditure for all middle-income countries is 5.8%. Based on these numbers, the level of healthcare spending did not appear to be South Africa's problem.

Though South Africa's private healthcare sector which is made up of a small number of large players that deliver quality globally competitive services and contribute 4.1% of GDP to the country's health spending, affordability remains a major barrier to about 82% of South Africans (Saville et al., 2020). For instance, while the average price for only consultation with a general practitioner in a private health facility is $27 (excluding medicine), the price to visit a public health clinic at state-run hospitals is about US$1 per person per visit. However, the public sector is severely under-resourced, highly inefficient and poorly managed. To access most primary health clinics for basic services requires a person to start queuing no later than 6.00 am only to be seen many hours later (if at all). As a result, South Africa's healthcare industry is a two-legged animal with a private sector that caters to a minority of the population through channels that are effective yet expensive and exclusive.

To address the challenges enumerated above, Quali Health was established to offer affordable but quality primary healthcare to the grossly under-serviced South African market. The facility employs a fully digital system to address the inefficiency of paper-based administration which was a legacy issue in both public and private healthcare that contributed heavily to wasted time and money. Patient information is captured biometrically using a tablet computer upon arrival. This information then "follows" the patient electronically as she progresses through stages of treatment. Relevant information is available to each caregiver at the touch of a button. Likewise, each caregiver can update information, such as doctors' notes, in real time. Granular, up-to-the-minute data enables monitoring of the system for blockages, customer pain points and stresses to costs. Longer term, electronic records of patient histories and reactions to drugs are powerful tools for building trust, managing a customer relationship and providing the customer-centricity sorely lacking in public health facilities (Saville et al., 2020).

Additionally, the health-related Sustainable Development Goals (SDGs) call for innovative ways of thinking about health systems. There is a vital need for high-quality health systems fostering a new dynamic in the traditional way of delivering medical care while optimising healthcare globally. In this regard, investment in sectors relevant to SDG 3 on good health and well-being decreased in 2020, whereas the needs in the health sector were increasing, underlining the importance of investment promotion in health using different mechanisms, including Investment Promotion Agencies (IPAs) (UNDP, 2023). As a result, the development of mechanisms to ensure investment promotion in health has a direct impact not only on existing firms in the healthcare ecosystem, but most importantly on the development of entrepreneurship in health sectors allowing smaller actors, from start-ups to SMEs, to develop their ideas, thus unlocking innovation in health. Digital health, including telemedicine, can provide essential access to quality health services in remote areas directly targeting the core of the SDGs principle of "leaving no one behind". It should, however, be mentioned that in countries where vulnerable groups still lack access to Information and Communication Technologies (ICT), the move towards digitalisation of healthcare can also marginalise them even further.

Health and Innovation

As stated earlier, the healthcare sectors around the world, particularly those in developing economies like Southern African countries, require a major rethink and overhaul following the changing healthcare landscape regarding customer needs. As demand for healthcare rises, it is obvious that governments alone cannot cope with the pressure to provide the needed health solutions to their citizenry demonstrating the need for private sector participation. While African-based researchers, scientists and innovators have the capability to make significant contributions towards building home-grown solutions, the continent lacks adequate financial investment in innovative pharmaceutical research and development (R&D). Therefore, the International Federation of Pharmaceutical Manufacturers and Associations (IFPMA) and Holistic Drug Discovery and Development (H3D) Foundation at the University of Cape Town are exploring how the African science and innovation community can be scaled up to capacitate the continent's R&D to play a more effective role in responding to local health challenges (Kibale, 2023). Through academic-led mentorship, H3D is striving to effectively expand the drug discovery community across the continent drawing on partnerships and industry collaborations to facilitate the development of home-grown medicines that solve African health problems. H3D is leveraging grant funding from United States Agency for International Development (USAID) to finance a pilot project that evaluates innovative technology for the cost-effective manufacturing of active pharmaceutical ingredients (APIs) in South Africa (Kibale, 2023). The partnership between H3D and Johnson & Johnson Satellite Centre for Global Health Discovery has harnessed the best scientific talent in Africa to mentor them in boosting H3D's antimicrobial resistance (AMR) drug discovery portfolio. In doing so, this has contributed to collaborations in African R&D innovation, showing the significance of the role of financial investment in providing access to resources that drive R&D, technology transfer and entrepreneurship. The work also demonstrates the role of mentorship programmes in fostering a culture of innovation and entrepreneurship that encourages the development of new technologies, products and services (Kibale, 2023).

Entrepreneurs of small and medium-sized enterprises (SMEs) and start-ups have a major role to play in contributing to health innovation which improves productivity, customer experiences and provides more affordable care as shown by South Africa's Quali Health. They can help advance the current trend towards networks of different value chain participants such as suppliers, platforms, service providers, and customers, integrated through common commercial models and data. A typical case of home-grown innovative solutions in the healthcare sector is how Jabulani Nyembe, a Bachelor of Business Science degree at University of KwaZulu Natal started Clinalytics, a healthcare-based start-up with co-founder and fellow student, Mr Muhle Ndwalane. Clinalytics gives healthcare professionals the tools to provide world-class healthcare services by providing a digital medical records software system that allows healthcare professionals to create, store, and analyse the medical records of patients. This solution is deemed to contribute to reducing the disadvantaged and the elderly's queuing for services due to poor monitoring and documentation of health-related ailments (Ngubelanga, 2023). This signifies the increasingly important role played by technology innovators and entrepreneurs of SMEs and start-ups in strengthening health systems in developing countries.

However, despite the increasing recognition of entrepreneurial involvement in the provision of innovative health solutions to deal with complex and demanding health issues, health entrepreneurs face several challenges including: (1) lack of scalability and sustainability of health innovation, leading to the failure of yet very innovative ideas. Though e-health entrepreneurial ecosystem is flourishing with a total number of 180 health-tech-focused start-ups currently operating in Africa, demonstrating that a strong potential exists for the development of digital solutions on the continent, one major challenge facing these enterprises is their ability to survive and expand to cover a greater population (Sharma et al., 2022). (2) Though there is an increasing recognition for collaborative effort by both private health entrepreneurs and public health to improve on health delivery, there is a general lack of effective integration of private sector innovation and public health. While private health entrepreneurs are more likely to innovate dynamic health solutions based on technology, the acceptance and integration of these innovative solutions into public health systems could be extremely challenging (UNDP, 2023). (3) Regulation and financial challenges—though entrepreneurs generally face a challenge in securing funds for their innovations, health entrepreneurs and start-ups in particular face a more heightened hurdle in securing the requisite regulatory support as well as higher levels of requirements to gain funding for their health innovations (Zahoor et al., 2022). Given the distinct nature of health innovations compared to other industries, investors who support or invest in health innovations will have wait for a prolonged period for returns on their investment. Similarly, since most traditional sources of funding like the banks lack understanding or familiarity with the health sector, they are also reluctant to support health innovations, resulting in a double-bound tragedy.

Entrepreneurship, Health, and Well-being

Though SMEs have been recognised for their significant contribution to poverty reduction, employment generation, and contribution to GDP, the employees within these enterprises are mostly subjected to poor working and less health-safety conditions usually due ineffective production mechanisms (Zahoor et al., 2022). As shown in the South African Quali Health example, most of these employees suffer significant psychological and emotional well-being challenges usually due to complex manufacturing and operational processes coupled with life pressures (Saville et al., 2020). The findings of Piao and Managi (2022), for instance, identified negative emotions which are usually linked to stress and anxiety as one of the critical factors influencing employees' psychological well-being. The findings of Saville et al. (2020) also show that one of the major reasons why South African workers defer treatment and do not seek early healthcare is the fear of losing their job if they take time off to join long queues to access healthcare. This suggests that SMEs need to identify innovative ways to improve employees' psychological well-being by building lean, effective and fast, healthcare delivery innovations. Ensuring the well-being of employees is paramount since they are an important resource entrepreneurs require to achieve their business objectives.

Research studies have shown that managers of SMEs have taken advantage of technological advancement such as machine learning, work automation, and artificial intelligence to improve on several aspects of their operations including work environment, employee productivity, knowledge sharing, and innovation (Nazareno & Schiff, 2021; Vrontis et al., 2022). Thus, in an era of technological advancement, SMEs could equally leverage on these technological tools to improve employee well-being, not just operational excellence. In other words, as alluded by scholars (e.g. Zahoor et al., 2022), in an era of technological advancement, just merely focusing on traditional human resource practices is not enough to achieve psychological well-being employees. For instance, building on prior research on innovation and organisational psychology, Zahoor et al. (2022) empirically examined how technological innovation can influence employee psychological well-being within SMEs' settings. Their finding shows that technological innovation has a significant linear effect on employee well-being. Their finding further shows that employee learning orientation and perceived organisational support are essential conditions that enhance the technological innovation-employee psychological well-being nexus suggesting that technological innovation might not always or necessarily be beneficial for the psychological well-being of employees.

The above discussions and empirical findings have shown that though health entrepreneurship is critical to addressing the challenges in the health sector particularly in developing economies like most countries in the southern Africa, technological innovation is equally important to achieve success in addressing such challenges in a technologically savvy environment as shown by the Quali Health example from South Africa.

Entrepreneurship and Innovation

Innovation, characterised by the creation and adoption of new ideas, products, or processes, is a driving force behind entrepreneurial success. Innovation and entrepreneurship are intertwined, with innovation serving as a catalyst for entrepreneurial success (Autio et al., 2014; Zhao,

2005). Though the two terms are sometimes used interchangeably by the general public and policymakers, innovation is not the same as entrepreneurship. Not all entrepreneurs are innovative and not all innovators are entrepreneurs. The survey finding of the Global Entrepreneurship Monitor (GEM, 2022/23) shows a majority of new, independent ventures (about 70%) are not innovative at all. Ever since the early work of Schumpeter (1934), scholars have consistently established a positive and significant link between the concept of entrepreneurship and innovation suggesting that the higher the innovation, the higher the success of entrepreneurial activities (Autio et al., 2014; Garud et al., 2014). This implies that entrepreneurs who embrace innovation or are innovation-oriented will be able to identify opportunities, create competitive advantage, adapt to change, enhance efficiency, and stimulate growth. Innovation also enables entrepreneurs to identify and seize opportunities in the market. By designing innovative solutions that address unmet needs or solve existing problems, entrepreneurs can create value and differentiate themselves from the competition. According to Autio et al. (2014), innovation plays a key role in gaining competitive advantage. Entrepreneurs that focus on innovation and continuously identify new opportunities and provide unique products, services, and business models or solutions are able to stay ahead of the competition and capture market share (Zhao, 2005).

In the wake of the COVID-19 pandemic, the importance of innovation in entrepreneurship has become even more pronounced (Akpan et al., 2021; Baporikar, 2021). Given the unprecedented levels of uncertainty and vitality the pandemic has brought, entrepreneurs who are innovative are better positioned to surmount these uncertainties by finding creative solutions, exploring new business models, and adapting to changing customer needs (Akpan et al., 2021). For instance, evidence from Dr Matshidiso Moeti, WHO Regional Director for Africa, suggests that during the COVID-19 pandemic the connection between entrepreneurship and innovation manifested in the development of innovative health solutions spanning disease surveillance, contact tracing, community engagement, treatment, laboratory systems and infection, prevention and control. Other ICT-based health innovations in Africa included WhatsApp Chatbots in South Africa, self-diagnostic toolkits in Angola, contact tracing applications in Ghana and mobile health information tools in Nigeria, and other home-grown innovations such as solar-powered automatic handwashing tools and mobile applications (Afro.WHO, 2020).

Therefore, entrepreneurship education must equally prioritise innovation to equip potential entrepreneurs with the skills and mindsets needed to innovate and thrive in a rapidly changing and competitive business environment. By focusing on creativity, promoting adaptability and resilience as well as embracing technological advancements, and encouraging an innovative creed, entrepreneurship educators will be adequately preparing future entrepreneurs to become innovative entrepreneurs who will effectively drive economic growth, reduce unemployment, and poverty.

To foster economic growth, numerous nations, regions, states, and universities have recognised the important connection between entrepreneurship and innovation and have implemented policies aimed at stimulating innovation within entrepreneurial firms (Akpan et al., 2021; Autio et al., 2014). These policies encompass various initiatives at the local, regional, and national levels, with a particular focus on promoting start-ups that emerge from universities. These initiatives include a range of measures including technology-focused economic development efforts like incubators and accelerators, along with formal government programmes such as the Youth Entrepreneurship Support Programme, and Start-up (Nigeria), National Youth Employment Programme (Ghana), The Presidential Youth Employment Initiative (South Africa), Zimbabwe's Youth Empowerment Programme and Poverty Alleviation (Zimbabwe).

As such, the extent to which SMEs in emerging markets can benefit from adopting digital platforms including the ways in which they deploy digital innovations to foster new value and revitalise their business models remains unclear (Xie et al., 2022). Yet, there is compelling evidence that, in distruptive environments characteristic of those experienced during COVID-19, entrepreneurs could no longer conceive digital technologies as appendages of their business models but rather as integral to their business development strategies and the development of their business models (Priyono et al., 2020; Purbasari et al., 2021). The harnessing of digital technology to support business model development has been hailed as a germane strategy for addressing disruptive environmental changes, especially where technology affordances are instrumental in the identification and exploitation of new business practices (Richter, 2020). This is particularly key in hostile environmental scenarios where fundamental changes are different from those stimulated by human innovations (Gupta & Bose, 2019).

3 Conclusion

Researchers have widely recognised the vital role of technology and innovation within the small business context. This recognition appears actuated by a set of related local and international drivers. These drivers include (and are not limited to) globalisation affecting business operations. Some have even argued that introducing technology within the business space is a new form of globalisation. However, as far back as the nineteenth century, calls to explore the role technology could play in leveraging business performance, especially among small businesses, began to take centre stage. This has led to growing calls for the need to understand how organisations may need to respond to this new form of globalisation.

The collection of research papers in this book has established that technological capability has become an important factor in entrepreneurial development as it has a significant impact on operational excellence, innovation, and customer satisfaction. These factors (customer satisfaction, innovation, and operational excellence) are key to achieving success in today's competitive business environment and technological capability plays an important role with this regard. The findings of Rambe (2022), for instance, shows the need for African governments to invest heavily in technological development of SMEs in particular to increase their efficiency in generating economic and social value in terms of creating new jobs through venture creation, and thereby, stimulating the entrepreneurial ecosystems and developing new solutions to supply and value chains.

The extensive closures of small businesses, their inability to respond effectively to the uncertainty imposed by social distancing and travel restrictions and their inability to craft flexible and agile business innovation models that accommodate the new realities of a pandemic environment, bear testimony to SME limitations. Essentially, business closures, contraction of SME operations during the COVID-19 pandemic weakened SME financial positions and exposed them to greater financial risk (Omar et al., 2020). Evidence of worker and production inputs shortages due to distortions of supply chains also negatively affected SME sales during the pandemic.

Consistent with these situated conditions, we argue that if African entrepreneurs anticipated such pandemic-based disruptions, they could have exploited the affordances of digital platforms and innovations to avail products and services, to create a new audience focused on obtaining reliable and real-time information in ways that augment digital entrepreneurship. Therefore, the capacity of African entrepreneurs to proactively respond to growing pandemic-imposed inequalities, future crises and their associated resilience in such contexts calls for greater scenario planning, futurist thinking and proactivity in anticipation of future adversities. This is because post-pandemic times such as those of COVID-19 exposed the significant inequality between developed and developing countries, imposed significant changes in lifestyles and access to basic infrastructure and compelled entrepreneurs to engage in greater collaboration and engagement with government, organisations, institutions and communities. These conditions further necessitate tapping into digital technologies, innovation and infrastructure.

References

Abisuga-Oyekunle, O. A., Patra, S. K., & Muchie, M. (2020). SMEs in sustainable development: Their role in poverty reduction and employment generation in sub-Saharan Africa. *African Journal of Science, Technology, Innovation and Development, 12*(4), 405–419.

Adeyemo, K. S. (2023). The status of digital innovation and data security in south african higher education. *South African Journal of Higher Education, 37*(2), 26–39.

Afro.Who (2020, October 29). *COVID-19 spurs health innovation in Africa*. https://www.afro.who.int/news/covid-19-spurs-health-innovation-africa

Ajide, F., & Soyemi, K. (2022). Oil rent, entrepreneurial start-ups, and institutional quality: Insights from African oil- rich countries. *Entrepreneurial Business and Economics Review, 10*(1), 35–49.

Akpan, I. J., Soopramanien, D., & Kwak, D. H. (2021). Cutting-edge technologies for small business and innovation in the era of COVID-19 global health pandemic. *Journal of Small Business & Entrepreneurship, 33*(6), 607–617.

Aldrich, H. E., & Waldinger, R. (1990). Ethnicity and entrepreneurship. *Annual Review of Sociology, 16*(1), 111–135.

Audretsch, D. B., & Belitski, M. (2021). Knowledge Complexity and Firm Performance: Evidence from the European SMEs. *Journal of Knowledge Management*, *25*(4), 693–713.

Audretsch, D. B., Belitski, M., Caiazza, R., & Phan, P. (2023). Collaboration strategies and SME innovation performance. *Journal of Business Research, 164*, 114018.

Autio, E., Kenney, M., Mustar, P., Siegel, D., & Wright, M. (2014). Entrepreneurial innovation: The importance of context. *Research Policy, 43*(7), 1097–1108.

Banks, M., Lovatt, A., O'connor, J., & Raffo, C. (2000). Risk and trust in the cultural industries. *Geoforum, 31*(4), 453–464.

Baporikar, N. (Ed.). (2021). *Handbook of research on sustaining SMEs and entrepreneurial innovation in the post-COVID-19 era*. Hershey, PA: IGI Global.

Beckert, J. (2015). The great transformation of embeddedness: Karl Polanyi and the new economic sociology. *SSRN Electronic Journal*. https://doi.org/10.2139/ssrn.2465810

Blimpo, M., Minges, M., Kouame, W., Azomahou, T., & Lartey, E. et al. (2017). *Leapfrogging: The Key to Africa's development -From constraints to investment opportunities*. World Bank. Third Investing in Africa Forum. Dakar, 25–27 September.

Block, J. Halberstadt, J.Högsdal, N., Kuckertz, A. Helle Neergaard, H. (2023). *Progress in Entrepreneurship Education and Training New Methods, Tools, and Lessons Learned from Practice*. Springer .

Bruno, R., Korosteleva, J., Osaulenko, K., & Radosevic, S. (2024). Sectoral digital capabilities and complementarities in shaping young firms' growth: Evidence from Europe. *Entrepreneurship & Regional Development, 36*(1–2), 115–135.

Bruton, G. D., Zahra, S. A., & Cai, L. (2018). Examining entrepreneurship through indigenous lenses. *Entrepreneurship: Theory and Practice*, *42*(3), 351–361.

Callon, M., Laredo, P., Rabeharisoa, V., Gonard, T., & Leray, T. (1992). The management and evaluation of technological programmes and the dynamics of techno-economic networks: The case of the AFME. *Research Policy, 21*, 215–236.

Chlosta, S. (2016). Methodological approaches towards context sensitive entrepreneurship research. In F. Welter & W. Gartner (Eds.), *A research agenda for entrepreneurship and context* (pp. 109–119). Cheltenham, UK: Edward Elgar Publishing.

Chomunorwa, S., Mashonganyika, E. S., & Marevesa, A. (2023). Digital transformation and post-Covid-19 education in South Africa: A review of literature. *South African Computer Journal, 35*(1), 91–100.

Daniel, A. D. (2016). Fostering an entrepreneurial mindset by using a design thinking approach in entrepreneurship education. *Industry and Higher Education, 30*(3), 215–223. https://doi.org/10.1177/0950422216653195

Ebewo, P., Ndlovu-Hlatshwayo, E., Mehlape, P., & Mlotshwa, S. (2023). Defining arts and cultural entrepreneurship. In C. Iwu & R. Shambare (Eds.), *Delivering entrepreneurship education in Africa* (pp. 33–56). Emerald Publishing.

Granovetter, M. (1985). Economic action and social structure: The problem of embeddedness. *American Journal of Sociology, 91*(3), 481–510.

Gupta, G., & Bose, I. (2019). Digital transformation in entrepreneurial firms through information exchange with operating environment. *Information and Management, 2019*, 103243.

Garud, R., Gehman, J., & Giuliani, A. P. (2014). Contextualizing entrepreneurial innovation: A narrative perspective. *Research Policy, 43*(7), 1177–1188.

GEM. (2023). *Global Entrepreneurship Monitor 2022/2023 Global Report-Adapting to a 'New Normal'*. London: GEM.

Hamad, H., Elbeltagi, I., El-Gohary, H., 2018. An empirical investigation of business-tobusiness e-commerce adoption and its impact on SMEs' competitive advantage: the case of Egyptian manufacturing SMEs. *Strategic Changement 27*(3), 209–229.

Hansen, D. (2023). *Informal Innovation in South Africa: An (invisible) force to be reckoned with*. Northglenn News story.

Hardie, B., Highfield, C., & Lee, K. (2020). Entrepreneurship education today for students' unknown futures. *Journal of Pedagogical Research, 4*(3), 401–417.

Harima, A. (2022). Theorizing disembedding and re-embedding: Resource mobilization in refugee entrepreneurship. *Entrepreneurship & Regional Development, 34*(3–4), 269–293.

Jack, S. L., & Anderson, A. R. (2002). The effects of embeddedness on the entrepreneurial process. *Journal of Business Venturing, 17*(5), 467–487.

Jafarnejad, A., Abbaszadeh, M. A., Ebrahimi, M., & Abtahi, S. M. (2013). Analysis of barriers to entrepreneurship in Small and Medium-sized Enterprises (SMEs). *International Journal of Academic Research in Economics and Management Sciences, 2*(4), 207.

Kanneganti, S. (2021). Unlocking the Power of the Private Sector to Build Resilient and Equitable Health Systems. World Bank Blog. https://blogs.worldbank.org/health/unlocking-power-private-sector-build-resilient-and-equitable-healthsystems

Kanyane, M. (2023). Digital work—transforming the higher education landscape in South Africa. In A. Shajek & E. A. Hartmann (Eds.), *New digital work: Digital sovereignty at the workplace* (pp. 149–160). Switzerland: Springer.

Kibale, K. (2023). Local Innovation Advances Health in Africa. https://healthpolicy-watch.news/local-innovation-advances-health-in-africa/ Inside View. Posted April 19, 2023.

Killingberg, N. M., Kubberød, E., & Blenker, P. (2021). Preparing for a future career through entrepreneurship education: Towards a research agenda. *Industry and Higher Education, 35*(6), 713–724.

Kim, S.-J., & Lee, J. (2019). Technological embeddedness as a determinant of techno-entrepreneurship. In F. Therin, F. Appio, & H. Yoon (Eds.), *Handbook of research on techno-preneurship: Ecosystems, Innovation and Development* (pp. 2–24). Cheltenham, UK: Edward Elgar.

Khurana, I., Dutta, D. K., & Ghura, A. S. (2022). SMEs and digital transformation during a crisis: The emergence of resilience as a second-order dynamic capability in an entrepreneurial ecosystem. *Journal of Business Research, 150*, 623–641.

Leke, A. & Yeboah-Amankwah, S. (2018). Africa: a crucible for creativity: lessons from the continent's breakout businesses. *Harvard Business Review*, November- December, 116–125.

Linton, G., & Klinton, M. (2019). University entrepreneurship education: A design thinking approach to learning. *Journal of Innovation and Entrepreneurship, 8*(1), 1–11.

Mutula, S. M., & Van Brakel, P. (2006). E-readiness of SMEs in the ICT sector in Botswana with respect to information access. *The Electronic Library*, *24*(3), 402–417. https://doi.org/10.1108/02640470610671240

Nabi, G., Liñán, F., Fayolle, A., Krueger, N., & Walmsley, A. (2017). The impact of entrepreneurship education in higher education: A systematic review and research agenda. *Academy of Management Learning & Education, 16*(2), 277–299. https://doi.org/10.5465/amle.2015.0026

Naidoo, V. (2021). SME sustainability in South Africa post-COVID-19. In *Handbook of Research on Sustaining SMEs and Entrepreneurial Innovation in the Post-COVID-19 Era* (pp. 419–437). Hershey, PA: IGI Global.

Nazareno, L., & Schiff, D. S. (2021). The impact of automation and artificial intelligence on worker well-being. *Technology in Society, 67*, 101679.

Ngubelanga, L. (2023). Young entrepreneur aims to revolutionise healthcare in South Africa https://clms.ukzn.ac.za/young-entrepreneur-aims-to-revolutionise-healthcare-in-south-africa/

Novotny, A., Rasmussen, E., Clausen, T., & Wickland, J. (2020). Helping birds to fly: Introducing start-up incubation ecosystems. In A. Novotny, E. Rasmussen, T. H. Clausen & J. Wiklund (Eds.), *Research handbook on start-up incubation ecosystems* (pp. 1–17). Cheltenham, UK: Edward Elgar Publishing.

Ogundana, O. M., Simba, A., Dana, L. P., & Liguori, E. (2021). Women entrepreneurship in developing economies: A gender-based growth model. *Journal of Small Business Management, 59*(sup1), S42–S72.

Omar, A. R. C., Ishak, S., & Jusoh, M. A. (2020). The impact of Covid-19 movement control order on SMEs' businesses and survival strategies. *Geografia-Malaysian Journal of Society and Space, 16*(2), 90–103.

Orlikowski, W. J. (2000). Using technology and constituting structures: A practice lens for studying technology in organizations. *Organisation Science, 11*(4), 404–428.

Osmundsen, K., Iden, J., & Bygstad, B. (2018). *Digital transformation: Drivers, success factors, and implications*. Mediterranean Conference on Information Systems (MCIS 2018), 37. https://aisel.aisnet.org/mcis2018/37

Piao, X., & Managi, S. (2022). Long-term improvement of psychological well-being in the workplace: What and how. *Social Science & Medicine, 298*, 114851.

Polanyi, K. (1944). *The great transformation*. Boston, MA: Beacon Press.

Portes, A., & Sensenbrenner, J. (1993). Embeddedness and immigration: Notes on the social determinants of economic action. *American Journal of Sociology, 98*(6), 1320–1350.

Priyono, A., Moin, A., & Putri, V. N. (2020). Identifying digital transformation paths in the business model of SMEs during the COVID-19 pandemic. *Journal of Open Innovation: Technology, Market, and Complexity, MDPI, 6*(4), 1–22.

Purbasari, R., Muttaqin, Z., & Sari, D. S. (2021). Digital entrepreneurship in pandemic Covid 19 era: The digital entrepreneurial ecosystem framework. *Review of Integrative Business and Economics Research, 10*, 114–135.

Rambe, P. (2022). *Understanding factors affecting technology entrepreneurship of university-incubated firms*. PhD Thesis. University of the Free State, Bloemfontein.

Rambe, P. (2023). The flipped classroom effect on entrepreneurship education: Applying critical pedagogy in digital environments. In C. Iwu & R. Shambare (Eds.), *Delivering entrepreneurship education in Africa* (pp. 1–31). Emerald Publishing Limited.

Roper, S. (2013). *Entrepreneurship: A global perspective*. Routledge.

Richter, A. (2020). Locked-down digital work. *International Journal of Information Management, 55*, 102157. https://doi.org/10.1016/j.ijinfomgt.2020.102157

Saville, A. D., Powell, P., Ismail-Saville, T., & Mthombeni, M. (2020). Quali health: Creating access to quality healthcare for South Africa's excluded majority. *Emerald Emerging Markets Case Studies, 10*(3), 1–34.

Schachtebeck, C., & Tselepis, T. (2023). Developing the competencies of envisioning and constructing through entrepreneurship education. In C. Iwu & R. Shambare (Eds.), *Delivering entrepreneurship education in Africa* (pp. 77–119). Leeds: Emerald Publishing Limited.

Schumpeter, J. (1934). *The theory of economic development: An inquiry into profits, capital, credit, interest, and the business cycle*. Harvard University Press.

Scott, J., Sinha, P., Gibb, J. & Akoorie, M. (2020). Introduction to the research handbook on entrepreneurship in emerging economies. In P. Sinha, J. Gibb,

M. Akoorie. & J. Scott (Eds.), *Research Handbook on Entrepreneurship in emerging economies* (pp. 1–25). Cheltenham, UK: Edward Elgar.

Shalley, C. & Breidenthal, A. (2021). Conducting rigorous research individual creativity. In J. Zhou, & E. Rouse (Eds.), *Handbook of research on creativity and innovation* (pp. 12–27). Cheltenham, UK: Edward Elgar.

Shajek, A., & Hartmann, E. A. (2023). *New digital work: Digital sovereignty at the workplace* (p. 291). Springer Nature.

Sharma, G. D., Kraus, S., Liguori, E., Bamel, U. K., & Chopra, R. (2022). Entrepreneurial challenges of COVID-19: Re-thinking entrepreneurship after the crisis. *Journal of Small Business Management*, *62*(2), 1–23.

Stamatović, J., & Zlatić, L. (2021). Entrepreneurship and the education of future teachers. *Journal of Elementary Education, 14*(1), 13–30.

Swartz, E., Scheepers, C., Lindgreen, A., Yousafzai, S., & Matthee, M. (2023). *Introduction: Technology leapfrogging and innovation in Africa: Digital transformation and opportunity for the Next Growth continent*. Edward Elgar.

Toefy, T., & Scheepers, C. (2019). *SweepSouth South Africa. Contextually intelligent female leadership of entrepreneurial domestic services*. Ivey Publishing.

Throsby, D. (2007). Modelling the creative/cultural industries. In*: New directions research: Substance, method and critique,* ESRC/AHRB cultural industries seminar network (pp. 11–12). Edinburgh: Royal Society of Edinburgh.

UNDP. (2023). Informal innovation in South Africa: An (Invisible) force to be reckoned With: https://www.undp.org/south-africa/blog/informal-innovation-south-africa-invisible-force-be-reckoned#:~:text=Making%20the%20Invisible%20Visible,-By%20surfacing%20as&text=In%20a%20country%20grappling%20with,that%20change%20is%20within%20reach. Retrieved December 27, 2023.

Ussif, R., & Salifu, K. (2020a). Contributions of small & medium to economic developments in sub-Saharan Africa. *International Journal of Academic Research in Accounting, Finance and Management Sciences, 4*(3), 63–78.

Uzzi, B. (1996). The sources and consequences of embeddedness for the economic performance of organisations: The network effect. *American Sociological Review, 61*, 674–698.

Vernon, P. (1989). The nature-nurture problem in creativity. In J. Glover, R. Ronning, & C. Reynolds (Eds.), *Handbook of creativity* (pp. 93–110). US: Springer.

Vrontis, D., Christofi, M., Pereira, V., Tarba, S., Makrides, A., & Trichina, E. (2022). Artificial intelligence, robotics, advanced technologies and human resource management: A systematic review. *The International Journal of Human Resource Management, 33*(6), 1237–1266.

Wafula, D. & Irungu. A. (2023). *Informal Innovation in South Africa: An (invisible) force to be reckoned with*. A Credit BBC Africa One Minute Story.

Wigren-Kristofersen, C., Korsgaard, S., Brundin, E., Hellerstedt, K., Alsos, G., & Grande, J. (2019). Entrepreneurship and embeddedness: Dynamic, processual and multi-layered perspectives. *Entrepreneurship & Regional Development, 31*(9–10), 1011–1015.

World Bank. (2017). *Africa's pulse: Focus on closing the infrastructure gap to increase growth*. World Bank.

Xie, X., Han, Y., Anderson, A., & Ribeiro-Navarrete, S. (2022). Digital platforms and SMEs' business model innovation: Exploring the mediating mechanisms of capability reconfiguration. *International Journal of Information Management, 65*, 102513. https://doi.org/10.1016/j.ijinfomgt.2022.102513

Zahoor, N., Donbesuur, F., Christofi, M., & Miri, D. (2022). Technological innovation and employee psychological well-being: The moderating role of employee learning orientation and perceived organizational support. *Technological Forecasting and Social Change, 179*, 121610.

Zhao, F. (2005). Exploring the synergy between entrepreneurship and innovation. *International Journal of Entrepreneurial Behavior & Research, 11*(1), 25–41.

Zhou, J., & George, J. (2001). When job satisfaction leads to creativity: Encouraging expression of voice. *Academy of Management Journal, 44*(4), 682–696.

Index

P. Rambe and R. E. Hinson (eds.), *The Future of Entrepreneurship in Southern Africa*, Palgrave Studies in Technology and Innovation in Africa, https://doi.org/10.1007/978-3-031-55935-8

SPRINGER NATURE

GPSR Compliance

The European Union's (EU) General Product Safety Regulation (GPSR) is a set of rules that requires consumer products to be safe and our obligations to ensure this.

If you have any concerns about our products, you can contact us on ProductSafety@springernature.com

In case Publisher is established outside the EU, the EU authorized representative is:

Springer Nature Customer Service Center GmbH
Europaplatz 3
69115 Heidelberg, Germany

The manufacturer's authorised representative in the EU is Springer Nature Customer Service Centre GmbH, Europaplatz 3, 69115 Heidelberg, Germany. If you have any concerns regarding our products, please contact ProductSafety@springernature.com

Printed and bound by CPI Group (UK) Ltd, Croydon, CR0 4YY
01/10/2026
02225903-0008